D0341780

Economics and the World around It

Economics and the World around It

Papers delivered at the
Centennial Symposium of the
Department of Economics,
The University of Michigan,
April 11-12, 1980

SAUL H. HYMANS, Editor

The University of Michigan Press

Ann Arbor

HB
21
E245
1982

EERL Withdrawn
ELMER E. RASMUSON LIBRARY
UNIVERSITY OF ALASKA
Surplus/Duplicate

Copyright © by The University of Michigan 1982
All rights reserved
Published in the United States of America by
The University of Michigan Press and simultaneously
in Rexdale, Canada, by John Wiley & Sons Canada, Limited
Manufactured in the United States of America

Library of Congress Cataloging in Publication Data

Main entry under title:

Economics and the world around it.

  Revised versions of papers presented at a symposium at
the University of Michigan, Apr. 11–12, 1980, held to mark
the centennial anniversary of the Dept. of Economics.
  Includes bibliographical references.
  1. Economics—Congresses. 2. University of Michigan.
Dept. of Economics—Congresses. I. Hymans, Saul H.
II. University of Michigan. Dept. of Economics.
HB21.E245 1982   330   81-21798
ISBN 0-472-08022-9   AACR2
ISBN-0-472-08021-0

For my wife Eileen,
who always understands

Preface

Part 1 of this volume contains revised versions of the papers presented at the symposium which marked the centennial anniversary of the Department of Economics of the University of Michigan. The symposium was a major component of the centennial celebration held in Ann Arbor on April 11–12, 1980. The editor's introductory essay attempts to put the substance of these important papers into perspective; I want here to express deep gratitude to the five authors—all former faculty members or students of the department—who cared enough both to celebrate with us and to respond to our call for their significant reflections on the state of our discipline. I am also most appreciative of the time and effort of my colleagues Gardner Ackley, Harvey E. Brazer, F. Thomas Juster, Glenn C. Loury, Shorey Peterson, and Peter O. Steiner, who have contributed as discussants of these papers.

Part 2 of this volume contains the proud and fascinating result of a labor of love undertaken by Marjorie C. Brazer—the writing of the history of the University of Michigan economics department. All of us who have been privileged to have a real association with the department feel an enormous debt to Marjorie Brazer. She reminded us in 1978 that we were approaching our hundredth year, she urged us not to let it pass unnoticed, and then she volunteered to research and write a history of the events, the people, and the discipline as they comprised the department. The result is historical scholarship, a picture of intellectual development, and human interest, all of the highest order. What is more, it is a delight to read.

The centennial celebration and symposium would not have been nearly as successful without the long and devoted labors of the centennial committee that I was privileged to chair. The committee members were my good friends and colleagues Robin Barlow, John G. Cross, Harold M. Levinson, William G. Shepherd, and our fine student colleague Marc Smith. The department's devoted administrative assistant Donna Henderson Smallwood and my caring and conscientious secretaries Bella Leach and Terri Bourton were of enormous importance to me as they kept control over the myriad details and tasks which accompanied all aspects of the celebration and the symposium.

I want to make special mention of Allan F. Smith, who served the university as interim president during the period in which the centennial was planned. We were trying to put together an event which would include a major publication, and we sought his help and advice. He gave both, including a significant financial contribution which really made everything possible. My colleagues and I are most grateful for the value he saw in the university's recognition of its Department of Economics. President Smith wanted the written record to be a major substantive publication; I hope that this volume is justification of his confidence.

I was already fully employed when I took on the chairmanship of the centennial committee. The extra time, the added concerns, the greater preoccupation, all produced spillover costs for my family. I thank Eileen and Steve and Amy and Staci for their gracious understanding and support.

Saul H. Hymans
Ann Arbor
March 1981

Contents

Editor's Introduction

Economics is what economists do. Some years ago Kenneth Boulding used that line (which he attributed to Jacob Viner) to lead off the "what is economics" part of his textbook. It is quite acceptable as a definition of economics, provided one is absolutely certain about who is and who is not an economist. Perhaps that is the reason why Boulding also went on to write about such things as limited resources.

The centennial committee, in arranging the symposium which produced the papers here published, wanted to use the occasion of the hundred-year anniversary of the University of Michigan Department of Economics to take a good hard look at economics. What is economics about now, how did it get that way, where does it seem to be heading, and what's missing—either about where it is, or where it seems to be heading? How does one solicit papers for such a lofty, ambitious, and very risky project without running the enormous risk of them turning out to be pedantic, pompous, or vacuous? Our control was to be absolutely certain of the credentials of those whom we asked to write for us. Happily, we had no difficulty in this regard even though the committee had restricted its choice by deciding that the symposium papers should be given by persons with a former, significant connection to the Michigan economics department. Perhaps that restriction was more help than hindrance. It may well have identified persons who not only could do what we wanted, but who could be talked into accepting so difficult a task for a very special purpose. I still have very warm memories of my initial telephone calls to each of the authors. So pleased were they at the prospect of returning to participate in the centennial event, that what we were asking of them seemed a small enough price to pay. Reality dawned as the deadline approached, but they came through magnificently.

Without anyone having willed it so, Richard A. Musgrave managed to set the tone and framework for the symposium. Writing alone and speaking first, he presented the very ideas which organized much of the analysis in the other papers, and thereby provided the basic framework into which all the papers fit. The title of Musgrave's paper is thus fittingly the title of this volume.

Musgrave tells us of three determinants of the development of economic theory: "(1) the internal logic of theoretical development, (2) the changing technical, institutional, and social setting in which the economy operates, and (3) the role of value or ideology." This framework is then applied to discussing the development of public sector economics, Musgrave's own special field. In the process, Musgrave has a good deal to say about market failure—a theme picked up quite naturally in Frederic M. Scherer's treatment of regulatory economics. Each author traces a similar pattern of analytical development which focuses first on the correction of market failure and ultimately on the issue of regulatory failure. Musgrave notes the coincidence of the recognition of regulatory failure and the emergence in the 1970s of a new generation of conservative intellectuals, thinly veiling the suggestion that the former might bear some causative relation to the latter. Musgrave expresses some optimism that in time the new "theory of government failure" might even improve our understanding of the public sector. Scherer concludes that deregulation is the wave of the present, largely because it may be less harmful than the regulation once thought to be the best available alternative to the inefficiencies inherent in natural monopoly.

The first two of Musgrave's determinants of theory development frame Sidney Winter's essay on production theory. Winter claims that production theory has been too much the product of the internal logic of its own development and far too little the reflection of the changing technical, institutional, and social setting of the economy. Winter fears that production theory may not be about much of anything that is of real interest (except to another production theorist) and may therefore be incapable of giving us answers to the questions that need asking—questions about the relationship of organization to production, of learning to production, of technology to production, and of the interrelations among these factors.

Musgrave also writes of macroeconomics, reminding us in fact that "for macro theory to be fun, there must be disturbances in the system. That is to say, *macro theory is essentially a theory of market failure.*" In one sense, this is a reference to the Great Depression which gave birth to modern macroeconomics. But it is even more the recognition that imperfectly competitive forces, market power, and the interactions of imperfect knowledge with shifting expectations are sufficient—without the extremes of the 1930s—to generate an important and meaningful role for macro analysis. James Duesenberry is quite aware of this in his penetrating discussion of the concurrent development of a reasonably stable (i.e., small amplitude) real economy along with a growing inflationary bias. Musgrave reminds us that our views about stabilization policy are value-based, and Duesenberry develops this notion to explain that inflationary bias is, in part, the result of a rational behavioral response to the knowledge that society has chosen to react "predictably to raise demand" early in, if not at the clear threat of, recession.

Econometrics—particularly macroeconometrics—also comes under Musgrave's purview. He claims that model building has gone beyond the implementation of short-run macro theory; it has in fact outrun the latter. Modern econometric techniques and computer technology have produced empirical lag structures, despite our apparent inability to derive theoretically based lag structures. Theory of a sort is then employed to rationalize sometimes shaky empirical results. Granting these and other evident difficulties, Lawrence Klein argues nonetheless that econometric forecasts do have real merit. In terms of "better promise on a repetitive, replicated basis . . . no challenger appears on the horizon." Nor do any other feasible techniques for forecasting "have simulation capability for dealing with 'what if' issues in a way that is meaningful to a wide variety of users." Klein is optimistic that econometric models will continue to improve as they reflect the economic understanding that accrues over time. The sharpest concern which Klein expresses is his growing fear that the econometric industry is straying too far from objective academic "monitoring of its professional content," that "special interest groups will use models, even if they are not up to standard, in order to establish points in support of their own special interests." Thus, he concludes, wholly independent, academically based econometric research teams must play a role of increasingly vital importance to society, just when the financial viability of such operations is becoming more tenuous.

PART ONE

Perspectives on a Discipline

Economics and the World around It

RICHARD A. MUSGRAVE

Economic theory, in Joan Robinson's phrase, is a box of tools. This makes a good beginning, but leaves open the question of what the tools are to be used for and who is to use them. During my years in Ann Arbor, I was too busy making tools to raise such epistemological questions, as were my colleagues. Ken Boulding completed the third edition of his magnum opus and was getting ready to disown it; Gardner Ackley and Warren Smith were revising the Keynesian model to allow for the eventuality of a sloping LM curve; Wolf Stolper had discovered that factors as well as products can move across borders; Bill Haber and Hal Levinson demonstrated that unions after all do raise wages; Dan Suits and Larry Klein were building the world's first man-sized econometric model; George Katona and Jim Morgan were dressing homo economicus in human clothing; Shorey Peterson was dispensing no-nonsense elementary economics; Bill Palmer was expounding Chamberlinian market structures; Harvey Brazer was exploring why governments act the way they do; and I was inventing my theory of public finance, interrupted only by occasional trips to Lansing to discuss the state of the state with Governor Soapy Williams. All this was to refurnish the box with a final set of tools, Michigan-made, ready to take care of any pipe that might burst or any wiring that might short-circuit. Thirty years later I am a bit more doubtful, as I suppose are my friends and comrades of those golden years. As one grows older it becomes more tempting to theorize about theories than to invent them, and I do not apologize for that. Both activities are needed and have their role.

Determinants of Economic Theory
Economic theory, so we tell our students, is to instruct us about the relationship between dependent and independent variables in the eco-

Richard A. Musgrave is H. H. Burbank Professor of Political Economy at Harvard University, and was a member of the Michigan faculty during 1947–59.

nomic system. But what about reversing the process and taking economic theory as the dependent variable? What then should we expect to find on the right side of the equation? The answer has to be catholic since single-cause explanations are sure to be wrong. To express this spirit while maintaining a workable framework for my paper, I shall distinguish between three lines of causation, including (1) the internal logic of theoretical development, (2) the changing technical, institutional, and social setting in which the economy operates, and (3) the role of value or ideology.

In the first place, economic theory, in the spirit of Schumpeter's *History of Economic Analysis*, may be seen as driven by an internal dynamics of scientific advance. Simple hypotheses turn into more concise formulations and provide deeper insights. Answers to old problems lead to new ones and an expanding theoretical structure emerges. To illustrate, follow the trail from early perceptions of diminishing returns, over the law of variable proportions to today's sophisticated production functions. Or consider the mutation of Quesnay's Tableau into multiple sector input-output models, the maturing of the Walrasian system into Arrow-Debreu theorems on the existence of competitive equilibrium, and the path from early wage funds to modern demand theories. While a continuing process, this refinement of analytical tools has proceeded at an uneven pace, with periods of slow progress along established lines (ordinary science in Kuhn's sense) interrupted by major breakthroughs (changes in paradigm if you wish). Identifying the paradigm changers is an attractive parlor game for economists (Smith, Ricardo, Marx, Menger, Wicksell, Schumpeter, Keynes, and who else?) which I shall not play here, but I should note that my concept of internal progress is not limited to puzzle-solving activity, but also includes the vision of new puzzles.

Secondly, refinement of analytical tools offers an important key to the history of economic thought but unfortunately (or happily, depending on where you stand) it is by no means the entire story. Surely, allowance must be made for the fact that economic activity (unlike the solar system) operates in a rapidly changing environment, this being one of the ways in which economics and astronomy differ. Such changes may be technical or demographic in nature, or they may involve the institutions, in which the economic process is conducted. The changing environment, by posing new problems, calls for new tools with which to resolve them. Adam Smith's concern with the division of labor was enlivened by the concurrent development of manufacture, Ricardo's interest in comparative advantage was linked to the debate over the Corn Laws, Keynes's macroeconomics responded to the experience of the Great Depression, theories of imperfect competition reflected the development of new market structures, the rising cost of energy now poses new problems in factor substitution, and so on. Many of the great contributors to economic theory were involved in the affairs of their time and even contributed to the course of events. The development of economic theory may thus be viewed as the manufacture of tools designed to meet demands derived from the course of changing events. When toolmakers lag behind changing demand (witness their default in the current debate over inflation) economics and economists suffer in reputation, and rightly so.

My third line of causation deals with the role of changing value systems. This might have been included as a further aspect of environmental change, but I prefer to consider it a distinct factor. The role of values, in my view, is not simply one of apologetic ideology or superstructure. That role exists, but beyond it values enter as a distinct variable with an exogenous quality of their own. Their effectiveness in shaping events depends on their holder's ability to promote them, be it by writing books, access to the media, or through political power. The marketplace of ideas is as imperfect (if not more so) as that for goods, but this does not reduce the importance of ideas. As time goes by, I have been increasingly impressed by the connection between the theories which particular economists produce and their values. Why otherwise could it be that the work of one set of theorists is directed at showing that velocity is more stable than the multiplier, that the Coase theorem takes care of externalities or that expectations are rational, while the work of another set aims to show that the multiplier is more stable, that Pigouvian taxes are required and that expectations are a matter of outguessing or of animal spirit?

By pointing to the importance of values, I do not mean to argue that economists cheat, although sometimes they do. Rather, I follow Max Weber's contention that it is quite proper for the investigator to let his or her choice of hypothesis be influenced by values, provided that the testing proceeds along objective lines. What matters, as Schumpeter put it, is whether the answers are right, not why the question was posed. Nevertheless, value considerations, by influencing the choice of problems under investigation, have much to do with how economic theory advances. Since ideological cycles are of the Kondratieff rather than the Kitchin type, this is an important factor, perhaps not over infinity but over quite substantial periods.

Having defined these three lines of causation, let me briefly respond to some objections which may arise. Some may wish me to stay with my first point; deal with the internal logic of theoretical development and leave it at that. External events should not be permitted to divert the pure theorist's concern with the true essence of economics, i.e., the efficient use of scarce resources, conceived as a formal proposition. Nor should economists feel called upon to address such amorphous concepts as value (excepting, of course, value in exchange) or distribution, a matter to be left to social philosophers or, even worse, to sociologists. I understand that message, but I disagree. Economics should be more than engineering and consulting training. If it is to be a social science, it cannot be sealed off from the world around it.

Others may well take the opposite view, pleased that I have added a second and third perspective, but disagreeing with my distinguishing so sharply between them. I am sympathetic, but plead inability to do better, at least in the context of this paper. The ultimate goal, to be sure, is to develop a general social theory in which various dimensions of the social process are linked in interaction. Economics has an important niche in such a system, but so do other aspects of the social sciences (psychology, social philosophy, politics) and no single perspective (not even economics) can claim to be the centerpiece. The Michigan tradition has not been unaware of this; and notwithstanding the current trend of the profession to the contrary, I hope that it will continue to be the case. At the same time it must be admitted that a general social theory is almost impossible to devise. Not because there would be too many equations but because there is no common unit of account, nor is there a common mechanism of interaction through which the various dimensions of the system can be linked. Some heroic attempts to do so have been made, including Adam Smith's in his *Theory of Moral Sentiments*, and Karl Marx in his theory of social change, but both present a vastly oversimplified and, in their own ways, biased view of how society really functions. Max Weber, wiser and aware of the multidimensional nature of the social process, avoided such oversimplification, but consequently failed to arrive at a workable system. However this may be, I shall for now have to focus on economic theory as if it were the centerpiece, and consider how its development has responded to my three forces.

More specifically, I shall apply this framework to examining the development of public sector economics. This has been closest to my own work and also one of the most lively and expanding areas of retooling. Since the twenties, when Lord Robbins declared economics the science of the marketplace, there has been a growing involvement of economic theory with nonmarket transactions. Public sector economics has become a major and integral part of economic theory. This development responded to a rapid growth of the public sector in western market economies, as well as to an ideological climate which (from the thirties to the early seventies) was supportive of governmental participation in economic life. Most leading economists during this period were in the liberal camp. In viewing this development, I will make use of my distinction between the allocation, distribution, and stabilization aspects of the public sector. Though much criticized, this tripartite approach has been widely accepted and remains, I believe, essentially correct.

Allocation Aspects
Beginning with the allocation aspects, the most important development of modern economics has been the theory of social goods. While dating back to Wicksell's writings of the 1890s and Lindahl's extension of 1919, the modern era begins with my retelling their story in the late thirties and with Samuelson's restatement of the mid-fifties. In this restatement social goods, i.e., goods involving nonrival consumption, were incorporated into the model of Pareto-efficient resource use, thereby establishing them as honorable members of the community of economic phenomena, and worthy of the theorist's attention. The principles of welfare economics were generalized to encompass the phenomenon of externalities, a fine illustration of how economic theory develops out of its internal logic.

But the linkage between stating efficiency conditions and reaching efficient outcomes (produced in the case of private goods through a market mechanism) remained undefined. Since social goods must be made available free of direct charge (marginal cost for additional users being zero) provision for such goods cannot be accomplished through the market mechanism. An alternative process is needed to secure preference revelation. To overcome the free rider problem, this has to be a political process, involving mandatory compliance. By disavowing this part of the problem as a hopeless morass, Samuelson's initial formulation placed social goods theory into a somewhat barren context, a context from which (notwithstanding my efforts and those of a few others) it has had difficulty emerging. Stating efficiency conditions for social goods was a fundamental first step, but tools are as good as their use and the payoff is in learning how to apply them. Budgetary provision based on mandatory implementation of a voting rule leaves some participants dissatisfied, so that the outcome will not be optimal. But this is no occasion for setting aside the issue. The real problem, in economics as in other aspects of life, is how to avoid tenth-best solutions if fifth-best outcomes can be obtained. The development of a theory of public choice has been helpful and recent models of cheat-proof voting systems may prove an important step. Nevertheless, much remains to be done along these lines.

As distinct from the endogenous nature of social goods theory, the development of cost-benefit analysis offers a prime illustration of demand-induced supply of economic tools. Though calling for the resolution of theoretical issues (e.g., how to derive the proper rate of discount) this enterprise has been an eminently practical one. While somewhat discredited by overly enthusiastic attempts at detailed application, it nevertheless offers a most useful step toward translating the theory of public economics into efficient practice. Such is the case even though the cookbook approach to cost-benefit can be applied only after the menu has been written. And to write the menu for social goods, the problem of benefit measurement must first be resolved. This qualification, however, is rendered less serious by the fact that public expenditures frequently, if not typically, involve provision for mixed rather than for pure social goods. Moreover, even in the latter case, cost-benefit analysis offers a useful framework in which to analyze the problem.

Since the sixties, there has been a shift in attention from the provision of social goods to the avoidance of social bads, such as those caused by environmental pollution, for example. External costs, like external benefits, are not accounted for by the market and hence in need of correction. Once more this is not an entirely new development, at least not to those of us who remember Pigou's *Economics of Welfare* with its proverbial smoke nuisance case. The principles are the same as for social goods theory; only the application differs. The sudden

growth of environmental concern and, with it, the growth of environmental economics may be seen as a response to the increasing incidence of pollution—another illustration of demand-induced tool supply.
Some such increase has occurred, especially with regard to automobile pollution, but there is more to the dramatic rise of environmental
economics than that. It also reflects the ideological antisystem mood
of the sixties, dwelling as it were on an inherent weakness of the
market with its neglect of external cost and the belief that there is a
common entitlement to, or sanctity in, the benefits of nature.

The trends in public sector economics which I have noted so far
support the proposition that action by the public sector is needed to
correct for market failure. While this has been the dominant trend
from the thirties to the sixties, the seventies have brought a sharp
reversal. Instead of viewing the government as acting efficiently in
correcting market failure, the dominant vision seems to be of government acting inefficiently and disturbing the functioning of the market.
The new theme is government, not market, failure. In part, this again
reflects the internal logic of theoretical development. As one com-
partment of the tool box is filled, the emptiness of another becomes
apparent and it cannot stay so for too long. Thus, in the wave of
theorizing about what efficient government should do, theorizing about
what makes government behave as it does is not neglected. While the
Marxist tradition in its concern with fiscal sociology and the role of
the state had always been aware of this aspect, mainstream analysts
had given it only minor attention. Government, so we had assumed,
would attempt to implement the wishes of the voters as well as it
could, especially if following our advice on what to do.

A positive theory of public sector behavior, though not necessarily a theory of public misbehavior, was thus in order. Yet it is not
surprising that the new development took the latter form, precisely
because it coincided with a sharp value shift in the ideological spectrum. The emergence of a new generation of conservative intellectuals
which we have witnessed over the last decade has been an important
event and has had a massive impact on public sector economics. Indeed, public sector economists have been in the vanguard of that development. As I see it, their modeling of government behavior in terms
of monopolistic bureaus and agenda setters takes a rather one-sided
view. Policy makers, like business men, may be expected to act as
maximizers, if that term simply denotes purposeful behavior. But it is

wrong to assume that the same purpose (i.e., profits) is the object of maximization in all cases. There is more than "one game in town" and to model government behavior in terms of profit maximization is to build government failure into the model. Moreover, such modeling leads to faulty policy prescription. Nevertheless, the new theory of government failure has been an important development which in time, and under a more balanced perspective, should contribute to a better understanding of the public sector.

Distribution Aspects

Turning now to the public sector's role in distribution, economic theory was quick to develop and to refine a theory of factor shares. At the outset, this theory was not without social content, as the relevant parties (land, labor, and capital) did reflect the then significant pattern of social stratification. But before long the theory of distribution became a theory of efficient factor pricing, interesting as a part of welfare economics and to some degree as a description of market behavior but only loosely related to the quite different question of how the fruits of economic activity are or should be distributed among the members of the community. Yet the latter issue plays a central role in what economic activity is about. Viewed from the perspective of the social scientist it may well be *the* central issue. However hard it may try, economic theory cannot for long neglect this half of the problem.

Under the old welfare economics (from, say, John Stuart Mill over Edgeworth to Pigou) the rationale of distribution policy, and its application to progressive taxation, was seen in terms of equal and comparable marginal utility of income schedules. Dan Suits used to tell me that this was a nonsense proposition since I would be unable to show him the laboratory where utility is measured. I never quite believed him, and still don't, but his came to be the view of the profession. The great retreat to Pareto-efficiency was underway, with distribution issues, somewhat like naughty children, banned from the professional table. But not for too long, since distribution soon reappeared in the guise of the social welfare function. (Let me note that my story here uses the novelist's license in somewhat distorting historical timing, but remains essentially correct.) This, however, was to restate the problem rather than to resolve it. Without telling us how the social welfare function is derived, and bedeviled further by Arrow's proposition that there is no consistent way of derivation anyhow, all this remained at a rather formal level. Nonetheless, distribution issues were readmitted and theorists were spared further embarrassment by the comparability assumption.

The social welfare function, after its triumphant entry in the late thirties, kept a rather low profile during the first three decades of its life, but has moved back into the forefront of discussion of late. Interestingly enough, this has come in response to the writings of social philosophers, mainly John Rawls's *Theory of Justice*. Justice as fairness, Rawls argued, requires a state of distribution in line with maximin, permitting inequality only to the extent that its retention improves the position of the least favored. Economists found much to criticize in this formulation (including the assumption of total risk aversion and the zero valuation of welfare losses from taxation incurred above the minimum) but it gave rise to an interesting debate over how the shape of the social welfare function could be derived from underlying value premises about social justice. I for one have found this a fascinating interaction between economic theory and theories of nonmarket value. Its timing was in line with the rapidly rising level of transfer payments by the public sector and the debate over such issues as the negative income tax and welfare reform.

A subsequent and recent development in the tool kit of distribution economics has been the application of optimal taxation theory to the income tax. This has also reflected a resumption of earlier themes. Edgeworth had qualified his conclusion in favor of equalization (the minimum total sacrifice rule) by reference to incentive effects; and Pigou, in his discussion of tax burden distribution, had pointed to the existence of what he called announcement effects. Moreover, it was Pigou whose queries induced the first formal statement by Ramsay. But only recently have efficiency costs of redistribution moved to the center of the discussion. Since continuing redistribution from A to B cannot be sustained by lump sum transfers (that least useful if most popular tool of welfare theory) the efficiency cost involved in such transfer must be allowed for. This development offers another illustration of theoretical advance driven by the internal logic of the system. My generation of tax theorists has paid much attention to the distribution of the tax burden, in terms of both horizontal and vertical equity, but we have tended to view the burden in terms of revenue collected, thus disregarding the efficiency cost of excess burden. Correction for this benign (or, as others might see it, malign) neglect was due. But the change in emphasis is also a good illustration of the ideological base from which questions are asked. For one thing, concern with the efficiency cost of redistribution appeals to a conservative position as it limits the scope for such policies. For another, the new generation of efficiency-oriented tax theorists shows little distress over the disappearance of horizontal equity from the analysis, a disappearance which follows from the assumption (shared by most optimal tax theory) of identical utility functions. My mathematical friends tell me that to allow for such differences would render the problem unmanageable. Yet this issue was central to the more equity-oriented analysis of my generation. I do hope that a mathematical genius who can reintroduce it will come along.

Stabilization Aspects

Turning to fiscal concerns with macro policy, we find perhaps the most dramatic and interesting story of continuing retooling. The macro vision of Adam Smith was one of economic growth, driven by accumulation and thrift. The state had a role in certain areas of public investment (bridges, harbors, canals) but that was all. Ricardian revisionism was less optimistic, with growth declining toward the stationary state and Malthusian subsistence. The state was assigned no role except as a spendthrift whose scope should be minimized. Both views involved a smooth journey along a predetermined path, with Say's law assuring the clearing of markets, and controlling traffic along the way. There was no occasion for stabilization policy in the modern sense. With Marx concern shifted to conflicts and contradictions, of both a short- and long-run nature, within the system. Stabilization would be called for but, by the nature of the capitalist state, could not be forthcoming in an efficient form. Wicksell's vision of the natural rate of interest focused on the equilibrating mechanism of the modern economic system and the role of financial markets therein, thus laying the groundwork for modern macro and stabilization theory. Robertson, and Keynes in his *Treatise*, continued in that vein, whereas business cycle theorists such as Hayek extended the structural tradition of Ricardo and Marx. Next came the Keynesian revolution, a piece of economic history for those who study now, but the dominant event of my generation's academic childhood. The *General Theory* obviously was a response to the policy needs of the Great Depression. But beyond this, so it seemed, it also offered a fundamental breakthrough in economic understanding. It had disproven the classical system and elevated deficit finance as *the* solution to the problem of macro policy. Later on, the neoclassical synthesis of the fifties provided a rapprochement between the Keynesian and the classical view, leaving the continuing battle between the two schools somewhat of a tempest in the theoretical teapot. Moreover, the neoclassical synthesis dislodged the expenditure side of the budget from its unique position as a stabilization tool, making it clear that aggregate demand control can be accomplished from either the tax or the expenditure side, or for that matter by monetary tools.

Since then we have witnessed a near replacement of short-run macro theorizing by econometric model building. This reflected the strategic role of lags in short-run economic change, a role first noted in Duesenberry's consumption lags (also a product of Michigan economics) and in Metzler's contribution to the Hansen festschrift. But when all is said and done, lag structures cannot be derived theoretically but are an empirical matter, making it difficult to construct useful models without an empirical base. Moreover, the econometric approach has been made possible by the development of computer technology, illustrating how the content of economic theory responds to changes in the technology of theorizing. The transformation of stabilization policy into econometrics has helped, but has also had its problems—not so much because it is the wrong way in which to go, but because as yet the tools are unequal to the task.

Another important development has been a renewed concern with the long-run issues of economic growth. This is not surprising. The short-run nature of the Keynesian model with fixed capital stock was inadequate and had to be amended to allow for capital accumulation and for growth, a factor which had been so central to the classical system. In the early phases of this development, as reflected in the Harrod-Domar model, there was a hope that reintroduction of growth could be combined with the insights of Keynesian economics, but this was not to be. Instead, growth theory returned the analysis to the context of a wholly flexible classical model, as if disturbances did not exist. With the Malthusian doom removed by the pill, society is free to choose its growth path into the future. Disturbances are considered irrelevant in the long run, which is not only wrong but also, as Keynes noted, of limited concern. All this has important bearing on the role of public policy. With the emphasis on growth, the impact of fiscal policy shifts from aggregate demand to the composition of output and in particular to the level of private investment. As I shall note presently, this has involved important implications for the politics of fiscal policy. Moreover, the nature of the growth model has direct bearing on what can be accomplished by fiscal policy. Given a growth model of the Solow type, fiscal policy can effect the level of output but not the long-run rate of growth, thus limiting its usefulness.

A painful parallel to the ultraclassical nature of modern growth theory is found in the current theory of inflation. Disregarding earlier models of inflation, which emphasized the dynamic aspects of adjustment lags, current models center on tracing a hypothetical adjustment to a nonexistent equilibrium rate of inflation, thereby missing the essentially dynamic nature of the problem. Economic theory progresses, but like other human endeavors, not necessarily along a straight line.

The most recent development in macro theory has been an emphasis on rational expectations, reflecting as it were a delayed reaction to the Keynesian emphasis on uncertainty and irrational behavior. Once more we see how in filling one section of the box the next one is discovered. Ordinary science then requires that it also be filled. The new tools need to be explored even if in the end they do not turn out to be very useful. I believe such to be the case when it comes to the application of the new approach to the role of fiscal policy. The proposition is that consumers' responses to tax and deficit finance will be the same because taxes needed for future debt services are capitalized. This seems to me a quite unrealistic assumption, so that the conclusion is not a particularly useful addition to our kit of tools. I should add in all fairness that there is a central assumption in traditional fiscal theory which is subject to a similar objection. This is the assumption, which most of us have been accustomed to use, that government adjusts tax and expenditure levels in a rational fashion. Thus, built-in revenue responses are taken to be stabilizing in an inflationary setting, as is an increase in tax rates, but such is not the case under an alternative and at times more realistic model, where government expenditures tend to move with tax revenues. One of the difficulties in recent years has been precisely this perverse type of behavior.

Enough has been said to show how the development of macro theory and of fiscal policy tools has responded to both the logic of internal development and to changes in the setting of the economy.

Once more a word may be added regarding the role of values. As a preliminary, what *is* macro theory, anyhow? After distinguishing between partial and general equilibrium aspects of micro theory, what remains there to be explored? Taking the model of a perfectly functioning market system, full employment prevails automatically and the market sets real wages so as to equate the demand and supply for labor. Similarly, the system automatically achieves an optimal rate of growth as the time preference of consumers is equated with the marginal product of capital. A policy issue arises only with regard to money supply. Economists in rare agreement reject the commercial loan theory and hold that a central bank is needed to control the money supply. But given a well-behaved classical system, this task is trivial. The central bank should simply let the money supply expand with real output. Macro theorists may investigate how the rate of growth would change if the time preference of consumers did differ, but that would be a limited pursuit.

For macro theory to be fun, there must be disturbances in the system. That is to say, *macro theory is essentially a theory of market failure*. As such, its link to ideological factors becomes evident. The exhilaration which early Keynesians experienced in proving Say's Law to be wrong is a good illustration. So is the almost touching satisfaction which marketeers derive from restoring the honor of their system by reference to the Pigou effect. If only wages and prices were perfectly flexible, there could be nothing wrong with "the system as such"—the working of the Pigou effect would, sooner or later, restore the economy to full employment. Essentially the same "as-if" argument reappears in postulating a long-run vertical Phillips curve with a constant equilibrium rate of inflation at full employment.

Value aspects also enter into how various instruments of stabilization policy are viewed. In the early stages of Keynesian economics, stabilization policy was directed at expanding demand. Moreover the instrument of expansion was seen in raising government spending. Celebration of the balanced budget multiplier came later, as did recognition that expansion can also be accomplished via tax reduction. The fiscal approach came thus to be associated with large budgets, with the liquidity trap a welcome excuse for expanding the public sector. Hence it is not surprising that fiscal policy advocates were to be found in the liberal camp. Now that the problem has become one of restriction, stabilization policy via expenditure adjustment (downward) emerges as a conservative cause. Checking inflation becomes a massive argument for cutting back the budget, notwithstanding the fact that demand restraint may contribute little to stabilization and that the primary source of demand expansion may be in the private sector—in consumer credit, for example.

Similar considerations apply to the rise of "supply-side economics," both in the context of long-run growth and in dealing with inflation. Having more in the future is, of course, to everybody's advantage, but the question is who gets less in the present. Growth-promoting policies in a market economy must strengthen incentives for saving and investment. Deterring effects of taxation upon incentives depend upon marginal rather than average rates, and the same applies with regard to the marginal tax rates which are implicit in transfers that decline with income. Incentive policies, therefore, tend to be antiredistributive and differ in this respect from stabilization policy which may be held distributionally neutral. The concern with growth and supply-side economics thus has strong political implications. These are evident for issues of distribution policy but go well beyond them. Emphasis on growth is in line with the ethos of capitalism, the heroic role of the entrepreneur and the entitlement to individual effort. What on the surface appears a purely economic issue—that raising the growth rate by x percent requires the rate of capital formation to be increased by y percent, for example—is but the tip of a much larger iceberg of political, social, and cultural change.

Conclusion

Looking back at the preceding discussion, it is not surprising to find that public sector economics lends itself especially well to exploring how economic analysis responds to the changing world around it. We have seen that the development of analytical tools in important respects follows its internal logic, but we have also seen that other factors such as changes in social or economic setting and in value systems must be allowed for as well. Failure to do so reduces what is inherently a social science to the much less interesting (if perhaps simpler) world of physics. Taking this view, it is unnecessary to add that I have misgivings about how our science has been moving. The growth of mathematical tools in recent decades has contributed greatly to the rigor of economic analysis, but it has also moved this analysis along lines to which mathematical rigor can best be applied. Technique and substance are not unrelated, nor are they without bearing on the role of values.

As noted before, I have been increasingly impressed with this role, not in the sense that its presence leads to false analysis, but in the sense that values pose the questions which are asked. In particular, I think that there are two value sets which are of key importance. One is how one relates to the phenomenon of the invisible hand. The other is how one views the issue of social justice. I begin with the former, the role of the invisible hand in securing an efficient outcome through the mechanism of a competitive market. Though commonplace in our thinking, this is a truly extraordinary concept. As an intellectual proposition, I still find it astounding, indeed mind-boggling, that the self-interested action of millions of individuals should automatically lead to a result which is efficient for the community as a whole. I have been told that this surprise is naive because efficiency is defined so as to reject the nonmarket outcome, but such is surely not the case. The phenomenon is extraordinary, especially since it does not hold in other spheres of social interaction. But it does not follow that a system, guided by the invisible hand, must be the best of all worlds. To some, it would appear a magnificent working of deistic design (as in Adam Smith's *Theory of Moral Sentiments*) while to others it poses a strange paradox. If the nature of things is such that man will be most social by being selfish, then how can a moral social order be established? The former will seek to demonstrate that most real world phenomena lend themselves to market solutions, thereby reducing the need for state intervention. The latter will be inclined to show that phenomena such as externalities do not permit solution by market process so that a political type of social interaction is required.

Similar considerations arise with regard to views of social justice. Some will hold that a person is entitled to the fruits of his or her labor, while others will hold that talents should be considered common property in the good society. The former will be inclined to verify the hypothesis that redistribution policies carry a heavy excess burden, while the latter hope to show the burden to be slight. And even after the cost has been agreed upon, as it should be in the course of objective analysis, observers will differ on the price which should be paid. No wonder, then, that value-based formulation of problems, combined with objective research in their resolution, has had a major effect on the development of economics, and in particular on the economics of the public sector.

Comments by HARVEY E. BRAZER

These are not the best of times for economists. On this Richard Musgrave and I are agreed. Nor should it surprise anyone that we agree as well on most other matters, in no small part because his thinking as embodied in his published works over the past forty years has contributed so much to the shaping of my views in the public policy area, and in part because I have been privileged to work closely with him, both here in Michigan and in John F. Kennedy's Washington. Over the years we have been close ideologically as well, believing that predominantly private capitalist markets were the best available means of marshaling and putting to use the nation's resources for the satisfaction of the wants of its people. But we were among the large majority of our generation who, influenced strongly by the experience of the Great Depression and the hope that the Keynesian revolution offered for avoiding such social catastrophes, recognized that the market system was prone to fail in a number of ways. It fails utterly with respect to public goods, it fails partially in the presence of externalities, it fails to maintain price and employment stability, and it falls well short of almost anyone's goals with respect to income distribution.

Thus as economists we saw our job as that of finding the appropriate correctives for market failure which, when properly applied, would save private capitalism and yield the best of all possible worlds. On this point I think that Musgrave and I remain in close agreement. Perhaps where we tend to part company most clearly is in our interpretations of what went wrong. How did we get to our present position, in which many of the liberal troops find themselves in disillusionment, if not disarray, while the ears and minds of power and authority are increasingly open and sympathetic to the views of those who would seem bent on taking policy back to pre-Pigouvian classical laissez-faire (cum supply-side "incentives")?

I would make several points, one or two of which perhaps are simply embellishments of Musgrave's positions, while others represent some departure from the views he has expressed here.

One source of our difficulties may lie in the strength and rigor of the central core of the discipline as it comes to us from Adam Smith through Ricardo and Malthus. The market paradigm was drawn so neatly and it functioned so magnificently that all efforts to improve upon its outcomes were doomed to failure. Malthus thoroughly established the dismal science. When, several generations later, neoclassical theory seemed to open the door, especially through Marshall, Edgeworth, and Pigou, to rational public intervention that would improve resource allocation and income distribution, we were brought up short by the "new" welfare economics. Interpersonal comparisons of utility were shown to be impossible, if not silly, and Pareto Optimality dealt the ultimate blow to any hope that economists might be able to demonstrate effectively that any policy was unequivocally better than no policy at all. Clearly, if the only policy change that can be justified is one that, while helping some, hurts no one, the scope for economic policy is narrow indeed. In came the Bergson-Samuelson social welfare function to the rescue, but Arrow brought up his impossibility theorem and shot this down too.

So we found ourselves prescribing micro policy positions with no really firm grounding for the structure of our theoretical framework. The result is that Henry Simons could justify redistributive taxation only because he saw the existing distribution of income as ugly. And Abba Lerner founded his predilection for redistribution of income on the notion that utility functions were probably randomly distributed among people, rich and poor, so if income were redistributed chances are total utility would increase. It turned out, of course, that only Ken Boulding had the answer—and it was love. If we are in disarray with respect to income redistribution it is because we have never developed the rational foundation for its justification that could come to terms with our basic market paradigm. It is this fact that has always made the liberal position tenuous. That position has now been assailed by the optimal taxationists, as Musgrave points out. But it was always vulnerable and had long been attacked by such as Harley Lutz, Dan Throop Smith, F. A. Hayek, and hosts of others. It just seems more vulnerable now than it did twenty or thirty years ago because it is no longer in tune with the political climate, as it was then.

In intervention with respect to resource allocation and in the matter of attitudes toward the role of government in micro budget issues, Musgrave's "Allocation Branch," the counterinterventionist views of Coase, Buchanan, Friedman, Niskanen, Tullock, Breton, et al. have been around for a long time. They clearly, in at least some of their major manifestations, predate the mid-1950s Musgrave-Samuelson developments. Again, I would say, if they seem to be on the ascendancy now it is not, I think, a consequence of value changes of the past decade. The interventionist theory was never that solid. While perhaps not as weak as the case for redistribution, it was, nevertheless, always on tenuous ground. What gives more currency to the policy implications of the conservative position is not so much a change in the values of economists as a swing in the political pendulum in American society, making for an atmosphere more receptive to that position.

If we look at where we have been in macro or stabilization policy we find once more, I think, that responsibility for changes in policy position lies not so much in a change in the values of economists as in the dominance of the politically feasible over the economically desirable. After all, monetarism is not all that new; even rational expectations go back some distance. We were doing well in the 1950s and 1960s when it was easy to do well. The Korean War may have saved us from a deeper post–World War II recession than the short-lived one of 1949 and, with a few planned fiscal policy adjustments and a more or less benign monetary policy, we averted both deep recessions and inflation while maintaining a very respectable rate of growth through the late 1960s. As economists in 1966 and 1967 we still knew what needed to be done and so testified before anyone who was listening. But the politics of representative government proved too much for a fiscal policy that called loudly and clearly for a major tax increase to pay for an unpopular war. And so what we now call the "underlying" rate of inflation began to grow. By 1970 "fine tuning," one of Walter Heller's well-turned phrases, was well behind the needs of the day. Now we are living what would have seemed to most of us a nightmare a little more than a decade ago—a developing recession accompanied by an inflation rate that promises to sustain itself at about 18 percent for at least a few more months.

What happened to "functional finance"? It has been buried, I believe, by the realities of politics that tell us that it is easy to combat recession and deflation, but that fiscal actions required to counter inflation are never popular and almost never politically acceptable. Too many oxen get gored. Now economists present a dismal picture and much respect for the discipline has been lost. We have turned our backs to the wind; we are not pushing tax increases that will curtail demand. Instead we find increasing support for tax cuts that will have supply-side effects, through providing incentives for saving and investment. But this is not new either. Through the 1950s and 1960s we saw investment incentives pushed through tax cuts costing tens of billions of dollars per year. It is just the circumstances and the pushers that have changed. Much as Musgrave and I may not like the look of impending developments in this area, neither of us is inclined to offer brave new alternatives. And if we were, I do not believe the Congress or the administration would be receptive to them, for it must be onward and upward with more investment to yield more growth.

It is hard to say whether the biggest failure in economic policy has been the failure to implement effective stabilization policy or the building and bursting of the bubble of unrealistic expectations held for the brave new social programs of the 1960s. In desperate efforts to do something about the crisis of the cities, the blight of poverty, the failures of our educational system, and a host of other social maladies, we embarked on the War on Poverty, a war in which we sought to destroy the enemy by throwing money at it. Unfortunately we rarely understood the underlying causes of the maladies we sought to cure and, not surprisingly, while suceeding in spending huge sums of money, we cured almost none of them. The cities are still decaying, many of them increasingly vulnerable to fiscal collapse, twenty-five million people are still poor, gaps between white and black incomes and unemployment rates are as high as ever, and so forth. And again economists, either responsible for or associated with programs that have been widely hailed as costly failures frustrating the expectations of the poor and the underprivileged, are held in low esteem.

For those of us who entered the profession in the thirty years including the mid-1960s there was considerable hope on all sides for implementation of rational, liberal policy in all three of Musgrave's budget branches. What do we tell our students now? For myself, I stopped telling them about the good old days under President John F. Kennedy as soon as I realized that some of them were not even born when Kennedy read his inauguration speech that January.

I have faith in pendulums. I don't think changes described by Musgrave in his paper are, as he would have us believe, a result of changing values among economists. Those who now seem in the saddle, or their forebears, have been ever with us. The temper of the times favors the views they espouse and their turn may have come. Are they really saying very much that wasn't being said in Secretary Mellon's day? It took the Depression, several years of it actually, for the pendulum to swing left, where it stopped for thirty years. As economists holding to the persuasions that dominated policy circles through those years, we were unseated by another swing in the political pendulum, to the right this time. And I find some of my best friends swinging right with it.

Public Regulation Economics Then and Now

FREDERIC M. SCHERER

The study of economic regulation—that is to say, active control by a governmental agency over market occupancy, pricing, and other aspects of private business enterprises' conduct—has consumed an appreciable fraction of scholars' energy since the early days of the University of Michigan's economics department. Michigan's economics faculty played a prominent role in the first identifiable surge of interest during the 1880s. Subsequent activity in the subfield of public regulation economics (or still more narrowly, public utility economics) has waxed and waned in Kondratieff-like cycles of forty to fifty years' duration. Recently the field has been experiencing another robust upswing. This conference, marking a century of economics scholarship at the University of Michigan, seems a fitting occasion for reflecting on where we are now and whence we came. I begin with an impressionistic survey of the current state of the art, loop back to compare how economists viewed the same set of problems during the 1880s, and then conclude by identifying certain continuing lines of tension.

Characteristics of the Recent Upsurge

From my perspective, the recent surge of interest in the economics of regulation has two paramount characteristics. One, in the realm of methodology, has been the triumph of rigorous mathematical methods over what had previously been a preponderantly institutional approach. The other, in the realm of policy, has been the strong and indeed remarkably unified support of economists for deregulation, or the substitution of competitive market forces for government controls as a regulator. The two developments are not unrelated, but let me begin with the former.

Frederic M. Scherer is professor of economics at Northwestern University, received his A.B. from Michigan in 1954, and was a member of the Michigan faculty during 1967–73.

The Mathemetical Analysis of Regulation

Establishing the turning points in cycles is a hazardous business, but I believe the evidence in this case is clear. The key event was the nearly simultaneous publication in late 1962 and early 1963 of articles purporting to show mathematically how the traditional approach to public utility price and profit regulation could induce profit-maximizing regulated firms to make economically inefficient input proportions and scale choices.[1] The essence of their analysis was as follows. When regulating monopolistic public utility corporations, governmental agencies commonly proceed by identifying a "rate base" more or less closely related to the firm's total capital investment. They also estimate a "fair rate of return" approximating (but, at least during the 1950s and 1960s, often exceeding by a small margin) the market cost of capital. They then approve a set of product prices expected, given predicted noncapital costs, to yield a return on capital equaling the "fair rate of return" times the value of the rate base. Averch and Johnson proved that when, under this scheme, the allowed "fair rate of return" exceeded the regulated firm's cost of capital, the firm had an incentive to choose inefficiently capital-intensive modes of production. There would be too much capital used relative to other inputs, and so costs would be driven up, leading to a restriction of output below the level a cost-minimizing but regulated firm would supply. In his parallel article, Wellisz proved that firms regulated in a similar manner, and subject to varying levels of demand at various times of the day or year, would tend to inflate their rate base by building too much peak-load capacity, encourage its utilization by charging inefficiently low prices to peak-time consumers, and make up the difference with high prices to off-peak consumers.

This so-called A-J-W thesis profoundly influenced the economics profession in two ways. First, it showed that regulatory instruments ostensibly designed to protect the public interest might actually serve the public badly by encouraging inefficiently high costs and the misallocation of resources. A rethinking of the relationship between regulation and efficiency was thus called for. Second, it demonstrated that the calculus of constrained maximization and other "advanced" mathematical tools, only beginning at that time to permeate the mainstream of graduate economic theory education, could be applied fruitfully and even excitingly to problems of public utility regulation.[2] Bright young economists began, first in a trickle and then in considerable numbers, to invade the field. So radical has been the transformation of what was once the almost exclusive province of institutionalists that young theorists with much knowledge of mathematics and almost none of the real world now consider public regulation a "fun" area in which to apply their tools. One trained, as I was, in both the old and new schools is unsure whether to applaud or despair.

An early consequence was an outpouring of work extending the original A-J-W results: determining the optimal tradeoff between regulation-induced inefficiency and the misallocation stemming from unfettered monopoly pricing, exploring dynamic ramifications, investigating how the effects might vary for firms maximizing some objective function other than profit, and extending the range of applications.[3] There has also been a fair amount of parallel, but thus far largely inconclusive, statistical research to test whether the A-J-W inefficiencies actually occur in real-world regulated industries.[4]

During the past decade, the application of mathematical methods to regulatory economics has spread to a much wider array of problems. The theory of optimal peak-load pricing, on which an important contribution had already been made in 1957 by Peter Steiner,[5] has been richly developed to cover complications such as uncertain demand and variable technologies (e.g., when electricity is produced using capital-intensive nuclear base-load capacity augmented by fuel-intensive gas turbine peak-load capacity).[6] Much work has been done on the theory of optimal pricing with uncertain demand for both storable and nonstorable commodities. Economists also achieved impressive success addressing the central pricing dilemma of natural monopoly: with long-run marginal costs below average cost, uniform marginal cost pricing leads to losses that may have to be subsidized, possibly inducing other distortions, while average cost pricing that allows the firm to break even is allocatively inefficient. Extending the pioneering "second-best" theorems of Lipsey and Lancaster and especially Boiteux,[7] Baumol and Bradford formulated the natural monopoly regulation problem as one of securing a set of discriminatory prices that maximizes consumers' surplus, subject to a constraint requiring prices high enough for the firm to break even.[8] They obtained the remarkable result that prices to diverse customer classes should be elevated above marginal costs more, the less price-elastic the demand of a customer class is. The result is remarkable both for its

simplicity and because it provides, from the theory of welfare economics, support for a pricing practice public utility industries had long
accepted and advocated—charging what the traffic will bear.[9]

Professor Baumol has also played an influential role in reinter-
preting what "natural monopoly" means when the regulated enterprise supplies multiple products.[10] Out of this work came elegant
mathematical theorems on the question of "sustainability"—that is,
whether there is any set of prices a regulated multiproduct natural
monopolist can charge to ensure that, absent regulatory inhibitions
on entry, the monopolist's domain will not be invaded by "cream-
skimming" competitors. There followed a still more remarkable result: discriminatory prices satisfying the Baumol-Bradford-Ramsey
constrained welfare maximization criterion will often do the job! In
this result, Baumol et al. have discovered the regulated industry counterpart of Adam Smith's invisible hand. By serving the interests of
society, the regulated monopoly also serves its own, protecting itself
from competitive entry.[11]

While some economists were studying how regulated natural
monopolists could defend themselves against potential competitors,
others were exploring how competition and regulation interacted and
how that interaction affected performance. There have been several
different thrusts, most of them less rigorous mathematically than the
developments surveyed thus far. One focused on the problem of in-
termodal competition—e.g., how Interstate Commerce Commission
(ICC) regulation of rates charged by such competing modes as rail
and truck affected shippers' modal choices. In a pioneering statistical
study, Meyer et al. found substantial resource misallocations as a result of ICC rules.[12] Second, it has been recognized that government
regulation often creates potentially profitable monopoly franchises for
which entrepreneurs may compete, in the process wastefully expend-
ing resources on legal fees, preemptive investment, and the like. This
is the subject of what is now called the theory of rent-seeking.[13] Third,
the relationships between monopoly, competition, regulation, and
product "quality" have been extensively investigated. Work blending
theory and statistical methods showed with unusual clarity that long-
haul rates under the existing system of airline rate regulation stimulated vigorous "service" competition, leading to a frequency of flight
schedules that overstepped the optimal balance between operating cost
and traveler inconvenience costs.[14] Other work in the same vein sug-

gested that regulated competition in the television industry yielded too little programming variety.[15] Encouraged in part by the theoretical and empirical findings from regulated industry studies, but partly simply because the time was ripe, there has been in the past decade a proliferation of research on "monopolistic competition," and specifically, on the blend of monopoly and competition that provides the socially optimal amount of product variety, quality, and durability.[16] The normative implications thus far are largely cautionary: neither free competition nor regulation necessarily leads to the "right" amount of quality.

One further development, although somewhat outside the mainstream of economics, deserves mention. During the past twenty years there have been impressive advances in the theory of how capital markets evaluate risk in determining a firm's cost of capital.[17] These have seen considerable application in regulated industries as regulators have sought to ascertain with greater precision the "fair rate of return" they would apply to their regulatees' rate bases. Although this must undoubtedly be counted as progress, it is not without an element of paradox. For one of the most surprising implications of the Averch-Johnson theory is that the closer the allowed rate of return comes to the regulated firm's cost of capital, the larger will be the resulting distortions in capital intensity choices.[18] In other words, the better job regulators do in setting the rate of return, the more inefficiency they encourage!

Growing Skepticism and the Campaign for Deregulation

An inescapable message emanating from the vast amount of theoretical and statistical work on regulation during the 1960s and 1970s was that regulation could under many circumstances lead to deficient economic performance and might even make things worse than they would be without regulation. This had much to do with economists' growing disenchantment over existing regulatory institutions.

Another quite different strain of scholarship also had an impact. One important event was the nearly simultaneous publication of three "revisionist" histories of early federal railroad regulation.[19] The authors of all three observed that railroad company leaders were distressed over the "rate wars" occurring among competing lines during the 1870s and 1880s. Price wars were often touched off by secret rate concessions to large shippers, and secrecy made it difficult to enforce cartel agreements. Railroad men recognized that the elimination of secrecy could help solve their problem. They lobbied Congress to include stringent advance notification and publicity provisions governing rate changes in the draft bill to regulate railroads, and having succeeded, they supported passage of the Interstate Commerce Act of 1887. The tactic worked. MacAvoy documents that, for at least a while, secret rate cutting nearly vanished and railroad profits rose. The implication was clear. The Interstate Commerce Commission, praised by generations of public regulation economists as the prototype of enlightened regulation in the public interest,[20] had in fact been "captured" by the regulatees even before its inception.

From this "capture" theory of regulation, originally articulated by political scientists and supported by the revisionist economists' studies of the ICC, it was but a short step to the new "Chicago School" theory of regulatory economics and politics.[21] This theory says in effect that regulation occurs because there are well-organized vested interests expecting to benefit. It goes on to observe that producers subjected to regulation are usually better organized and more able to manipulate political levers than consumers. Therefore, the principal beneficiaries of much regulation are said to be the regulated producers, not consumers and not in any clear sense of the word "the public."

I have painted a one-sided picture in the last three paragraphs because I believe it is the picture most professional economists, and especially the younger ones, have seen. The result has been an extraordinary degree of unanimity among economists in favor of deregulation. Like all movements, this one has its coattail-hangers and opportunists who have found the deregulation theme a lucrative magnet for research and institutional support funds. But the main manifestation has been an outpouring of solid research and effective advocacy. I believe economists can claim much of the credit for airline deregulation. We played a smaller but not insignificant role in the less dramatic steps toward deregulation of communications, railroading, trucking, natural gas, and (still less) securities markets. Our efforts have been far from uniformly successful. There are both compelling rationales and (not necessarily consistent) strong political pressures favoring many kinds of regulation, and one might say that for every element of regulation struck down recently, seven new ones have appeared. It remains also to be seen how correct our view of the alternatives to regulation has been—whether, for example, the quality and availability of airline, trucking, and rail service will not deteriorate after the transition to deregulation has been completed. I, for one, look forward with some apprehension to what events will reveal. Yet I am prepared to call the 1970s, at least from the perspective of economists interested in industrial affairs, the decade of deregulation.

Economists and Regulation in the Late Nineteenth Century

If the 1970s were the decade of deregulation for the economics profession, the 1880s were the decade of regulation. Economic regulation was scarcely new. Americans have always had "the governmental habit," as my colleague Professor Hughes calls it.[22] Our founding fathers, who carried the habit with them from postfeudal Europe, regulated the prices and service conditions of toll roads, bridges, inns, public warehouses and markets, bakeries, breweries, and much else. But the nature of the problem began to change as the nineteenth century moved toward its final years. Until then, the scale of the business ventures regulated was characteristically small, and traditional local governmental institutions were relied upon to exercise the desired control. Then a series of technological changes altered both the scale and character of business-government relations. This occurred first with the railroads, leading in 1871 to the first state railroad regulatory commissions with power to control maximum rates. Next came such important developments as the distribution of artificial gas for lighting (in the early 1870s), central electric power and light systems (circa 1885), and the electric traction street railway (1888). Local governments, it was widely acknowledged, were unable to cope with these new forms of private enterprise.

Economists took notice too. They perceived that competition could not be counted upon to effectively regulate the performance of enterprises whose monopolistic position was attributable more to the technological imperatives of large-scale, capital-intensive operation than to the governmental franchise grants blamed for market failures by Adam Smith and his followers. A leader in this new American school of economists was Henry Carter Adams, who was the University of Michigan's first specialist in economics. In 1887, in an influential paper published in the first volume of the American Economic Association's proceedings, Adams offered both a rigorous definition of natural monopoly and a coherent principle to guide public intervention.[23] A natural monopoly, he said, was an enterprise that conformed "with any degree of intensity" to the law of increasing returns to scale—i.e., when a doubling of inputs leads to more than a doubling of outputs.[24] Where an industry's technology mandates natural monopoly, Adams argued, "the principle of free competition is powerless to exercise a healthy regulating influence."[25] If his analysis were correct, he continued, it was clear where the line demarcating the proper realm of state intervention lay: "The control of the state over industries should be co-extensive with the application of the law of increasing returns in industries" (p. 524)—i.e., with the existence of natural monopoly.

In expressing these views, Henry Carter Adams was no voice crying in the wilderness. Rather, he was mainstream new American economics. The volume in which his "State and Industrial Action" paper appears also contains the minutes of the meeting at which the American Economic Association was founded. With Richard T. Ely, Adams was a principal cofounder. He chaired its organizational meeting and was elected its first vice president. The founding economists' beliefs about industrial problems of the time were reflected in the first plank of a platform drafted by Professor Ely.

> 1. We regard the state as an educational and ethical agency whose positive aid is an indispensable condition of human progress. While we recognize the necessity of individual initiative in industrial life, we hold that the doctrine of *laissez-faire* is unsafe in politics and unsound in morals. . . .[26]

To this position Adams was not unsympathetic philosophically. Nevertheless, as the first recorded speaker after Ely, he suggested that it be amended because it might be misinterpreted to imply lack of appreciation for the work of earlier economists or endorsement of a German statist philosophy. Therefore, the criticism of laissez-faire was deleted and other language was softened. Yet the platform adopted continued to speak of the state as an indispensable contributor to progress, to note the "vast number of social problems" stemming from conflict between labor and capital, and to urge an open-minded but progressive development of economic conditions and legislative policy.

There were other reasons why, in the view of the American Economic Association's founders, markets could fail and public intervention might be appropriate. Many believed that competition could be excessive or ruinous as well as deficient, or that, especially in naturally monopolistic industries, it could oscillate between those two extremes in a wasteful manner. Professor Adams's main concern, as articulated in his 1887 paper, was with the competition that drove wages and working conditions to the unacceptably low common denominator imposed by the most unscrupulous employer.[27] Product quality might similarly suffer, he argued, although he admitted exceptions.[28] His description of excess capacity among cartelized Buffalo grain elevators reveals a keen understanding of how the competition for a monopoly position (in modern jargon, rent-seeking) could lead to substantial waste.[29] Similarly, Professor Edmund James of the Wharton School, second vice president of the infant American Economic Association, observed that in the naturally monopolistic municipal gas supply industry, high prices charged by an incumbent firm tended to attract competitive entry, precipitating a rate war which was followed by merger or a territorial agreement under which "two supply the market at greater cost than the one, and the additional cost is paid by the public."[30] The only acceptable solution, James concluded, was to grant gas companies a monopoly in the territory they supplied and then to implement a system of regulation that would "prevent such shameful exploitation of consumers . . . and such shameful waste of capital."[31] The belief that competition could be excessive in natural monopolies was also not unique to early American Economic Association (AEA) joiners. Professor Hadley of Yale, the leading authority on railroad economics, whose name is conspicuously absent from the 1886 list of AEA members, wrote in 1889 that in the absence of pooling agreements, rates would be set by "the most reckless manager. . . . Under such circumstances," he continued, "the question of protecting railroad investors becomes a matter of the highest practical moment."[32]

Given their concern about the dangers of ruinous competition, scholars of that earlier era could hardly have viewed the tendency for rate wars to be discouraged under the Interstate Commerce Act's provisions with the alarm of modern revisionists. To Professor Hadley, what happened was certainly no revelation. In what must have been the first evaluation of the act's implementation published in a professional economics journal, he observed that the act's provisions against secret discriminatory rate cuts were opposed by no railroad managers and welcomed by the most intelligent of them.[33] "When the Act was first passed," he went on, "the railroads made a strong and, on the whole, surprisingly successful effort to do away with personal discrimination in some of its worst forms. . . . Direct, personal discrimination in rates almost ceased."[34]

Economists of the 1880s might have been surprised by the conclusions of our modern "capture theory" revisionists, but only for their historical naiveté. They knew about the pervasive corruption of regulators and legislators. James put it graphically:

> The revelations in the reports of the New York Senate Committee of Investigation are sufficient to convince any but the most obstinate or stupid that the mere fact the gas business is in the hands of private companies, does not guarantee that it is therefore no force in city politics. . . . [Nor does a gas company] confine itself to gas questions and leave other questions alone. . . . The gas company can always be relied upon to assist the water company, for example, in all attempts to resist the law and plunder the public. . . . Our American communities are ordinarily delivered bound hand and foot into the power of the enemy where gas and water companies manage to unite with . . . the industrial and commercial monopolies . . . in our midst.[35]

The real problem, as the AEA founders saw it, was not that governments were corruptible, but that business interests saw to it that corruptible governments were installed. One of the three main evils of a strict laissez-faire policy, Professor Adams wrote, was its insistence that public power be restricted within the narrowest possible limits. "Public corruption . . . is no accident. It is the necessary result of the idea that the best thing to do with a public official is to lay him on the shelf out of harm's way."[36] The solution in their view, characteristic of the late-nineteenth-century progressives, was not to abandon hope of regulating business effectively, but to strengthen the government so it could do the job it had to do. To them, I suspect, the Interstate Commerce Commission represented an ideal opportunity to achieve meaningful reform. Professor Adams believed sufficiently in its prospects that he served part time as its chief statistician from 1887 to 1911. In hindsight, one is forced to conclude that he too was excessively naive, for the reform, if achieved at all, did not endure. If he were here today, he would probably be sadder than any of us and wonder if there is any hope for America. With the background of his postgraduate days in Germany leavened by continued observation, he would know that it *is* possible to have a competent and honest, even if occasionally petty, civil service. And he would undoubtedly be wiser than I in proposing a remedy to rescue the American political and regulatory system.

It hardly needs to be said that the views of economists in the 1880s were formulated with little recourse to the mathematical methods distinguishing modern regulatory economics. To be sure, Professor Adams's statement of the principle of increasing returns was given in the same algebraic form that many modern price theory textbooks use. Professor Hadley's 1886 book, *Railroad Transportation* (New York and London: Putnam's) contains an appendix using calculus to show that the profit-maximizing freight rate for a commodity varies with what we would now call the elasticity of demand. And on pages 76 and 77, there is a discussion of how value of service pricing can combine with a farsighted policy of keeping rates low enough to discourage new entry, thereby giving the public "the benefits of competition without its disadvantages." It is remarkably prescient of the Baumol-Bailey-Willig "weak invisible hand" sustainability argument. But one should not push such comparisons too far. Mathematical analysis was not the strong suit of our forefathers a century ago. Since then, there have been vast gains in the clarity and precision of our insight into the problems of regulated monopoly.

Another noticeable difference between then and now was the much greater openness of 1880s economists toward solving the problem of natural monopoly through government ownership. The early volumes of the American Economic Association's publications contain well-balanced analyses of the pros and cons.[37] Today in America, those who study public enterprise are a small and lonely group. The explanation appears to be the same one that economists emphasized nearly a century ago: American governmental entities seem incapable of managing a complex enterprise competently and honestly. Now, as then, European governments do the job much more successfully in their more extensive array of public enterprises.[38] Again, if he were here, Professor Adams might be able to tell us why our governmental entities are so inept.

Perhaps the most striking difference of all concerns the views of what it is that public agencies regulating monopolies, natural or unnatural, are supposed to be accomplishing. The founding fathers of the American Economic Association knew what they wanted—fairness, prevention of monopolistic exploitation of consumers, and the just price. Should this seem unduly vague, they were willing to elaborate. To Henry Carter Adams, for example, a public utility ought to operate at the lowest price consistent with efficient service, and this meant the absence of excessive profits, and managerial salaries exceeding those that would be paid under competition for services of the same grade.[39] To a modern regulatory economist, "fairness" is less attractive as a criterion because it is much less certain how one measures or defines it without making value judgments that economists have been trained to shun as unscientific or undemocratic. Instead, the emphasis is first, foremost, and virtually exclusively on efficiency. This frequently leaves economists vulnerable to the criticism that we spend our time worrying about rather unimportant things, for most statistical studies show the "deadweight loss" triangles attributable to monopolistic pricing to be quite small—not much more than 1 or 2 percent of gross national product.[40] Students of regulatory economics can take some solace from evidence that the inefficiencies resulting from clumsy regulatory rate setting—e.g., because of Averch-Johnson-Wellisz effects or the distortion of rail-truck modal splits[41]—could at least in principle be much larger. Even if we moderns are right in our emphasis, which is less than certain, it would be inappropriate to criticize the 1880s economists for their differing views. The notion of the deadweight loss attributable to distorted pricing did not enter the mainstream of Anglo-American economics until 1890, when the first edition of Marshall's *Principles* was published.[42] For understandable reasons, then, there is a sizable gap in views about what regulation is supposed to accomplish.

The Continuing Tension: Second-Best versus Third-Best
All this has, I believe, much to do with the differing policy emphases between economists of the 1880s and those of the 1970s, and also with the differences among economists of diverse persuasion today. By 1887, it was clear that industry conditions conducive to natural monopoly made it impossible to secure what we would now call a first-best competitive solution. The question was, what to put in its place? The logic of second-best—maximizing efficiency subject to the condition that the public utility firm break even—was unknown to scholars of that era. The choice then had to be among third-best policies.[43] One was simply letting the market muddle through unfettered,

which to the vanguard of 1880s American economists was plainly unsatisfactory. The only remaining alternative (other than government enterprise) was regulation, and it was accepted. It was recognized that maintaining incentives for what we now call X-efficiency under regulation would not be easy. Yet there was optimism that the problems could be solved, and it was at least thought that the X-inefficiencies resulting from monopoly rent-seeking and overcapitalization could be reduced. The allocative distortions which regulation might induce were unknown. And regulation went far toward solving the most blatant inequities arising under natural monopoly—a consequence to which our forefathers attached considerable weight.

A century later, we have better theory, we know more about the distortions that regulation itself can cause, the economy in which regulation must function is more complex, and the choice is harder. First-best is still unattainable in many industries. Government enterprise tends to be ruled out because we have not discovered how to sustain incentives for bureaucratic efficiency. At least for industries with a tendency toward natural monopoly, the feasible policy choice is reduced to that between regulation or deregulation.

Now, however, the arsenal of regulatory instruments is better stocked. We know about second-best, and we have made a good deal of progress toward developing the theory relevant to squeezing as much allocative efficiency as possible out of an inherently imperfect situation. I confess to some puzzlement at the vigor with which those instruments have been shaped in what I have called the decade of deregulation, when, one might suppose, the need might be considered less pressing. The key remaining question is, can our regulatory agencies amass the skill, information, and sense of mission needed to impose second-best pricing policies on the naturally monopolistic enterprises with whose oversight they have been charged? I for one am skeptical. Getting regulators who are competent and well-motivated continues to be difficult. Information remains a critical problem. How, for instance, will regulators determine the demand elasticities and (when relevant) cross elasticities needed to enforce Baumol-Bradford-Ramsey prices?[44] Without the requisite information and competence, the best one can expect is third-best—a rough equating of revenues with costs and a crude approximation to an efficient price structure. And matters could be worse. If A-J-W or similar biases induced by regulatory instruments intrude, the pricing efficiency attained under even the most successful second-best approach might be frittered away by other allocative and X-inefficiencies.

The other main alternative is deregulation (or resisting the temptation to begin regulating). When an industry tends toward natural monopoly or perhaps even natural oligopoly, this is admittedly a third-best approach. We know, however, that except when barriers to competitive entry are very high, the allocative inefficiencies attributable to monopoly pricing are modest. If we then accept efficiency as our paramount goal, there is much to be said for letting the market work, and indeed helping it work as well as possible by ensuring that barriers to entry (stemming either from governmental action or the conduct of incumbent firms) are kept as low as possible. I would not suggest that this is the proper solution for all traditionally regulated industries. Among other things, a strong public preference for equity and "just" prices over efficiency could lead to its rejection. Such a preference, I believe, underlay much of recent United States energy price policy, and it continues to be evident even as gas and oil price deregulation proceeds. Among economists, however, there appears to be something approaching a consensus favoring third-best policies combining a minimum of regulation with as much competition as scale economies allow. In this respect, we have departed far from the views of the American Economic Association's founders.

NOTES

I am indebted to Gerald Goldstein and Ronald Braeutigam for valuable suggestions.

1. Harvey Averch and Leland L. Johnson, "Behavior of the Firm under Regulatory Constraint," *American Economic Review*, December 1962, pp. 1052–69; Stanislaw H. Wellisz, "Regulation of Natural Gas Pipeline Companies: An Economic Analysis," *Journal of Political Economy*, February 1963, pp. 30–43.
2. Harvard—to be sure, no leader in the pedagogy of economic theory—first imposed a requirement of mathematical training including constrained maximization in 1962.
3. For a survey, see Elizabeth Bailey, *Economic Theory of Regulatory Constraint* (Lexington: Lexington Books, 1973).
4. For surveys of the literature, see Paul M. Hayashi and John M. Trapani, "Rate of Return Regulation and the Regulated Firm's Choice of Capital-Labor Ratio," *Southern Economic Journal*, January 1976, pp. 384–98; and

Derek McKay, "Has the A-J Effect Been Empirically Verified?" Social Science Working Paper No. 132, California Institute of Technology, 1976.

5. Peter O. Steiner, "Peak Loads and Efficient Pricing," *Quarterly Journal of Economics*, November 1957, pp. 585–610.

6. See the symposium on peak-load pricing in the *Bell Journal of Economics*, Spring 1976, pp. 197–250.

7. R. G. Lipsey and Kelvin Lancaster, "The General Theory of Second Best," *Review of Economic Studies* 24, no. 1 (1956): 11–32; and Marcel Boiteux, "Sur la gestion des monopoles publics astreints à l'équilibre budgétaire," *Econometrica*, January 1956, pp. 22–40.

8. William J. Baumol and David Bradford, "Optimal Departures from Marginal Cost Pricing," *American Economic Review*, June 1970, pp. 265–83. As Baumol and Bradford point out, their paper had many antecedents, among which that of Frank Ramsey, "A Contribution to the Theory of Taxation," *Economic Journal*, March 1927, pp. 47–61, is so prominent that economists often speak of Ramsey-Baumol-Bradford pricing rules.

9. As in other cases of third-degree price discrimination, the simplicity fades when there are interaction effects—e.g., in the form of finite demand cross elasticities—among the demand classes.

10. See William J. Baumol, "The Proper Cost Tests for Natural Molopoly in a Multiproduct Industry," *American Economic Review*, December 1977, pp. 809–22; and John C. Panzar and Robert Willig, "Free Entry and the Sustainability of Natural Monopoly," *Bell Journal of Economics*, Spring 1977, pp. 1–22.

11. William J. Baumol, Elizabeth Bailey, and Robert D. Willig, "Weak Invisible Hand Theorems on Pricing and Entry in a Multiproduct Natural Monopoly," *American Economic Review*, June 1977, pp. 350–65.

12. John R. Meyer, M. J. Peck, John Stenason, and Charles Zwick, *The Economics of Competition in the Transportation Industries* (Cambridge, Mass.: Harvard University Press, 1959). The latest and theoretically best-grounded contribution in the extensive literature that followed is Ronald R. Braeutigam and Roger G. Noll, "The Regulation of Surface Freight Transportation: The Welfare Effects Revisited," California Institute of Technology working paper.

13. Early contributions were Gordon Tullock, "The Welfare Costs of Tariffs, Monopolies, and Theft," *Western Economic Journal*, June 1967, pp. 224–32; and Richard A. Posner, "The Social Costs of Monopoly and Regulation," *Journal of Political Economy*, August 1975, pp. 807–27.

14. See, especially, George W. Douglas and James C. Miller III, *Economic Regulation of Domestic Air Transport* (Washington, D.C.: Brookings Institution, 1974), chaps. 6 and 7; and George C. Eads, "Competition in the Domestic Trunk Airline Industry," in *Promoting Competition in Regulated Markets,* ed. Almarin Phillips (Washington, D.C.: Brookings Institution, 1975), pp. 16–39.

15. See, for example, Roger Noll, M. J. Peck, and John McGowan, *Economic Aspects of Television Regulation* (Washington, D.C.: Brookings Institu-

tion, 1973); and Michael Spence and Bruce Owen, "Television Programming, Monopolistic Competition, and Welfare," *Quarterly Journal of Economics*, February 1977, pp. 103–26.

16. The literature is enormous. For citations, see the revised edition of F. M. Scherer, *Industrial Market Structure and Economic Performance* (Chicago: Rand McNally, 1980), pp. 258–61 and 394–403. Hindsight suggests that Michigan's Fred M. Taylor may have been right when he advised Edward Chamberlin to work on a dissertation topic other than monopolistic competition, which Taylor considered too intractable. The theoretical tools needed to cope successfully with the problem have only been worked out recently, a half-century later. See Chamberlin, "The Origin and Early Development of Monopolistic Competition Theory," *Quarterly Journal of Economics*, November 1961, pp. 519–20.

17. For a survey, see Michael Jensen, "Capital Markets: Theory and Evidence," *Bell Journal of Economics and Management Science*, Autumn 1972, pp. 357–98.

18. See the first edition of my *Industrial Market Structure and Economic Performance* (Chicago: Rand McNally, 1970), pp. 533 and 552–55; and William J. Baumol and Alvin Klevorick, "Input Choices and Rate-of-Return Regulation," *Bell Journal of Economics and Management Science*, Autumn 1970, pp. 162–76.

19. See Gabriel Kolko, *Railroads and Regulation, 1877–1916* (Princeton: Princeton University Press, 1965); Paul W. MacAvoy, *The Economic Effects of Regulation: The Trunkline Railroad Cartels and the Interstate Commerce Commission Before 1900* (Cambridge, Mass.: MIT Press, 1965); and George W. Hilton, "The Consistency of the Interstate Commerce Act," *Journal of Law and Economics*, October 1966, pp. 87–113.

20. This was certainly the view of Professor Sharfman, dean of public regulation economists during the 1930s and 1940s. Thus, the last sentence of his monumental work concludes: "The Interstate Commerce Commission has achieved a high degree of effectiveness in its own sphere and has contributed substantially to the development of the general essentials of sound regulatory practice." (I. Leo Sharfman, *The Interstate Commerce Commission*, 5 vols. [Commonwealth Fund, 1931, 1937], 4:388.) That is also the impression I retain from having been a student in Professor Sharfman's last course on regulation during the 1953–54 academic year. Sharfman discusses at length the opposition to pooling (i.e., the epitome of cartelization) under the act, but deals only casually with the notice provisions, their enforcement, and their economic effects. See *The Interstate Commerce Commission*, 1:17 and 23, and 3A:83.

21. See George J. Stigler, "The Theory of Economic Regulation," *Bell Journal of Economics and Management Science*, Spring 1971, pp. 3–21; Richard A. Posner, "Theories of Economic Regulation," *Bell Journal of Economics and Management Science*, Autumn 1974, pp. 335–58; and Sam Peltzman, "Toward a More General Theory of Regulation," *Journal of Law and Economics*, August 1976, pp. 211–40.

22. Jonathan R. T. Hughes, *The Governmental Habit: Economic Controls from Colonial Times to the Present* (New York: Basic Books, 1977), especially chap. 2.
23. H. C. Adams, "Relation of the State to Industrial Action," *Publications of the American Economic Association* 1 (January 1887):495–528, especially.
24. Ibid., pp. 523–24. Compare Arthur T. Hadley's much clumsier 1886 definition: "A natural monopoly is where competition is physically impossible." *Railroad Transportation* (New York and London: Putnam's, 1886), p. 64. Cf. Richard T. Ely, *Monopolies and Trusts* (New York: Macmillan, 1912), pp. 59–60, who cites Adams's paper as the still seminal definition of natural monopoly.
25. Adams, "Relation of the State to Industrial Action," p. 524.
26. *Publications of the American Economic Association* 1 (1886):6–7.
27. Adams, "Relation of the State to Industrial Action," pp. 502–11. For expressing his views on labor in 1886, Adams lost his professorship at Cornell.
28. Ibid., pp. 503–4.
29. Ibid., pp. 482–83.
30. "The Relation of the Modern Municipality to the Gas Supply," *Publications of the American Economic Association* 1 (1886):75–78.
31. Ibid., pp. 115–16.
32. Arthur Hadley, "Railroad Business under the Interstate Commerce Act," *Quarterly Journal of Economics*, January 1889, p. 177. Hadley, unlike the AEA founders, was skeptical of regulation as a solution. See for example his perceptive analysis of the near impossibility of setting "reasonable rates" by commission in *Railroad Transportation*, pp. 143–44.
33. Arthur T. Hadley, "The Workings of the Interstate Commerce Law," *Quarterly Journal of Economics*, January 1888, p. 163.
34. Ibid., p. 170. Or at p. 184: "One thing they [the railroad men] knew,— that they were tired of fighting, and were glad to make the law for the time being a pretext for the cessation of rate wars."
35. "The Relation of the Modern Municipality to the Gas Supply," pp. 92–93.
36. Adams, "Relation of the State to Industrial Action," pp. 528–29 and 539. For a similar view twenty years later, see the report to the National Civic Federation of the Commission on Public Ownership and Operation, *Municipal and Private Operation of Public Utilities* (New York: National Civic Federation, 1907), 1:38–39. Members of the commission included such business leaders as Samuel Insull and V. Everit Macy as well as economists John R. Commons and Jeremiah Jenks.
37. See the report of the AEA committee on municipal government and public works in *Publications of the American Economic Association* 2 (1888):501–81. It was chaired by Professor Adams.
38. Compare the views of the 1888 Adams committee; the 1907 National Civic Federation transnational study of *Municipal and Private Operation of Public Utilities*; and Juergen Mueller and Ingo Vogelsang, *Staatliche Regulierung* (Nomos, 1979), especially chaps. 7 and 8.

39. Adams, "Relation of the State to Industrial Action," pp. 514 and 527–28. In "Municipal Government and Public Works," *AEA Publications* 2:531–32, he recognized that an arbitrary legal ceiling on dividends could impair incentives for efficiency.

40. See the second edition of my *Industrial Market Structure and Economic Performance*, pp. 459–64.

41. See the first edition of *Industrial Market Structure and Economic Performance*, pp. 531–33 and 540. Compare Braeutigam and Noll, "The Regulation of Surface Freight Transportation," who find earlier loss estimates to be biased.

42. Alfred Marshall, *Principles of Economics* (London: Macmillan and Co., 1890), p. 447 n. 1. An obscure English-language precursor was Fleeming Jenkin, "On the Principles Which Regulate the Incidence of Taxes," originally published in 1871, reprinted in Richard Musgrave and Carl Shoup, eds., *Readings in the Economics of Taxation* (Homewood, Ill.: American Economic Association, 1959), pp. 227 and 233.

43. On the logic of second-best and third-best policies, see the second (i.e., first-best) edition of my *Industrial Market Structure and Economic Performance*, pp. 24–28.

44. On the information problem, see my "Statistics for Governmental Regulation," *American Statistician*, February 1979, pp. 1–5.

Comments by SHOREY PETERSON

The century we are celebrating was 40 percent gone when I arrived in Ann Arbor as a graduate student in 1920. I should perhaps recall the passing of that period during which—according to Mike Scherer—utilities and regulation had been "the almost exclusive province of institutionalists." I do not, and perhaps Scherer and I use the word "institutionalist" differently, since there was then a school of economists who bore that name. Veblen stood out. We at Michigan were students of Fred M. Taylor, a leading neoclassicist, and were inclined to look down on people we thought less analytical. Some of us, including Ben Lewis and me, worked closely with I. Leo Sharfman; and as we turned from Freddie Taylor to Leo Sharfman, we felt no break in theory or in analytical approach. Taylor used hypotheses

Editor's Note. Professor Peterson retired from the Michigan faculty in 1967 and remained in close contact with the department until his death in June, 1981. He never lost his interest in economic scholarship, especially in his own area of industrial organization. The comments published here were edited from a personal communication which he sent to F. M. Scherer several months after the centennial symposium.

extensively, told us why, and explained their dangers; Sharfman was down to earth in dealing with regulated industries, and institutions were among the phenomena that were considered. The basic problem of regulation was one of devising procedures which would yield results close to those of competitive markets, as we understood them. The market simulation involved in applying the idea of "fair return on a fair value of the property" was not easy to work out. How does land value enter the rate base in railroad regulation when it is due to the presence of railroads? Ben Lewis wrote his thesis on a piece of the problem, the place of "going value" in the rate base. So I am startled a bit when Scherer mentions the recent "triumph of rigorous mathematical methods over what had previously been a preponderantly institutional approach." Half a century ago we thought we were becoming good neoclassical economists working properly in one of the applied fields.

As to the mathematical part of rigor, we would have thought it just an extension of the logic we employed. Now I might add that if the user got off the track in order to be mathematical, the rigor would vanish. Scherer recognizes the danger, at least for "bright young economists . . . with much knowledge of mathematics and almost none of the real world," who find "regulation a 'fun' area in which to apply their tools." I might add, as an outsider, that rigor in handling the model is for the technician; that for the economist it lies more in the fit of the model to reality and in the adaptation of method to the purpose of the analysis, which should not lie in the exercising of tools. Even within the clear province of mathematics, I have long wondered how assured we should be that seemingly precise results represent good thinking. I raised this question once with a professor of aeronautical engineering; and he said that when he wanted to give a really tough examination in a mathematical course of his, he required that students use words only in their answers.

Perhaps the most striking thing Scherer says about the "modern regulatory economists" is that in their work they decided to change the objective of regulative policy. He says of the "founding fathers" — of the American Economic Association, that is — that to them the goal in regulating utilities was "fairness, prevention of monopolistic exploitation of consumers, and the just price." In context the statement is acceptable, but these recent scholars did not find it "attractive," so they changed it. Such ideas as "fairness" got them into "value judgments," and these were likely to be "unscientific or undemocratic." Anyway, I take it, they preferred to work with the concept of the efficient market and to consider the effect of regulation on the efficiency of resource use. They sensed the presence of "inefficiencies resulting from clumsy regulatory rate setting," and this area is what they would investigate. It would be interesting to compare such inefficiencies with those from unfettered monopoly; and their inquiry would get them into the policy area, perhaps in supporting the move toward deregulation. With it there might even be "substitution of competitive market forces for government controls as a regulator." Scherer reports the "remarkably unified support of economists for deregulation." I marvel even more at these "modern regulatory economists." For purposes of their research they not only change retroactively the purpose of regulation; they also remove the reason for it, since only by eliminating natural monopoly, which had the honor, could they have competition as the regulator. And their activities influence economists!

This may be caricature, and it may be unfair to Scherer since he did not write his centennial piece with such handling in mind. But when he suggests that good thinking triumphed in analysis of utility regulation with the coming of these mathematical people, I must recall what went on before and remark that his *reservations* about the triumph are what seem most persuasive. I wouldn't have thought it possible for scholars to transform a policy to fit their preferred analysis of it had I not attended a conference some years back at which it happened. Some lawyers and economists joined to appraise experience under the securities laws and the Securities and Exchange Commission, and the papers of economists dealt almost entirely with the bearing of policy on the efficiency of the securities markets in the allocation sense. To the older of us, the reports of Senate hearings were still echoing, and the graphic reports of scandals and chicanery, and Congress enacted laws, mainly of the "full disclosure" sort, to clean up the markets. Appraisal that dealt with the essential policy would focus on the cleaning up. It might look also for dubious side effects. Those who administer policy can be overzealous or unwise, and Congress may be also. Whether or not these participants were in this case, they at least did not convert the problem from skulduggery into misallocation.

Is it not in the area of side effects that the modern economists have done most of their work on regulation? Permitting a return on too much capital, the usual example, is not so much a weakness of regulation in protecting customers, as wastefulness in the process of doing so. This waste, I infer, may lie either in a wrong proportion of capital to other factors or in unwarranted addition to capacity. Discovery and analysis of such side effects is a useful pursuit in economics as in medicine; but it should be seen for what it is. In neither discipline do practitioners throw good treatments out because of side effects unless they are serious and ineradicable; and if the analyst is making a case for action, he must look into both of these dimensions of performance. Allowing a return on capital that is excessive seems a correctible mistake, and legislative bodies should watch their agents. Whether inducing or permitting excessive use of capital by utility companies is an actual condition, I do not know; but I would think that much work beyond inferences from models would be needed in showing it. There may have been such work. The low ratio of labor to capital in power plants may have reasons beside economy and operability by supervisory personnel in time of strike. The large shift from labor to capital in telephone exchanges could have an explanation beside lower cost and better service. If excessive use of capital means excess capacity, a crucial factor is an acceptable standard of needed reserve capacity. Does this require an index of toleration for blackouts and brownouts? Having just gone through four days without electricity, I'll testify. A long observed feature of the reserve problem is the ratio of peak to average use, and rates may enter here. The worst side effect, it has seemed to me, is a possible dampening of progress. Why spend money on research and development, why install better equipment, if rate cuts will parallel cost reduction? But there is progress, due largely, I suspect, to the fact that regulation is loose and slow. And of course that better equipment comes from unregulated firms, and they have good salesmen. And if the modern economists are developing cures for the defects they find, they too should remember that regulation is loose and slow. And though the point is plain, some of them, I am persuaded, should repeat the refrain: these matters bear not on the need for regulation, nor whether it meets the need.

Scherer makes deregulation a part of this new era of analysis. I'll comment a little on the basis of early experience and casual observation, trying to relate deregulation to the policy it seems to reverse. That policy was well rooted. Leo Sharfman connected it with the old doctrine of businesses "affected with a public interest" because the customer was peculiarly dependent on a particular supplier and might be exploited. Common law imposed special obligations on such sellers: to serve, to serve well, to charge reasonably. In the much later period when our Supreme Court found many kinds of intervention unacceptable, it accepted quite drastic control in such cases of special dependence. In the modern setting the cases appeared most clearly in production processes where producers attached customers to them physically by means of wires, pipes, and tracks. The odd label "public utility" came into use. My residence is thus attached to Detroit Edison, Michigan Consolidated Gas, and Michigan Bell. Products are important; my dependence complete. If these firms overcharge me, I may use less of their products, and I may have either more or less to spend on other products, so there will be a little shifting in resource use, some distortion of the allocative mechanism. But this outcome does not arouse me or my neighbors, nor would it lead to legislative action. What bothers is the deprivation of real income, for business buyers the unwarranted increase in costs. Everyone dislikes the enrichment of monopolists. Perhaps these utilities, long cowed by regulation, would be little immediate threat without it; but I prefer to stick with the general view of economists of normal monopoly behavior. So in this important segment of the utility industry, I have not joined that consensus of economists Scherer mentions. I still want my protection.

Perhaps in common usage the word deregulation may lack the sharp meaning that scholars would give it. It may mean a little reduction in control, a substantial reduction, or complete abandonment of it. It may refer to utilities getting rid of any controls to which they are subject, whether or not related to their monopoly nature. Perhaps some of the industries called utilities do not belong there in the traditional sense. Possibly I can do a little clarifying here. I'll speak of transportation, since most of my experience is there, mostly during about two decades from the mid-1920s. The field of transportation is an interesting one in various respects. Abandoning another thesis topic, I turned to highway transport, which was developing tremendously at the time. I did my thesis on the economics of highway development itself and then, with the freedom of a postdoctoral fellowship, spent several months looking into the regulation of motor carriers, first in some state capitals and then in the Interstate Commerce Commission (ICC) library, which was accumulating material in anticipation of the control of interstate motor transport, to come in 1935. While there I did an article that the *Quarterly Journal of Economics (QJE)* published on the beginnings of regulation in this field. It was my first professional product.

The states followed the general pattern of regulative laws, with little concern apparently over the need of regulation. The answer was implicit: motor carriers were transportation; transportation was regulated; therefore motor carriers should be regulated. But differences among modes of transportation could be critical, and the most critical seemed obvious. A railroad company uses a set of rails that are part of its plant, and towns along its lines are likely to depend on it, but a dozen trucking companies can compete on the same improved highway without interfering physically with each other. This way of viewing the monopoly aspect of utilities made the distinction clear and sharp. Without going further on the deregulation issue, one may notice that decontrol has gone furthest in the cases of road and air transport. Airways are like highways in their capacity to accommodate rivals. As long-distance telephone service operates via radio and satellite, the Bell System is having to adjust to increasing competition. One might add to the "laws" of public intervention: Regulation of the public utility type tends to disappear when the business in question has ceased to be, or never was, a public utility. But it is seldom good to base analysis on a semantic stance.

The public might think it was witnessing an extension of railroad laws to motor carriers, especially after the ICC got involved, when it was really seeing a reversal of regulation. There were no farmers crying for fair grain rates, but others knew what was happening. Railroads and railroad unions provided the political push for regulation in Wisconsin, I was told. The certificate to operate was the heart of the new control. At a hearing in Madison I watched three railroad lawyers deploy their skills to keep a fellow with a bus or two from operating them from there to Milwaukee. For ease of entering, the motor carrier business was about the best there was. With a truck or bus bought on credit, you were in business; you didn't have to be a businessman to be a commercial carrier. There was rate control too, but now it was minimum rates. For the first time the power over minimum rates, granted the ICC in 1920, became important. Established carriers, rail and motor, wanted price protection and they got it. Regulation's shift of purpose, from customers to producers, resulted from motor carrier competition of course, but not altogether. This was the period of the 1930s, when policy consisted largely in putting floors under everything; and transportation, with laws available, was a very suitable case. It seems that the new direction has continued for the most part. In speaking of a current measure for trucking decontrol, a reporter writes of removing the ICC's "rate- and route-protecting authority." President Carter spoke of the same measure as getting rid of controls that were designed for threatened industries during the Depression. Might it be suitable to ask anyone who favors deregulation whether he has power companies or motor carriers in mind and just what he objects to? Indeed government's impact on business is so diverse that the speaker should always state his specific interest. Here rigor begins.

For the person who uses the word regulation more loosely than I do, full deregulation may have more sweep than he intends. Transportation is an unusual industry in various ways and control has been of various sorts. It is usually dangerous in some degree, and the customer who entrusts his person or his property to a carrier takes a risk. The old doctrine of common carriers covered the matter of liability in the case of goods, and a more extensive policy is effective now. With motor carrier operation so easy to enter, it is arguable that a policy of controlling entry is desirable, quite apart from competition. At the opposite extreme, the exclusive franchise has point for the natural monopoly in fixing obligations and lessening investment uncertainty. In the case of common carriers that undertake to accept a wide variety of traffic, usually with fixed routes and perhaps schedules, the carrier accepts a situation in which not all routes and kinds of traffic will be equally profitable. A monopoly can handle this situation but a competitive firm is likely to have trouble, especially in facing rivals like anywhere-for-hire truckers that can pick and choose their traffic. Trucking is common carrier, contract carrier, or private, but the trucker may move from one to another unless compelled to pick his role and function in it. So protective control for producers meant a rigid categorizing of operators, with procrustean requirements reducing efficiency. Doubtless the waste has been considerable, and it has been a weighty element in the case for deregulation, or more properly, for a certain feature of decontrol. There is room for particularity and choice in judgments of control.

The most serious difficulty in deregulating railroads was likely to come, I thought, in handling the rate structure. Economists were saying that regulation had had its day since the monopoly that caused it has disappeared. But casual knowledge of regulation is not enough. I was more sensitive to these observations, I suppose, because after my postdoctoral fellowship year I worked with Leo Sharfman for several years on his ICC volumes, and my biggest single job was to research and draft the long chapter on the structure of charges. There is nothing comparable in the other public utilities. Railroads carry several thousand types of traffic between a very large number of pairs of points. Rates are in numerous classes, differing widely by weight, and special commodity rates cover most heavy movements. With high fixed costs and usual excess line capacity, and with considerable market latitude, railroads could charge "what the traffic would bear" over a wide range above incremental cost. Traffic management tended to take too immediate a view of such costs. With freight rates a large element in the cost of many products, railroads had considerable influence in the development of industries and areas—a leading reason for regulation, viewing it in the large. Such pattern as might have emerged in combining cost and traffic factors was prevented by the spotty presence of competition, especially in port areas, between large centers connected by parallel lines, and among lines serving a market center from different producing areas. The ICC, from its analysis in reports, seemed balanced in its approach. It avoided disturbing change if it could; it saw the reduction of average cost and it allowed the flexibility that would add to traffic; and it pursued its primary goal of restoring cost to its proper place as the basis of economy and of fairness, as the public viewed rates. Its rule seemed to be to *permit* traffic considerations to operate within limits, but to *compel* recognition of cost factors where seriously neglected. Highway carriers have a quite different cost structure, and their competition has doubtless moved rates somewhat toward a basis of fully assigned cost. But motor carriers don't meet the lower range of railroad rates for high-density and bulk traffic, especially for long distances. Absolutely these rates are low, but they are high in relation to railroad costs, and much important traffic is involved. I notice that congressional discussions of a current deregulation bill for railroads have included this matter (July, 1980). This is old stuff, but I mention it partly because I am rather shocked at Scherer's statement that economists are generally joining the deregulation parade. I lean toward maximum feasible decontrol, but I don't know enough to know what is feasible.

I must react to the "revisionists," as Scherer describes them. I'd heard of them before, but hadn't read them. One who has worked closely with regulation as reported by the ICC for its early years must be startled with the idea of having missed the main thrust of it. Of course I do not accept the idea. Apart from the closer evidence, the Act to Regulate Commerce fitted with the Sherman Act into the broad reaction to big business for which, as Scherer explained nicely, Henry Carter Adams was a leading academic spokesman. Looking closely I recall the early case, before 1890, in which railroads insisted that, in a proper interpretation of Section I, rates could be unreasonably low as well as unreasonably high. The ICC was firm in its view that Congress had not meant to protect the railroads against their folly in pricing; and the judgment held until Congress granted minimum-rate authority in 1920. Business is not expected to dislike every feature of laws that control it; and here an acceptable feature was the requirement that railroads charge the published rate. It seemed the best way to prevent personal discrimination; and who wants to pay rebates to big firms to get their business anyway? But mainly the companies battled the ICC, and successful suits restricted its control of rates in their major aspects. Amendments in 1906 and 1910 gave it the authority it thought it needed. Perhaps it was too ardent in its pursuit of abuses; at least many thought so when the railroads failed to handle World War I traffic acceptably and government took them over and operated them for two years. Congress was sympathetic and in 1920 directed the ICC to be more concerned with their financial health. The minimum-rate authority was part of this change of emphasis. The idea of a better way to serve the public is not to be confused with a shift in political power to the railroads; they were still in public hands.

Beside regulation, government has been involved in transport in two other important ways, both of which, I think, should enter a study of the industry and of its place in a market system. One is through subsidy, variously conferred and on various grounds; the other through participation, as a kind of junior partner, in supplying essential facilities of the transportation industry. Highways, developed waterways, airways have remained generally in the province of government, though their use has been private. Railroads come closest to being an entirely private industry. My dissertation on highways was a study of this second connection of government. By the mid-1920s, as I recall, the total bill for motor roads in this country approached a billion dollars a year. I treated the problems of development and use of highways as questions of market simulation—though the phrase was not then current. I just followed the engineers, who were leaders in the development on both the technical and economic sides. And I did most of my reading in engineering journals in our transportation library. There were two distinguishable problems beside the technical, one in guiding investment and the other in financing it. The latter lay mainly in working out a system of charges for road use. Tolls were rejected as the general means of charging for use of a million miles of motor roads. By the time I wrote, dependence was already mainly on license fees and fuel taxes. Observers were calculating how close the proceeds came to meeting the full cost, especially because of the railroad's charge that their competitor was being subsidized.

But does one just assume that public roads, a traditional function of government, should be treated merely as a subordinate part of motor transportation—including, of course, the use of private automobiles? The doctrine of the "king's highway" could be thought of as a basic right, that of mobility for people and their animals. Land in England was owned publicly, privately, and by monastic orders; but free men should have the right to move about without guilt of trespass. Fixed rights of way might follow. For centuries roads served farmers mostly, and probably were their responsibility. There was the toll road period, with a different theory and a different road use, but the old view of rural roads persisted. Then came motor vehicles, and a new era of road building and road policy emerged. Roads were built with a new technique to serve the needs of motor traffic, which was part of the private economy—a very conspicuous part. It seemed to me that the engineers just took it for granted that the quid pro quo of markets should govern thinking about public highways. A society whose leaning toward private enterprise was dominant accepted the approach. I don't know whether any political scientist has studied this event. It seems momentous. What a marvelous pork barrel highway funding could have been! I have always thought we should be deeply grateful to the engineers, though I could question details of their simulative analysis. I had some chance to say so later.

Engineers liked to work on costs and benefits, though the vogue of cost-benefit analysis lay some years ahead. They went into detail and they measured all they could. One small dissent of mine concerned the bearing that the measurability of a factor seemed to have on its weight; roadside beauty rated low. Research was extensive on aspects of investment guidance and on adaptation of special charges to vehicle types and features of road use. The result was of course a crude simulation of the market, but the focus of judgment was on the right things. The market operates through decisions that take account of imponderables. I put some of my findings on investment guidance into an article that the *QJE* published. W. Z. Ripley, then editor, asked me to do another on the payments for road use, but I had got so involved with Sharfman's research that I didn't get to it.

Intervention in transportation has been important also in the form of subsidy. The forms vary, and so do the reasons, as we look at railroads, airlines, inland and ocean water transportation. I don't know why barge lines enjoy free waterways, but that is their good fortune. Transport gets this attention because of its special place in the economy. Does not the current word infrastructure cover its role? It is the basis of the specialized organization of production, both in its geographic sweep and the internal division of tasks that underlies scale and need for markets. But transport is part of production cost, and its net effect is what counts. So, under the presumptions of a market system, subsidy needs a special justification, as in the longer-run offset of its cost or some collective gain of which ordinary market demand does not take account or does not meet through the by-product service of ordinary output. The social interest in a wide range of goods is met adequately in this incidental way; so collective throw-off is not itself a reason for subsidy. We do not pay partly for motor roads with general tax money because school buses and military vehicles run over them. Now leading reasons for subsidy, as seen by the public, are the need for urban mass transportation and for continuing support of rail service that has suffered loss of patronage but communities continue to need. It bothers me that editorial writers and others seem often to view transport subsidy as a normal role of government. At least the immediate issue is one of allocation, but one may not get far with it without a value judgment or two. Some of the purer economists should dirty their hands with it. It would be a sorry state if hang-ups on such grounds should make the talents of economists unavailable where they are needed. Do specialists in industrial organization stay away from such policies as agricultural adjustment and rent control? But what still puzzles me is that anyone should feel squeamish about the straight market simulation of the regulation of utilities.

Comments by PETER O. STEINER

I am pleased with this paper; it has the four things that every discussant looks for. It has a clear, crisp thesis, so that in order to criticize it one does not first have to create it. Second, it is scholarly, informative, and not too witty. Third, it has an unresolved problem. And fourth, it has at least one significant error.

Let me take a moment to restate baldly what I take to be Scherer's thesis. It is (1) that the attitude toward regulation of society is a function of the tenets of faith of those studying the phenomenon. And (2) that those tenets were sharply reversed between the decade of the 1880s when regulation became the fashion and the 1970s when deregulation won the day.

His underlying belief is that in the 1880s economists, legislators, and students of the problem discovered the possibility of market failure, both with respect to natural monopoly and with respect to the possibilities of excessive competition. They believed government to be (potentially at least) both fair and efficient. Thus government was a potential solution to those forms of market failure. But government was subject to corruption, and the political process was a dangerous one. The legislators of the 1880s thus sought to correct market failure by creating an independent regulatory commission, insulated to a substantial degree from political pressures. Scherer sees in that environment the birth and flowering of regulation.

The 1970s, according to Scherer, present a sharply different situation. First, there is now a new theory, mathematical not institutional, which exposes what was not known in the 1880s—regulation, however fair, will not be efficient. Second, by the 1970s efficiency had triumphed over equity as the relevant goal. Third, we now recognize that the original regulators guarded against the wrong problem. They worried about corruption, when the real danger was capture. The independent regulatory commissions, honest though they may be, have been captured by the regulated. These changed insights have led, according to Scherer, to a new consensus for deregulation.

I wish to quarrel with some of this. My first question is, were the 1970s really the decade of deregulation? The answer to that is yes if by regulation one means the regulation of natural monopoly. It seems to me, however, that regulation is broader and more important than that. *More new regulatory agencies and activities were started during the 1970s than during any decade of our history,* more even than in the 1930s. Without reciting numbers, let me point out that both the Environmental Protection Agency (EPA) and the Occupational Safety and Health Administration (OSHA) were progeny of the 1970s. The Equal Employment Opportunity Commission (EEOC), the third of the modern regulation giants, was not; it was a product of the 1960s. My purpose here is not to deny a deregulatory trend in some areas, but to point out that regulation is a multifaceted, some would say multifarious phenomenon, and that one can speak of a changing emphasis concerning regulation, rather than of a loss of faith in regulation itself. There is a declining sector of regulation, but there is also a growth sector. Economists and lawyers interested in regulating, or in studying regulation, need not worry about structural unemployment just yet.

My second and more serious quarrel with the Scherer thesis regards the sector in which deregulation is growing. What has led to second thoughts about the efficacy of prescriptive regulation? Scherer's paper suggests two main reasons for this change in attitude. The first is the new theory, the mathematical theory, about the perverse incentives of regulation. The regulators are mere mortals, who fail to find the elusive second-best solutions. Second is the capture thesis. Regulators in fact prove to be defenders of the regulated rather than protectors of the public interest.

I want to offer two alternative explanations of the phenomenon of a tendency for deregulation. One of those has almost nothing to do with regulation itself. I suggest that much of the force for deregulation comes from our inability to understand and cope with inflation. Inflation, I suggest, has proven to be a great instrument toward social reform of things that did not cause it—things such as the Fair Trade Laws and macroeconomics! It seems to me much of the deregulatory pressure comes from people who are frustrated about their inability to cope with inflation in other ways. These include, but are not limited to, members of the Council of Economic Advisers. Regulation makes a nice scapegoat, and deregulation is doing something, despite the fact that if one looks at the short-run correlations, deregulation has not helped all that much.

My second alternative hypothesis is more subtle and more important. I think the loss of faith in regulation arises not from the fact that there is too subtle a theory of how to regulate effectively, but from the fact that we now recognize that governments as well as markets can fail. It is not the lack of subtlety of government, but inherent forces in the regulatory area that lead governmental regulation to fail. Three points are worth emphasizing in this regard, and they have been made in a different part of the literature than that reviewed by Scherer. These things, I suggest, are more important aspects of the regulatory failure than Averch-Johnson effects, and the like.

(1) There exist, as James McKie has shown, massive boundary problems both between the regulated and the nonregulated sector, and between the jurisdictional and the nonjurisdictional activities of regulated firms. To some of these there is no realistic sensible solution. As one example, jurisdictional limits force regulators to allocate the unallocatable. It takes no subtle theory to prove that when you attempt to allocate the unallocatable, you fail.

(2) Regulatory regimes which develop in one state of technology often prove particularly inappropriate as that technology changes. But the freedom of even honest, wise, and subtle regulators to adapt to changed situations is likely to be severely limited by the property rights that the regulators and past regulations have themselves created. There is, in short, a real constitutional problem of sequential adaptation to a series of changes unanticipated at the times the precedents were set.

(3) There is what is sometimes called the bureaucratization of regulation, or what I call the legalization of regulation. The unavoidable result is red tape and long delays, largely because the regulation involves not only what gets done, but who gets to do it. The need for a regulator to decide who as well as what requires hearings and all kinds of procedural due process. This makes the process inherently very expensive and raises the transactions costs.

Let me turn finally to the unresolved problem in the paper, what Scherer calls his "puzzlement." He says

Now [in the 1970s], however, the arsenal of regulatory instruments is better stocked. We know about second-best, and we have made a good deal of progress toward developing the theory relevant to squeezing as much allocative efficiency as possible out of an inherently imperfect situation. I confess to some puzzlement at the vigor with which those instruments have been shaped in what I have called the decade of deregulation, when, one might suppose, the need might be considered less pressing.

Let me offer Scherer the "solutionment." The loss of faith, I submit, was in the pattern of regulation and in the performance of some specific regulations, *not in the fact of regulation nor in the need for regulation itself.* Three Mile Island certainly reflects regulatory failure on a massive scale. It has not led, nor will it lead, to deregulation; it will lead to more regulation. That airline rates have been subject to deregulation does not lead to a sense that we should leave to the free market the question of whether the DC-10s' engines are attached in a proper way. We are today comparing, at long last, imperfect regulation (which we now know to be imperfect) with imperfect markets. The alternatives to present imperfect regulation, as it is, include more regulation, different regulation, less regulation, and no regulation. There are some advocates of each of those kinds of activities. But most students of this problem do not think a single answer is right with respect to all aspects of the regulatory area. The consensus today, if there is one, is not on no regulation, but on the need, market failure by market failure, regulatory failure by regulatory failure, to reconsider the alternatives and see if we cannot come closer to a better mix of the free market and regulation.

An Essay on the Theory of Production

SIDNEY G. WINTER

My purpose in this paper is to explore the question, "Is economic theory 'about something'?" I wish particularly to address this question as it relates to the theory of production. Implicit in the asking of such a question is at least a mild skepticism concerning the degree of relationship between economic theory and the reality it attempts to interpret. I find that, in the case of production theory, such skepticism is amply justified.

Motivation

My interest in the question, and the approach I take in trying to answer it, are motivated by three considerations. The first is a concern with the problem of providing a concrete interpretation for production theory as it presently exists. By this I mean that it would be good to be able to explain to an intelligent and skeptical listener, initially unfamiliar with the theory, how the theory relates to economic reality and why its central constructs and propositions constitute a valid and fruitful approach to understanding that reality. Because of the theoretical naiveté of the hypothesized listener, the explanation would have to be cast largely in everyday language and supported by reference to examples of productive activity that form part of common knowledge and experience. Because the listener is skeptical, the explanation should anticipate and deal with a wide range of probing questions that can be raised about the theory. It will not suffice to remark that it is customary among economists to think in these particular theoretical terms, or to claim that this way of thinking has made possible great, but unspecified, accomplishments. Because the listener is intelligent, he or she will certainly accept the inevitability of abstractions and approximations in any scheme that attempts to provide a unified and

Sidney G. Winter is professor of economics, Department of Economics and Yale School of Organization and Management, Yale University. Professor Winter was a member of the Michigan faculty during 1968–76.

55

logically structured account of a diverse range of phenomena, and will respond sympathetically to the observation that, after all, it is not possible to solve all the problems in the area at once.

This emphasis on the desirability of "concrete interpretation" is itself not customary among economists, and a brief defense of it may therefore be in order. There is, first of all, a case based on the requirements of effective pedagogy. Economists are in fact frequently called upon to expound economic theory, including production theory, to audiences of varying degrees of intelligence, skepticism, and innocence of previous contact with economics. Various sorts of benefits derive from successfully overcoming skepticism and imparting understanding in these encounters, ranging from increased enrollments in economics courses through more generous support for economic research to enhanced influence in the formulation of public policy at the highest levels. Thus, even if skeptical demands for concrete interpretation could otherwise be dismissed as irrelevant to the scientific progress of the discipline, there would still be reasons to try to respond convincingly to those demands.

But, in my view, such a response is called for on methodological as well as pedagogical grounds. Although abstraction and approximation are inevitable in scientific theorizing, it is better to be aware of the aspects of reality that have been omitted or misrepresented. Such awareness is an indispensable source of guidance in identifying the empirical arenas in which the theory might be expected to display predictive power; in its absence only a reckless cut-and-try and hope-for-the-best approach is possible. The attempt to explicate the basic commitments of a theory in concrete terms can reveal the sense and circumstances in which those commitments might be strained, and thus help to demarcate its valid claims to predictive and explanatory strength.[1]

The second motivating consideration for this essay is recognition of the challenge that technological change presents to production theory and to economic theory generally. Familiarity may in this case have bred a dulled awareness of the problem, but one has only to focus one's attention squarely on it to appreciate anew what a gross embarrassment it is. On one side lies the assumption that the state of technology is a given datum, a part of the definition of the economic problem as it confronts an individual actor or an entire system. In its commonest form, the assumption is that technology is not merely exogenous, but constant. This assumption permeates vast reaches of economic research. It shapes the discipline's most profound, comprehensive, and sophisticated attempts at explaining why prices are what they are, and it is equally fundamental to much applied work of narrower focus, including work that is seriously intended to be of direct policy relevance. On the other side are the arrayed facts of technological change. There are simple facts, like the behavior of pocket calculator prices or death rates from poliomyelitis, and complicated facts like measured values of total factor productivity in various industries. To put the matter plainly, these facts render the constant technology assumption untenable. I believe it is also clear that the exogenous technology assumption is untenable. Consider, for example, the attention now focused on the technologies of alternative energy sources—fission, fusion, solar, geothermal, "biofuel," and "synfuel"—and ask whether the pace and level of that activity has not been shaped significantly by the appearance a few years back of an effective crude oil cartel.

Mediating between the given technology assumption and the facts violently opposed to it are a host of dubious expedients and partial adaptations. The most dubious expedient of all is the one that conditions all the relevant propositions on the statement, "*if* technology is constant . . . ," but then offers no suggestions at all as to when, where, and whether technology is constant. Thanks essentially to this device, a distressingly large fraction of the discipline's intellectual business manages to get conducted as if technological change did not exist. Of course, a few economists have made creditable attempts to accommodate the phenomenon of technological change within the standard framework of economic analysis,[2] and superficial or mechanical efforts in this direction have been relatively abundant. But most of these attempts have been encumbered, in greater or lesser degree, by conceptual difficulties whose sources lie at the foundations of standard production theory.[3] An examination of those difficulties is undertaken here, with the idea that even proposals for quite radical reform of the theory would deserve serious consideration if they offered some prospect of alleviating the serious tension between the theory and the manifestly important realities of technological change.

Another sort of tension informs the third of my motivating considerations. This is the tension that exists in the analysis of the individual productive organization, i.e., the "theory of the firm." It is still standard practice, in the textbooks and in much contemporary research, to represent the business firm abstractly by the productive transformations of which it is capable, and to characterize these productive transformations by a production function or production set regarded as a datum. In this theory, the focus is on the way market conditions affect the choices made among possible productive transformations; there is no attempt to explain why those transformations are what they are. This standard approach seems to be in latent but serious conflict with a quite different perspective that has gradually emerged in the literature concerned with explaining the very existence of the phenomenon known as the business firm, and with the related problem of the scope of the individual enterprise. Coase, in a classic article, posed the question of why some economic activities are organized through markets and others are organized within firms.[4] To pose such a question is to place firms in an institutional role that parallels that of markets, whereas in the standard view firms are unitary actors and are in a role roughly parallel to that of consumers, but not at all like that of markets. This alternative approach has been employed with great success in the analysis of particular problems, particularly by Williamson in his discussion of vertical integration.[5] But the extent of its departure from the standard approach has not been emphasized, and neither the promise nor the problems of the alternative have been well described.

These three considerations are linked together, in my view, by the fact that they all involve a single peculiarity or defect of standard production theory. The theory is supposed to be about *productive knowledge*; such is the role it plays in larger constructs of economic theory. But, beyond the briefest sort of mention as the basic concepts are introduced, it is not discussed and developed in terms of knowledge. Indicative of the situation is the fact that the everyday vocabulary that one would expect to crop up in any sort of theory of knowledge does not play any significant role in standard production theory. Words like "teaching," "learning," "skill," "practice," "memory," and "understanding" are almost entirely absent.[6] The suggestion that follows from this diagnosis is that it might be possible to do better on all three fronts—to make the theory concretely interpretable, to integrate the analysis of technological change with the theory, and to better describe the role of the individual productive organization—if production theory were recast more explicitly as a theory of knowledge and developed further in that direction.

In the following section, I briefly survey the development of production theory, highlighting issues relevant to the discussion later in the essay. The section following that one ("Toward a Theory of Productive Knowledge") examines a key consideration that an adequate theory of productive knowledge should accommodate—the fact that "states of knowledge" are usually not sharply defined. The next section displays some of the novel views of familiar production-theoretic concepts and issues that the knowledge perspective affords. The final section reviews and concludes the argument.

Origins and Varieties of Production Theory

The topics that we now count as part of the theory of production were, over much of the history of the subject, addressed primarily in the context of the problem of distribution, which was itself viewed as the problem of explaining the division of the social product among the classic "factors of production"—land, labor, and capital. The major uses that we now find for the theory of production—in analysis of the role of production possibilities in the determination of relative prices, and in the efficient allocation of resources—only began to acquire something like their present importance with the advent of neoclassical economics late in the nineteenth century. In classical economics, it was the marginal productivity schedule, and not the production function or the cost function, that was the focus of attention. The question was not, "how much output can be obtained, at a maximum, from this list of inputs?" but rather, "by how much will output increase if the amount of this particular input is increased some, with all other inputs held constant?"

From our present-day theoretical standpoint, we recognize that the latter question is not well posed unless there is some understanding about how the increment of the variable input is to be used. Our standard resolution of this problem is to understand both the original input list and the augmented list to be used in such a way as to produce a maximum output given the "state of the arts"—i.e., to refer back to the first of the two questions just stated. In the classical treatments, however, the discussion of the "laws of returns" is not so clearly founded on the concept of technical efficiency. Rather, the propositions are advanced more as observational laws characterizing the results of experiments actual or imagined, natural or planned. These experiments involve simple incremental modifications of familiar methods for producing output. The increments of input are apparently conceived as being applied in a reasonable way, but there is little suggestion that the matter requires or receives careful consideration. The important point is that the quasi-empirical marginal productivity schedule involved in the classical conception does not raise any troubling questions of how it is known that the methods involved actually yield maximum output for given inputs. To put it another way, the conception does not challenge the theorist to develop the idea of a "state of the arts" with the care appropriate to the importance bestowed on that concept by the modern interpretation of the production function.

The primacy of the distribution problem and of the quasi-empirical conception of the marginal productivity schedule persist in early neoclassical discussion of production. Particularly significant here is Wicksteed's 1894 work, *An Essay on the Coordination of the Laws of Distribution*. His title names his task, which was to show that separate laws of distribution, involving a classical application of marginal productivity principles to each factor in turn, are mutually consistent in the sense that the resulting factor shares exhaust the product. It was in introducing this problem that he made the notion of the production function explicit in economic analysis for the first time, in the following terms:

The Product being a function of the factors of production we have $P = f(a, b, c \ldots)$[7]

Neither in this statement nor in Wicksteed's subsequent analysis is there any hint that there is anything conceptually problematic about the idea of such a function; it is merely a mathematically explicit expression of the long-familiar idea that if the input quantities vary, the output quantity will vary as well, and in certain characteristic ways.

Even today, introductory treatments of the production function and of factor substitution in textbooks and lectures often follow much the same Ricardian path, with the same agricultural examples. The strength of the approach lies in the plausibility of variable proportions production in the agricultural context, and in the simple, common-sense arguments that establish the general character of the response of output to variation in a single input. A casual acquaintance with a relatively simple and commonly encountered production technology is the only prerequisite for understanding. But this strength is also a source of weakness of the sort suggested above; the loose way in which the technology is discussed tends to leave obscure the conceptual connections among productive knowledge, the production function, and technical efficiency.

No sooner had the production function made its explicit appearance in economic analysis than it was immediately—in the lines immediately following the above-quoted line from Wicksteed—specialized to being homogeneous of the first degree. This was the basis of Wicksteed's coordination of the laws of distribution, i.e., his demonstration that the product is precisely exhausted when inputs are paid according to their marginal products. In beginning his examination of the validity of the constant returns to scale assumption, Wicksteed stated:

> Now it must of course be admitted that if the physical conditions under which a certain amount of wheat, or anything else, is produced were exactly repeated the result would be exactly repeated also, and a proportional increase of the one would yield a proportional increase of the other.[8]

Elaborating this statement, Wicksteed made clear that the replication had to be understood to involve a replication of the inputs in exact detail; otherwise one would not be exactly repeating the original condition. He then went on to deal, in a somewhat confused way, with the fact that the economic laws of distribution must involve something more than the physical conditions of producing the "mere material product." What he did not pause to explain—but probably had in mind—was that the replication whose result he considered obvious involved the same production method. This supposition does make the result obvious in the sense that a replication of a given physical experiment, hypothetically perfectly controlled, necessarily yields the same result. What is noteworthy in the present context is (a) that this interpretation is inappropriate given the modern understanding of the production function, which presumes that there is a choice of method, and (b) that Wicksteed's discussion manages to slide past the problem of characterizing the set of available methods, or "state of the arts."

At some point, and I am not clear just when, the connection between the production function concept and technical efficiency began to be emphasized. A clear statement may be found in Sune Carlson's 1939 book, *A Study on the Pure Theory of Production*.

> If we want the production function to give only one value for the output from a given service combination, the function must be so defined that it expresses the *maximum product* obtainable from the combination at the existing state of technical knowledge. Therefore, the purely *technical* maximization problem may be said to be solved by the very definition of our production function.[9]

To whatever historical depth some awareness of this point might be traced, it seems clear that its salience was vastly enhanced by the advent of new approaches to production theory that gave explicit consideration to production methods *not* "on the production function." These new approaches comprised the members of the family of linear models of production, including linear activity analysis, linear programming and input-output analysis, and also such descendants and relatives of this family as process analysis, nonlinear programming, and game theory. They made their appearance in the work of von Neumann, Leontief, Koopmans, Kantorovich, Dantzig, and others over the period 1936 to 1951.[10]

The linear activity analysis framework, as developed by Koopmans, is most relevant here.[11] This contribution introduced into economics a workable abstract representation of what the classics called the "state of the arts"—what Carlson calls "the existing state of technical knowledge" in the passage cited above. Productive knowledge was described first of all by "basic activities," formally represented by vectors of technical coefficients, but conceived as corresponding to identifiable, concrete "ways of doing things." Further, the theory adduced a set of principles that described how the productive knowledge represented by the basic activities could be extended in scope, combined, and modified. Central to these principles were the assumptions that activities could be scaled up or down at will while maintaining the same proportional relations among inputs and outputs, and that the results of activities performed simultaneously would be additive. If these assumptions were true, then the whole scope of technological possibilities could be characterized in relation to the basic activities involved. This would mean, in particular, that in the case of a single-output production process, the numerical specification of all basic activities would make it possible, in principle, to determine the maximum output that could be produced from a particular input combination. And if the problem were not too large relative to the computation budget, linear programming solution algorithms would make such a determination possible not merely in principle, but in practice.

Still another mode of abstract representation of technological possibilities became common in economic theory with the development of modern general equilibrium theory by Arrow, Debreu, and others.[12] This approach generalizes the earlier ones by going simply and directly to the abstract heart of the matter. Commodity outputs in amounts represented by the list $q = (q_1, \ldots, q_M)$ may or may not be producible from input commodities in amounts represented by the list $x = (x_1, \ldots, x_N)$. If q is producible from x, then the input-output pair (x, q) is "in the production set" (or "production possibilities set"). Whatever is known or considered plausible as a property of the structure of technological knowledge is, in this representation, treated as a postulate about the properties of the production set. For example, the linear activity analysis model is recovered as a special case if it is postulated that the production set comprises a finite set of basic activities, plus the combinations and modifications permitted under the activity analysis assumptions.

It is useful to note what is gained and what is lost in going from linear activity analysis to a general production set. What is gained is generality—there is a simple abstract representation for states of knowledge whose structure may not conform to that postulated by activity analysis. What is lost, naturally enough, is specificity—and potential empirical content. No longer is there the suggestion that it might be possible to fully characterize an actual state of technological knowledge by looking in the world for "basic activities." In particular, there is no guidance as to how one would test the claim that a specific input-output pair not actually observed in the world is "not possible given the existing state of technical knowledge." Thus, to refer back to earlier discussion, the concept of a production function that expresses the "maximum product obtainable" from each input combination is once again left without any direct empirical interpretation.[13] This is not to say that its status as a purely logical construct is impaired; given additional mathematical restrictions that are commonly imposed, it is logically possible to define such a function on the basis of an underlying production set representation of the state of technical knowledge. The construct thus defined may be employed in further theoretical development and perhaps in that way be related, ultimately, to empirical data.[14]

The situation may be summed up in the following terms. It is the production set concept that stands, in contemporary formal theory, for the classical idea of a "state of the arts" or for an "existing state of technical knowledge." Arrow and Hahn concisely say

> [Thus,] the production possibility set is a description of the state of the firm's knowledge about the possibilities of transforming commodities.[15]

To assume that the production set has certain properties—for example, those that correspond to the linear activity analysis model—is thus an indirect way of imputing analogous properties to the "state of knowledge" that the production set describes. I have proposed here that this indirectness of approach may be understood as a reflection of the historical development of the theory, in which the marginal productivity schedule preceded the production function which preceded the production set. In the "finished" structure of modern theory, the concepts that developed later are logically antecedent to those that appeared earlier. And the development of the more recent arrivals has been strongly influenced by their logical role in an already extant theoretical structure; they have not had much chance to develop a life of their own.

Thus it happened that it became much easier for the theorist to describe the logical connection between the production set and the production function than to explain the substance of what the production set represents—a state of knowledge. This neglect of the independent conceptual anchoring of the production set idea has inhibited both the recognition of its limitations and the development of alternative and complementary theoretical treatments of productive knowledge. In the following section, I suggest what might be involved if, at this late date, we were to give the idea of knowledge its proper place in production theory.

Toward a Theory of Productive Knowledge

Put aside, for the time being, the wealth of useful concepts, techniques, and insights represented by the traditional theory of production. Suppress, so far as possible, the thought that any proposed alternative approach to productive knowledge must ultimately confront the issue of how best to make use of that inherited fund of intellectual capital. Imagine that we have a clean theoretical slate, except that the word *knowledge*, underscored, appears at the top. The task is to theorize usefully about the phenomena associated with the fact that individuals and organizations "know how to do things." The objectives include those served by the traditional theory of production, but also an improved understanding of technological change. The available resources comprise whatever we understand about knowledge and "know-how," whether drawn from personal introspection and experience, or from systematic inquiry in economics, engineering, psychology, or other disciplines.

From this determinedly open-minded point of view, the first thing seen is a major fact that the traditional theoretical apparatus keeps hidden: A "state of knowledge" does not have sharply defined limits. Surveying available knowledge is like surveying a landscape on a hazy day. Some things are close enough to be seen clearly, others remote enough to be totally invisible. But the intermediate conditions cover a broad range and are complex to describe. To define the limits of visibility, or the visibility status of a particular feature, requires reference either to an arbitrary standard or to a very precise statement of the objectives of observation.[16] Is a building visible if its profile can be discerned? If you can count the windows? If you can tell whether it is gray or green? It depends on what definition of "visible" is chosen from the range of plausible available alternatives. Similarly, whether something is to be regarded as "known" or not will often depend on what one chooses to mean by "known," and particularly on the degree of indefiniteness concerning details that is regarded as consistent with a thing being known. There is nothing fuzzy about this proposition itself; it is as clearly factual as the experience of viewing a hazy landscape or grading an essay question.

The validity of this point is extremely robust with respect to the scope and content of the knowledge involved. Consideration of types of knowledge whose limits seemingly are sharply defined yields, on reflection, further examples of significant ambiguities. Consider, in particular, the image that is implicit, and sometimes explicit, in discussions of production theory—the image of a state of knowledge defined by some sort of symbolic record of possible techniques, a "book of blueprints" for capital goods or a file of "recipes" for basic activities. Even this image loses its apparent sharpness when considered concretely. A symbolic record does not have to be very large before considerations of access time take on practical significance. Although a particular item is, unambiguously, either in the file or not in the file, whether it is usefully available from the file or demonstrably unavailable is often less clear.

Some ambiguity thus arises, as a practical matter, even in situations that seemingly correspond ideally to the production-theoretic notion of a sharply defined "state of knowledge." More importantly, however, the types of knowledge involved in actual productive activity do not lie anywhere near the extreme of relatively sharp definition illustrated by symbolic records. It is useful here to distinguish the knowledge applied in the actual performance of productive activity from the related knowledge invoked in the planning of such activity. Under each heading, there is a major source of haze covering the landscape of productive technique.

Performance Knowledge

Actual productive performances involve the exercise of individual skills, and of organizational routines that are, at the multiperson level, the counterpart of individual skills. This observation has many significant implications for the theory of productive knowledge; here I emphasize its relationship to the "hazy limits" of such knowledge.

Skills are formed in individuals, and routines in organizations, largely through "learning by doing." They are developed in particular environments, and meet pragmatic standards of technical and economic adequacy that are characteristic of those environments. The effectiveness of a skill or routine shaped by such a learning process is typically dependent in a variety of ways on features of the environment in which it developed. Many of these dependencies may not be obvious and go unremarked in the learning process—particularly in the case of dependence on conditions that are constant over time in the environment of learning but vary over the environment of application. Contrast this sort of pragmatic, output-oriented learning with the development of a new scientific experiment in a particular laboratory. It is as if the only objective were to get a specific experimental result, and since understanding of mechanism is of no immediate use, the problem of experimental control is ignored. Of course, the process of scientific inference from experimental results is subject to well-known hazards, even when a strong theory of what might affect the result guides a diligent effort at control. The hazards of inference from "this has worked up to now" are notably larger in the context of productive knowledge, where the dominant motivational focus from the very start is on *whether* something works, and not why. Quite rational satisficing principles dictate that investment in the quest for understanding be deferred until there is a symptom of trouble to deal with.

There is thus a plausible economic logic behind the fact that the world of productive activity seems to contain many individual and organizational capabilities whose effectiveness is quite real but not at all well understood, and is hence a world of uncertain scope. Among the familiar sorts of contingencies to which productive activity is subject are changes in characteristics of material inputs (e.g., mineral ore grades, or impurity levels in industrial chemicals), work load imbalances arising from demand-induced changes in the composition of output, variations in skill levels and attitudes toward work in the labor force, changes in the production environment involving air pollution, noise or vibration, electromagnetic radiation, and so forth.[17] The mix of relevant contingencies obviously differs greatly from one type of productive activity to another, but the fact that all production systems are "open"—that they involve interaction with an environment—has the corollary that all are subject to disruption if the environment starts to behave in novel ways. Such disruptions may be the occasion for a round of troubleshooting, learning, and adaptation—or they may destroy the viability of the productive organization.

Because the effectiveness of individual skills and organizational routines depends on the environment "cooperating" in ways that are imperfectly understood, there is an inevitable ambiguity about the limits of this sort of applied productive knowledge. The discussion above points out that this ambiguity extends to the simplest sort of inference one might want to make, that productive performances actually accomplished in a particular organization in the past will continue to be possible performances in the future. Such a prediction is conditioned by "relevant conditions remain unchanged," but, in contrast to the case of scientific knowledge, there is little reason to think that the relevant conditions have even been identified, let alone that their future constancy has been assured. The chance that significant difficulties will appear is of course much greater when the objective is not the mere continuation of a successful productive performance, but rather a replication in a new locale, a modification of the method, or a new adjustment to other activities in the same environment. Such attempts at deliberate change obviously entail a risk of violating un-identified preconditions for the success hitherto achieved; the greater the change attempted, the more likely that an acute form of some latent difficulty will be triggered.[18]

Planning Knowledge

Productive knowledge of a more intellective sort is involved in the planning and problem-solving activities of managers and engineers. In this context, the idea of a sharply defined state of knowledge trans-lates into the notion that the universe of production problems divides sharply into those that can be clearly seen ex ante to have solutions, and those that equally clearly cannot be solved. One obvious objection to this notion derives from the previous discussion—insofar as the quest is for solutions that will work in practice, all the ambiguities surrounding the scope of productive practice also infect the planning process.

But there is a more serious objection. Any field of problem-solving activity whatsoever could be used to illustrate the point that the knowledge employed includes a range of techniques for seeking solutions, including techniques for patching together solutions of old problems to solve new ones. Knowledge of this sort cannot yield any clear ex ante distinction between problems that can be solved and those that cannot, such as would exist if the knowledge consisted merely of an easily accessible file of achieved solutions. Rather it permits a range of judgments of widely varying reliability as to the likelihood that available problem-solving techniques will prove effec-tive in the various cases posed. At one extreme are trivial problems, which can be judged solvable with very high confidence, while at the other extreme are problems that can be classed as impossible for some clear affirmative reason. In between is a continuum in which uncer-tain appraisals of the feasibility of solution are complexly related to uncertain judgments of the time and effort required for such success. This generalization is valid across an enormous range of activity, from recreational puzzle solving, through theoretical economics, to the de-velopment problems of the new biological technologies or fusion power. Its validity is rooted in the simple fact that practical knowledge in all spheres consists in large measure of knowledge of how to *try* to find solutions to previously unencountered problems.

The theory of heuristic search provides a quite general framework for thinking about the scope of such problem-solving knowledge.[19] A "problem," in the formulation associated with heuristic search, is something broadly analogous to the task of finding a path through a maze. There is an initial element, or starting point, and a desired element(s), or goal. There is a set of operators that convert elements, i.e., positions in the maze, into neighboring elements; one operator is "turn right and go to next junction point," another is "go back to previous junction point." A "solution" is a path through the maze from starting position to goal, and it may be specified by a corresponding sequence of operators—the operator applied at the starting position, the operator applied at the position resulting from that operation, and so on. Depending on the problem, the search for solution may be like the physical search of a labyrinth (operators are applicable only at the current position generated by the sequence of previous operators), or like solution of maze puzzles that display all maze positions simultaneously and permit arbitrary choices of position for the next operation. Of course, the length of the search for a solution may be profoundly affected by anything that constructively guides the choice of operators, even something as simple as the ability to recognize previously explored dead ends. A *heuristic* is "any principle or device that contributes to the reduction in the average search to solution."[20] Some heuristics are applicable across very wide ranges of problems— "work backward from the goal"—while others are relevant only in highly specific problem contexts—"convert $\tan\alpha$ to $\sin\alpha/\cos\alpha$ wherever it appears."

One way to understand what goes on in the hazy boundary regions of planning knowledge is to examine some of the problem-solving heuristics employed there. Such an approach affords a novel perspective on standard production theory, since that theory appears as one among many specialized "theories of production" that could be constructed within the general framework of "production planning as heuristic search." Each such specialized theory focuses on a small subset of the available heuristics, exaggerating their efficacy, and disregards the others. Standard theory is distinguished by its (implicit if not explicit) focus on recourse to information stored in symbolic records, and also on the possibility of linear scaling of independently operating basic activities. It abstracts from the uncertainties and difficulties that afflict these problem-solving approaches in practice, and also from the availability of other approaches. In particular, it ignores a wide range of options for querying various sources of information about feasible production schemes, including calling a meeting of the key personnel, trying a small test run, consulting a trade journal, retaining a consultant, or hiring a key employee away from a competitor.

Quite a different specialized "theory of production" is embodied in a simulation model I developed in collaboration with Richard Nelson and Herbert Schuette while at the University of Michigan.[21] The firms in that model have no files in which they store productive knowledge that is not currently needed; at a given time they possess only the single technique they are actually using. Our modeling of the probabilistic technique-change process may be interpreted as an abstract representation of the heuristics "look for incremental improvements in the current technique," and "copy the superior techniques of other firms." The definition of "improvement" (or "superior") in this scheme is "cost reducing"; for this reason, the firms of the model respond to changes in relative input prices in the usual way, though not for the usual reason. Of course, this model goes too far in denying any role at all to symbolic information storage. And, just as standard theory exaggerates the ease with which plans from the file can be implemented, this model exaggerates the ease and accuracy of imitation. Its virtue lies in the fact that the processes and considerations it emphasizes are ones much neglected by standard theory. Also, it serves to illustrate the point that the concept of a sharply defined "state of the art" is not an inevitable constituent of a formal production theory.

An example of theory that is much more narrowly specialized, but even more clearly subsumable in the heuristic search framework, is the recent development of computer-aided synthesis and analysis of chemical processes.[22] This work is both a theory of and a tool for the solution of production problems, and includes the development of new technology as well as the use of known methods in existing facilities. The computer program draws upon a store of basic chemical knowledge, and manipulates this knowledge by heuristic methods that parallel those of human designers. One account summarizes the approach as follows:

To simulate the long-run adaptation of the industry by the synthesis of new technology we must first examine the economic forces that cause the industry to focus on a particular new technology to bring into being, and then we must simulate the mental activities of the research engineers who bring the technology into existence. . . . To simulate technology synthesis, we must engage in technology synthesis.[23]

Obviously, there are a great many heuristics that are relevant to the solution of production problems, particularly if one counts all the subject-specific ones such as those involved in chemical reaction path synthesis. What sense can be made, then, of the notion of a sharply defined "state of the art" or "state of knowledge," given that the knowledge in question includes such a diverse array of more or less effective problem-solving methods? A narrow interpretation, focusing on solutions actually achieved, is unappealing because of the plain existence of easy but hitherto unattempted problems. To broaden the definition, on the other hand, is to risk encompassing in the "state of the art" the solution of problems that may be very difficult, or even impossible.

Implications

One can think of a variety of possible theoretical responses to the problem posed by the ambiguous scope of productive knowledge. At one extreme, the issue could be left hidden under the "theory must necessarily be abstract" rug. At the other, some suggestions implicit in the above characterization of the problem could be taken as the basis for a program of radical theoretical reform. It would be accepted that economists need to found their theory of production in a basic, operational understanding of what it means for individuals and organizations to know how to do things, and that the help of disciplines long active in this area might prove useful in acquiring such understanding. Personally, I find the proposal for such reform attractive and quite plausible. Without some such reform, I do not think that there will be fundamental progress toward understanding the forces of economic change that are reshaping our world at such a drastic pace. But I recognize that the case for this proposal cannot be made persuasive by reference to conjectured possibilities of achieving remote goals, however important those goals may be. More to the point are the prospects for achieving some significant immediate gains in understanding, while avoiding the costs of a complete break with the familiar tradition. The following section makes a case of this sort. It attempts to show that, pending the radical theoretical reform that is probably needed, there is value in simply approaching familiar issues in production theory with the idea in mind that it is supposed to be about knowledge.

The Knowledge Perspective: Illustrative Examples

Production Sets Reconsidered

The straightforward implication of the discussion in the preceding section would seem to be that, since states of knowledge do not have sharp boundaries, there is no realistic basis for the theoretical concept of a sharply defined production set. A more fruitful conclusion, however, is suggested by the analogy with the problem of defining "visibility." The concept does not lack practical value merely because the world does not exemplify the sharp binary distinction it connotes. Effective use of the concept merely depends on an awareness that it can be sharp only to the extent that it is sharpened by a definition that is, to an important degree, arbitrary. Furthermore, a single conventional definition is unlikely to serve well in all the different contexts in which some such concept might be useful; there will be a need to modify the definition in an expedient fashion, according to the problem at hand.

A thoroughgoing reassessment of the production set concept from this point of view would be a major task. I suggest, however, that a useful start can be made simply by noting the (metaphorical) relevance of a familiar idea from the theory of statistical hypothesis testing, in which any particular criterion for locating the boundary of the production set is subject to two types of error. It may represent techniques as "known," thus implying that they are immediately usable with negligible additional problem-solving costs, when in fact their feasibility is far from established and they might become available only after the expenditure of considerable time and money. Or, it may represent techniques as "unknown" when the actual situation is just that nobody knows (or remembers at the moment) precisely how they might be used, and a moderate amount of problem-solving effort could change that. To adopt a stringent definition of "known" is to make the former error unlikely, at the expense of making the latter very likely. The reverse situation arises if the standard for something being "known" is very undemanding.

Because economists have consistently reified the boundary of the production set, they have not had the occasion to discuss what standard of "known" they had in mind, or to examine the sensitivity of their conclusions to these two types of error. The fact is that the propositions of economic analysis present widely differing sensitivities—or, to put it the other way, some are likely to be valid on one extreme interpretation of what "known" means and some on the other. Consider the basic idea, on which depends so much of our understanding of real markets, that certain sorts of price relationships are likely to prove ephemeral. Individual propositions of this sort are derived from an affirmative claim that particular techniques (e.g., buy here, ship from here to there, and sell) are widely known. They do not involve any claim about what is *not* known. Such propositions are therefore strong if the techniques in question meet a stringent standard for being (widely) known, but are weak if the standard is undemanding. On the other hand, consider the claim that technological change is a strictly exogenous influence on economic activity,—where "technological change" is understood as involving the discovery of methods of production not previously known. If it has any merit at all, this proposition may be approximately valid only for an extremely broad definition of "known"—the sort of definition that would classify nuclear fusion as a known technique for generating electric power as of the mid-1950s. For any moderately restrictive definition of "known," the evidence indicating that economic forces shape the course of technological change is overwhelming.

It would, I think, be a significant step forward if economists would devote more attention to the problem of defining "known," and recognize that the element of arbitrariness in any specific definition entails vulnerability to errors of two types. It is conceivable that such an effort might yield operational definitions of "known" that, in realistic cases, would substantially justify formal description of the knowledge state by a production set with a sharp boundary. (These would be cases analogous to the situation when the air is crystal-clear except where the landscape is obscured by a dense fog bank.) A more likely or typical result would be a heightened sophistication concerning the qualifications to analytical results that inhere in the representation of a complex, ill-defined, and changing knowledge state by the stark and simple apparatus of standard production theory. Such a rise in sophistication would have the effect of affixing warning labels to many familiar propositions of positive and normative economic theory, indicating that they are not safe for use in the vicinity of an active knowledge margin. In a society in which efforts to solve novel technological problems are a commonplace phenomenon, such warnings are badly needed, though the producers of the sorts of propositions in question often seem oblivious to their hazards.

The Repositories of Productive Knowledge

I turn now to the question of who or what it is that possesses the sort of productive knowledge represented by a production set, and where that knowledge is stored. This question seems inescapable if one views production theory as a theory of knowledge and also tries to think in concrete terms about what is going on. Whatever society's total inventory of productive knowledge at a given time may be, it can presumably all be accounted for, in principle, by considering in turn all of the forms of storage that are actually available—human memories, books, magnetic tapes, blueprint files, and so forth. All of these modes of storage clearly involve real costs of one sort or another, and this fact raises some difficulties for standard theory. In particular, it is hard to reconcile standard theory with the notion of an inactive or potential firm—a firm whose capabilities for transforming inputs into outputs are merely latent possibilities, awaiting the call of the proper price signals to spring into reality. Such a notion is fully explicit in many renderings of general equilibrium theory, and is sometimes used in other contexts as a surrogate for a more substantial theory of entry. The obvious question is, who pays the storage costs for such a package of idle knowledge?[24] More fundamentally, if the functioning of firms as repositories of productive knowledge presupposes the existence of economic arrangements for information storage, how can it be appropriate to view firms and their production sets as data of the economic problem?

This puzzle is closely related to the tension, described earlier, between the standard theory of the firm and the transactional approach of Coase, Williamson, and others. The issue is nicely framed in this passage from Graaf, one of the few authors to confront the problem squarely in the course of an exposition of standard theory.

> When we try to construct a transformation function for society as a whole from those facing the individual firms comprising it, a fundamental difficulty confronts us. There is, from a welfare point of view, nothing special about the firms actually existing in an economy at a given moment of time. The firm is in no sense a 'natural unit.' Only the individual members of the economy can lay claim to that distinction. All are potential entrepreneurs. It seems, therefore, that the natural thing to do is to build up from the transformation functions of the men, rather than the firms, constituting an economy.
>
> If we are interested in eventual empirical determination, this is extremely inconvenient. But it has its conceptual advantages. The ultimate repositories of technological knowledge in any society are the men comprising it, and it is just this knowledge which is effectively summarized in the form of a transformation function. In itself a firm possesses no knowledge. That which is available to it belongs to the men associated with it. Its production function is really built up in exactly the same way, and from the same basic ingredients, as society's.[25]

Clearly, this view of individuals as the "ultimate repositories of technological knowledge" is highly complementary with a view of firms as institutions akin to markets, distinguished from the latter by the prevalence of distinctive forms of contracting and related governance arrangements. And these conceptions together dispose of the problem of who is minding the knowledge store of the inactive or potential firm—there is no such store. The firms actually observed are held together only by the thin glue of transaction cost minimization, and are only a bit less accidental and ephemeral than the particular pairings of buyers and sellers that occur in a market for a perfectly homogeneous commodity.

This is in some ways a satisfying solution to the puzzle. It should certainly appeal to anyone with philosophical leanings toward reductionism. Also, it is highly consistent with the individualistic traditions of economics. I suspect that it fails to be the dominant view only by a curious twist of doctrinal history, namely, the fact that the concept of the "firm" has been so dominated by the image of the single proprietorship that the conflict with individualism has not been explicit. However, as Graaf noted, this individualistic viewpoint is extremely "inconvenient" empirically. For those pursuing the econometrics of production, there is a monster specification problem lurking in the idea that the production function of a firm exists only as an aggregate consequence of its transactions. And most students of industrial organization, or of corporate strategy, will probably resist the implication that the distinction between entry by acquisition and de novo entry is fully reducible to transactional difficulties in the various input markets. For the naive listener, however, the problem will be that the story is simply not convincing. The likes of Exxon, General Motors, and IBM just do not look accidental and ephemeral. Such a listener will probably argue that the textbooks are closer to being right—it is the firms, not the people who work for the firms, that know how to make gasoline, automobiles, and computers.

That there is a large measure of validity in this naive view is a proposition that can, I believe, be defended effectively. There is indeed a sense in which the capabilities of an organization are not reducible to the capabilities of individual members. To explain this in detail is a larger undertaking than I can attempt here.[26] The preceding section's discussion of performance knowledge that is the result of learning by doing suggests a large part of the explanation. The coordination displayed in the performance of organizational routines is, like that displayed in the exercise of individual skills, the fruit of practice. What requires emphasis here is that, in the organizational case, the learning experience is a shared experience of organization members, particularly those who have an extended tenure with the organization. Thus, even if the contents of the organizational memory are stored only in the form of memory traces in the memories of individual members, it is still an organizational knowledge in the sense that the fragment stored by each individual member is not fully meaningful or effective except in the context provided by the fragments stored by other members. Knowledge possessed by the organization as such is implicit in the coherent structure of "idiosyncratic knowledge" or "firm-specific human capital" held by the members. In addition, of course, an organization may maintain a variety of forms of symbolic records which, because of their interrelationships and their relationships to distinctive interpretive powers reposing in the memories of human members, are another form of organizational knowledge.

The importance of learning phenomena, at both individual and organizational levels, receives much more emphasis in the literature of business behavior and strategy than it does in theoretical economics. In airframe production, the "learning curve" has long been used as a planning tool, and it is from this source that the "learning by doing" idea entered the economic literature.[27] A particularly dramatic example of the importance of learning (and forgetting) is part of the record of the Convair 880/990 fiasco. Convair pulled its 880 jets off the production line in various stages of completion as a result of difficulties in its contractual relations with Howard Hughes. When the difficulties were straightened out, and production resumed, learning had to begin anew. It was hampered by a lack of records that detailed the stage of completion of each aircraft, and by continuing design changes. The result was that production costs ballooned to many times their planned level, contributing to the nearly half billion dollar loss that Convair suffered in the episode.[28] On the positive side, the Boston Consulting Group (BCG) has centered a simple applied theory of business strategy on the concept of the "experience curve," to the considerable profit of itself and presumably of its clients. (The experience curve in BCG's terminology relates to all costs, not just to the direct labor time input involved in the original conception of the learning curve.)[29]

Some recent work in industrial organization has begun to pay more attention to learning effects and the resulting distinctive patterns of technical competence that differentiate firms and shape their strategies. Prominent examples are the "mobility barriers" analysis of Caves and Porter, and Teece's work on technology transfer and on the scope of the enterprise.[30]

A strong case can thus be made that firms, or at least some firms, are significant entities, not accidental or ephemeral transacting patterns. The standard theoretical representation of a firm by a production function or production set is partially justified. But, in light of the foregoing account, one can still agree with Graaf that the firm is not a "natural unit." One can object to the standard framing of the economic problem in general equilibrium theory, or to the theory of the firm in the textbooks, in which the productive knowledge attached to firms is viewed as given data. And one can certainly object to the idea of a production set associated with an inactive or potential firm, a firm that possesses no files, no magnetic tapes and no experienced employees in which specifically organizational knowledge might reside. What is defensible is a conception of a firm as a significant and persistent but historically contingent entity, a repository of specifically organizational productive knowledge that is a reflection of its evolution as an organization.

I conclude that there is much merit both in the view that individuals are repositories of productive knowledge and in the view that business firms and other organizations are such repositories. There being no conflict between the two views, the question arises as to why economic theory cannot accommodate them both. Perhaps it might even contribute something to an understanding of the distinctive roles of these repositories in the economic system. Such understanding could be helpful in a number of ways, particularly in the analysis of public policy issues involving the creation, merger, restructuring, or support through adversity of productive organizations. I have no doubt that a useful contribution of this sort can in time be made. But the immediate problem is that most of formal economic theory now occupies a very awkward middle ground, is often merely obscure about the nature of the technological repositories, and largely ignores the literature on the "nature of the firm." It cannot illuminate what it is that firms do for us that individuals and markets could not do; up to this point it has not even framed the question.

Land, Space, and Additivity

The question of returns to scale has been the focus of one of the most significant and protracted discussions of production possibilities to engage the attention of economists. It is easy enough to understand the interest shown in this question, since it is central to the theoretical appraisal of several important issues in political economy,—among them the determination of the functional distribution of income, and the viability of competitive organization. The discussion divides into two parts, the first relating to considerations allegedly tending to produce increasing returns to scale (up to a point), and the second relating to considerations allegedly tending to produce decreasing returns to scale (after some point). In neither branch has there been any noticeable emphasis on the fact that it is states of knowledge to which these notions of returns relate, since it is states of knowledge that production sets and functions describe. Under the present heading, my purpose is to show that some issues in this area come into sharper focus when viewed from the knowledge perspective.

Formal axiomatic treatments of production set properties typically include an assumption called *additivity*. This says that the sum of feasible production plans is itself feasible. If it is known how to produce output q^a from input x^a, and also how to produce q^b from x^b, then it is known how to produce $(q^a + q^b)$ from $(x^a + x^b)$. In the special case when $x^a = x^b$ and $q^a = q^b$, the conclusion is that $2q^a$ is producible from $2x^a$—a doubling of a feasible plan yields a feasible plan. It is this form of the proposition that has often been advanced in less formal discussion, as in, for example, the Wicksteed passage about exactly repeating a particular production plan for wheat, or in the following statement by Hahn:

> The common sense proposition that the duplication of a given industrial process (together incidentally with a duplication of entrepreneurs or entrepreneurial function) will lead to a doubling of the output is unassailable. . . .
>
> If two identical entrepreneurs set up two identical plants, with an identical labor force, to produce an identical commodity x, then the two together will produce twice the amount of x that could be produced by one alone.[31]

In a similarly confident vein, Arrow and Hahn have more recently said "the assumption of additivity . . . can always be defended and indeed made essentially tautologus."[32]

The considerations I want particularly to explore here involve the relationship of additivity to knowledge and to the spatial distribution of productive activity. Note first that the image suggested by Hahn's two identical plants or Wicksteed's notion of conditions exactly repeated is of spatially distinct but otherwise identical production activities. Since production is understood to involve input and output flows, or amounts over a designated time interval, doubling of production must be understood as a concurrent replication of activity. It is then plain enough that a second manufacturing plant or a second wheat field cannot be in precisely the same location as the first, and also that nothing resembling a replication of the original activity could be accomplished by trying to squeeze twice the activity into the same physical space. In short, the additivity axiom relates to the aggregation of the results of activity occurring in different places.

A difficulty arises here, because it is not in general legitimate to aggregate commodity amounts over space. Particularly in formal theorizing of the sort in which the additivity axiom is explicitly set down, it is customary to treat an arbitrary number of commodities and to treat distinctions of location in space and time as implicit in the basic scheme of commodity definitions. As Debreu says, "a commodity is a good or service completely specified physically, temporally and spatially."[33] Thus it appears that Hahn's two identical plants cannot actually produce an identical commodity x, because physically identical units in different locations are not units of the same economic commodity. And even if Hahn's "common sense proposition" is correct apart from the location issue, it does not strictly correspond to the standard formalization of additivity, with its component-by-component vector operation.

An interpretive device that affords an escape from this conceptual box is to admit that the formal theory must be understood as neglecting spatial and temporal distinctions beneath some threshold level. Within this perspective, the thrust of the foregoing argument is simply that there is a limit to the fineness of the distinctions of space and time that can be made if the mathematical operation of adding commodity amounts is to be interpretable. Debreu is, characteristically, explicit and clear about his employment of the device, but does not actually mention the problem to which it is the response. He considers time divided into "elementary intervals" and space into "elementary regions" that "are chosen small enough for all the points of one of them to be indistinguishable from the point of view of the analysis."[34]

The virtue of this device is that it permits the theorizing to go forward at a high level of abstraction and generality, in which distinctions over space and time are treated as though on exactly the same footing as all other distinctions among commodities. However, for the purposes of a theory of productive knowledge, the physical characteristics of commodities and the physical circumstances of production are clearly *not* on the same footing as distinctions in time and space. The theorist faces no temptation to assume that knowledge of how to make pins implies knowledge of how to make pig iron, but, in spite of some qualifications and cautions already mentioned, it will often be a reasonable approximation to assume that the same productive knowledge can be applied with identical effect in different temporal and spatial contexts. And even when this approximation is unacceptable, it will still be convenient to think of the content of a state of knowledge as specified independently of spatial and temporal restrictions, and thus to isolate for separate examination the problem of its transferability across time and space.

Of course, the physical circumstances of production do vary with geographical location. It is this fact, rather than considerations of location per se or of transportation cost, that needs to be reflected in a theory of productive knowledge. While all production activities occupy physical space of some sort, the range of environmental situations presented by production sites is diverse. Consider Iowa farmland, Malaysian rubber plantations, the 110th floor of the World Trade Center, the deep tunnels of South African gold mines, the ski slopes of the Alps, the orbital paths of communication satellites. Each sort of site is naturally equipped with characteristic values of physical parameters such as its spatial configuration, the force of gravity, exposure to solar and cosmic ray radiation, wind velocities, humidities, and temperatures. It is obvious that these physical characteristics are an important determinant of the sort of production that takes place at particular sites, and are intimately related to the technological knowledge that makes such production possible. (In each of the examples cited, a large part of the problem that technology solves is under the heading of either "taking advantage of" or "overcoming" the specific physical characteristics of the site.)

The influence of these conditions on production is closely related conceptually to the classical factor of production, "land."[35] For example, implicit in the bundle of conditions characteristic of a production site is a limit on what can be accomplished in the way of production at that site, that is to say, limitations of spatial extent and other attributes are responsible for the eventual appearance of diminishing returns to other inputs. But the appropriate concept is broader than merely considering a portion of the land surface of the planet and more complex than merely considering a region of physical space, involving as it does all the physical features of the environment of a region of physical space. And it is worth noting that these physical features often constitute as much a part of the problem to be solved by the application of productive knowledge as they are an aspect of the solution.

There is, I think, something to be said for giving theoretical recognition to a generic input category corresponding to classical "land," though it is not for the purposes of the theory of distribution that this seems useful. Because the connotations of "land" are too narrow and too suggestive of a nonexistent homogeneity, I will call the inputs in this category "site-use inputs." The generic trait that defines the category is that these inputs involve the services of a region of physical space with its attendant environmental conditions. Two related considerations make it helpful to distinguish such inputs, collectively, from other sorts of inputs.

One is the fact that, whatever the specific institutional arrangements under which the use of specific sites for production may be allocated, the entire bundle of environmental conditions characteristic of a site is acquired willy-nilly with the use of the site itself. However complex may be the role of these various conditions as influences on the production activity that takes place, there is no need to think of them as factors of production distinguished from the spatial region to which they relate. If, for example, the feasibility of replicating a production activity is at issue, a useful and relatively concrete initial focus for such discussion is on whether a second site, technologically equivalent to the first, exists and can be identified. A large part of the airy discussion of whether all factors have been identified and suitably doubled can be supplanted by such a focus on the site-use input.

The second consideration involves the relation of productive knowledge to the environment in which it is applied. While the ability to transfer technological knowledge from one site to another and produce corresponding results does depend on the existence of a technologically equivalent site and on the ability to recognize it as such, it certainly does not depend on the ability to purchase or otherwise manipulate the associated environmental conditions individually. Neither does it require an understanding of the ways in which those influences operate. Effective methods, learned by doing at one site, may be effective at a second site without ever being understood in any depth.

It would not be difficult to accommodate some of the foregoing observations within standard production theory, with minimal disruption of its basic framework. For example, it could be assumed that there are finitely many different types of production sites, i.e., different technological equivalence classes of sites. An individual site of a particular type might best be thought of as an indivisible unit of standard spatial configuration. The familiar assumption of "impossibility of something from nothing" could be specialized to "impossibility of output without a site-use input of some type." Additivity would not be assumed to prevail at an individual site; indeed, it would be sensible to assume that the output attainable from an individual site is bounded. Technology would be described, not in terms of feasible transformations of economic commodities, but in terms of the transformations of physically specified commodities that are feasible at sites of each given type (plus a separate characterization of transportation technology). The effect of additivity would arise in this model of production to the extent that there are many sites in each technological equivalence class, and that it is for some reason meaningful or useful to neglect the necessary locational distinctions among sites. (The Debreuvian "elementary regions" device is optional.)

Such is the plan for a formal theory that would accurately capture the point about the feasibility of replication made by Wicksteed, Hahn, and others. Implicit in the plan is the message that it is impossible adequately to discuss questions of returns to scale in production without straying into the intellectual territory of location theory—a message that I find entirely plausible.[36]

Of course, the notion of a "technologically equivalent site" is a theoretical abstraction that will not be much help to anyone who is actually trying to find a new site that is "similar enough" to the original one. Real land does not come posted with signs saying, "This is a Type 27 site," any more than other commodities come tagged with the names of homogeneous aggregates to which they belong. To recognize that real attempts at technology transfer do not have the benefit of these signs and tags is to begin to appreciate the fact that the replication idea operates in reality as a heuristic—a useful but fallible approach to the problem of getting additional output roughly equal to that produced in an existing facility.

I conclude this discussion of land, space, and additivity with an example that underscores both the similarity and the difference between my conception of site-use inputs and the classical conception of land. There is one choice orbital track for a communications satellite, 22,300 miles above the equator. In that orbit alone, a satellite hangs stationary above a point on the turning Earth. Within that orbit there are better and worse locations, depending on the communications traffic densities in the areas below. Thus there are a limited number of production sites particularly appropriate to the production of communication satellite services; even in empty space, "land" is scarce. (In principle, those choice sites give rise to Ricardian land rents.) Because sites are scarce, efforts to get more output must focus on either the "intensive margin" associated with currently occupied orbital positions, or the "extensive margin" of inferior orbital positions and tracks. In neither case, however, is there a preexisting production function along which to move; the engineers invent it as they go along. With forty-four satellites now in geosynchronous orbit between 4 and 150 degrees west, and with a doubling expected within five years, the spacing requirements imposed by existing technology are incompatible with the numbers. According to a recent *New York Times* story, "engineers are focusing on technologies to increase communication capacity through the use of higher radio frequencies and more sophisticated satellites that make more efficient use of their place in orbit."[37] Presumably, the force of diminishing returns will ultimately deflect attention to the extensive margin, if, indeed, it is not already doing so.

On the one hand, this example testifies to the universal relevance of some basic ideas of economic theory. On the other, my somewhat dubious invocation of diminishing returns in the context of a discussion of changing technology is a reminder that we have a considerable distance to go in linking production theory to an adequate conceptualization of states of knowledge and the changes therein.

Summary and Conclusion

I have attempted in this essay to suggest the probable fruitfulness of an effort to put the idea of knowledge in its proper, central place in production theory. A wide range of familiar issues can be seen in a clearer light by taking this point of view. From it may be derived helpful guidance for the empirical application of standard production-theoretic concepts and a promising menu of projects for incremental theoretical improvement. Partial substantiation of this claim is provided, I hope, by the examples in the preceding section. There are other examples that would serve at least as well. I have omitted discussion of divisibility, the counterpart of the discussion of additivity.

Together these analyses lead to a focus on the design heuristic "increase the physical dimensions of individual productive units" and thus to an appraisal of the important phenomenon of scale-augmenting technical change.[38] But this will have to be left to another time.

Of course it is probable that if the leads offered by the knowledge perspective were diligently pursued, the ultimate result would not be a mere accumulation of refinements and improvements of standard production theory, but would also involve the construction of a broader and more flexible theory of productive knowledge. Such an alternative theory would fit uncomfortably with some other parts of the conceptual apparatus that economists bring to the study of economic behavior and organization. For example, the idea that firm behavior is optimizing threatens to become a cumbersome or ineffective theoretical device when the constraints of the supposed optimization reflect knowledge states with ambiguous and shifting boundaries—though the more basic idea that firm behavior is largely motivated by the quest for profit remains as viable as ever. Similarly, analysis of the ways in which firms draw upon the advances in productive knowledge taking place in other firms and in the broader social environment can hardly fail to be profoundly at odds with theories that view firms as independent, preexisting repositories of knowledge, behaviorally linked only through markets.

It is no accident that standard production theory fits so well with the remainder of the structure of economic theory, whereas awkward problems ensue when the substantive realities of productive knowledge are allowed to influence the conceptualization. Production sets, with their nonoperational linkage to states of knowledge, form a foundation that was constructed after the shape of the superstructure was already largely known. The foundation performs the support function well because it was designed to do so. If it is less than adequate as an abstract representation of the reality to which it supposedly refers, it is probably because that reality was never the primary influence shaping the choice of abstractions.

My inquiry into what our familiar production theory is about thus leads back to the question of what it is for. Most of modern economic theory displays an admirable coherence and consistency, in which production theory participates. The same concepts and much the same formalisms that appear in the abstract parables about the normative appeal of competitive capitalism are also central to work that aims at scientific understanding of economic reality. In fact, the existence of a clear link to the shared conceptual structure at the core of the discipline is often employed as a simple quality criterion for empirical work. Unfortunately, however, the commitments associated with that conceptual core tend to impede understanding of the many dynamic and important aspects of reality that involve the turbulent boundary areas of productive knowledge. Dramatic struggles to advance, control, and exploit new knowledge take place in some areas, while in others, society's productive capabilities seem to be decaying as a result of poorly understood social and economic forces. Standard production theory is just not about these phenomena, not even in the sense of providing a helpful platform for some future intellectual launching in their direction. They will remain relatively neglected and poorly understood at least until economic theory grants them a status higher than that of deferrable difficulties and awkward complications at the periphery of the discipline. Such a change can only come about if theorists display a willingness to reconsider, at a fundamental level, the conceptual structure appropriate to a theory of productive knowledge.

NOTES

1. Philip Wicksteed, whose work figures significantly in the "Origins" section of this essay, endorsed this methodological view with the following eloquent statement: "It is true, of course, that every transformation of the mathematical expression of an economic fact or hypothesis must be ideally capable of direct expression in economic terms, and therefore every step of the mathematical argument is ideally capable of being translated into a logically cogent economic argument. Moreover, to effect this translation will usually be in the highest degree instructive, throwing all manner of side lights upon the subject of discussion, leading the student into the inner recesses of the hypotheses on which he is working, and not seldom revealing some suspected weakness or inconsistency in his premises." (*An Essay on the Coordination of the Laws of Distribution* [London: Macmillan & Co., 1894], p. 5.) Even Milton Friedman, in an essay generally considered hostile to this sort of inquiry, acknowledged that the assumptions of a theory "are sometimes a convenient means for specifying the conditions under which the theory is expected to be valid," and also that "our aim should be to formulate the rules (for using a model) explicitly in so far as possible and continually to widen the range of phe-

nomena for which it is possible to do so." (*Essays in Positive Economics* [Chicago: University of Chicago Press, 1953], pp. 23 and 25.)

2. My former Michigan colleague Mike Scherer has made a major contribution in this area, in theoretical and empirical works too numerous to mention here. And a recent paper by Glenn Loury, currently at Michigan, is prominent in an important new body of literature that attempts to formalize Joseph Schumpeter's theories of innovation and competition. ("Market Structure and Innovation," *Quarterly Journal of Economics* 93 [August 1979]: 395–410.)

3. Neoclassical growth theory is the leading example of a substantial literature in which technological change has been treated in a manner that is minimally disruptive of standard production theory, but as a result fails to make much contact with the real phenomenon. There is very little attention to such questions as whether isoquants are well defined at factor proportions remote from historical experience, or whether there is really a meaningful distinction between factor substitution and technical change when factor proportions are changing essentially monotonically over time. Atypical in this regard is the 1969 paper which serves to illustrate the high marginal payoff to loosening the constraints of the standard framework: A. Atkinson and J. Stiglitz, "A New View of Technical Change," *Economic Journal* 79 (September 1969): 573–78.

4. R. H. Coase, "The Nature of the Firm," *Economica* 4 (November 1937): 386–405.

5. See O. E. Williamson, *Markets and Hierarchies: Analysis and Antitrust Implications* (New York: Free Press, 1975), chap. 4; idem., "Transaction-Cost Economics: The Governance of Contractual Relations," *Journal of Law and Economics* 22 (October 1979): 233–61. In the latter paper Williamson is explicit that "unified governance" and the associated "relational contracting" model is an alternative to "market governance" of "classical contracting," and that each mode dominates for transactions of a characteristic type (see fig. 2, p. 253, and related discussion). The business firm, as conventionally understood, is an example of "unified governance." But Williamson's focal example under the "unified governance" heading is not "firms" but "vertical integration." Thus, he apparently views the problem in terms of incremental changes in a given situation, and does not explicitly indicate whether his transaction-cost analysis provides a full rationale for the existence of the firm.

6. A related feature of the theory is that it bears the stamp of its original intended use in the analysis of equilibrium in informationally perfect markets. Instead of having a theory of productive knowledge that is applicable to that case among others, we have a theory applicable in that case only—when most of the significant knowledge problems have been assumed away.

7. Wicksteed, *An Essay on the Coordination of the Laws of Distribution*, p. 4.

8. Ibid., p. 33.

9. Sune Carlson, *A Study on the Pure Theory of Production* (New York:

Kelley and Millman, 1956), pp. 14–16, emphasis in original. Carlson notes F. Y. Edgeworth (*Papers Relating to Political Economy* [London: Macmillan & Co., 1925], 1:61–69) on the point, but it is not clear that the credit given is credit due. Edgeworth says in the quoted passage that entrepreneurs maximize profits to the best of their ability, but the issue is whether the implications of that for the appropriate definition of the production function were recognized.

10. Citations to these works and a brief discussion of the subject may be found in the published version of Koopmans's Nobel Prize address: T. C. Koopmans, "Concepts of Optimality and Their Uses," *American Economic Review* 67 (June 1977): 261–74.

11. T. C. Koopmans, "Analaysis of Production as an Efficient Combination of Activities," in *Activity Analysis of Production and Allocation*, ed. T. C. Koopmans (New York: John Wiley and Sons, 1951), chap. 3.

12. K. J. Arrow, "An Extension of the Basic Theorems of Classical Welfare Economics," in *Proceedings of the Second Berkeley Symposium on Mathematical Statistics and Probability*, ed. J. Neyman (Berkeley: University of California Press, 1951), pp. 507–32; K. J. Arrow and G. Debreu, "Existence of Equilibrium for a Competitive Economy," *Econometrica* 22 (July 1954): 265–90; G. Debreu, *Theory of Value* (New York: John Wiley and Sons, 1959).

13. There is, of course, empirical content in the hypothesis that a collection of observed input-output pairs are all optimizing choices from the same production set under competitive conditions. And specific postulated properties of the production set may be testable as well. See G. Hanoch and M. Rothschild, "Testing the Assumptions of Production Theory: A Nonparametric Approach," *Journal of Political Economy* 80 (March-April 1972): 256–75. My point is that there is no empirical check on the correspondence between the production set revealed by choice and some independently assessed "state of knowledge."

14. If the focus of this essay were on the empirical applications of production theory, production sets would receive little attention and production functions, cost functions, and profit functions would receive a great deal. Recent years have seen the development of a whole body of econometrically oriented research in production theory, shaped by a quest for empirical methods that are simultaneously as true as possible to the central commitments of the underlying economic theory, and as free as possible of restrictions that are peripheral or extraneous to that theory. See M. Fuss and D. McFadden, *Production Economics: A Dual Approach to Theory and Applications* (Amsterdam: North-Holland, 1978), vols. 1 and 2. But the focus here is on the conceptual underpinnings of the theory, and in the modern view the production set provides that underpinning for the production function.

15. K. J. Arrow and F. H. Hahn, *General Competitive Analysis* (San Francisco: Holden-Day, 1971), p. 53.

16. On the definition of "visibility," *Van Nostrand's Scientific Encyclopedia*,

(5th ed., pp. 2288–89 says the following: "In United States weather-observing practice, the greatest distance in a given direction at which it is just possible to see and identify with the unaided eye (*a*) in the daytime, a prominent dark object against the sky at the horizon, and (*b*) at night, a known, preferably unfocused, moderately intense light source. . . . After visibilities have been determined around the entire horizon, they are resolved into a single value of prevailing visibility, which is the greatest horizontal visibility equaled or surpassed throughout half, though not necessarily a continuous half, of the horizon circle."

17. A recent report in *Science* describes the ambiguities of productive knowledge in making microcircuits: "Despite the fact that the semiconductor silicon is likely the most intensively studied and well-understood solid material on earth, when it comes to making integrated circuits in large quantities, the pure white gowns and caps of production line workers might as well be covered with moons and stars of the type that bedeck the robes of the conjuror . . . the causes of defects are not always understood, nor are they easy to control when they are understood." (A. L. Robinson, "New Ways to Make Microcircuits," *Science* 208 [May 1980]: 1019.

18. There are many anecdotal accounts of unexpected and sometimes inexplicable difficulties affecting attempts to transfer "familiar" technology from one place to another. See., e.g., Michael Polanyi, *Personal Knowledge: Toward a Post-Critical Philosophy* (New York: Harper Torchbooks, 1962), p. 52.

19. I am drawing here on the work of Herbert Simon and his collaborators. See., e.g., A. Newell, J. C. Shaw, and H. A. Simon, "The Processes of Creative Thinking," in *Contemporary Approaches to Creative Thinking*, ed. H. E. Gruber, G. Terrell, and M. Wertheimer (New York: Atherton Press, 1962), pp. 63–119; A. Newell and H. A. Simon, *Human Problem Solving* (Englewood Cliffs, N.J.: Prentice-Hall, 1972); H. A. Simon, "On How to Decide What to Do," *Bell Journal of Economics* 9 (Autumn 1978): 494–507.

20. Newell, Shaw, and Simon, "The Processes of Creative Thinking," p. 85.

21. R. R. Nelson, S. G. Winter, and H. L. Schuette, "Technical Change in an Evolutionary Model," *Quarterly Journal of Economics* 90 (February 1976): 90–118.

22. G. J. Powers, "Modelling Discrete Adaptive Behavior in the Chemical Process Industries," and Dale F. Rudd, "Modelling the Development of the Intermediate Chemicals Industry," in *Adaptive Economic Models*, ed. R. H. Day and T. Groves (New York: Academic Press, 1975), pp. 391–452.

23. Rudd, "Modelling the Development of the Intermediate Chemicals Industry," p. 446.

24. Of course, there is no difficulty in the notion of a firm being in *short run* equilibrium at zero output and maintaining its productive knowledge along with its plant and equipment. The question is how information storage is financed in a firm that is forever waiting in the wings.

25. J. de V. Graaf, *Theoretical Welfare Economics* (Cambridge: Cambridge University Press, 1957), p. 16.
26. Nelson and I do attempt a detailed explanation in our book, *An Evolutionary Theory of Economic Capabilities and Behavior* (forthcoming).
27. See K. J. Arrow, "The Economic Implications of Learning by Doing," *Review of Economic Studies* 29 (June 1962): 155–73, and the references cited therein.
28. An entertaining account of the entire affair may be found in R. A. Smith, *Corporations in Crisis* (New York: Anchor Books, 1966), chaps. 3 and 4.
29. A prudent executive should probably have a discussion of antitrust law with his corporation counsel before committing himself wholeheartedly to a BCG-recommended strategy, as the following concise summary suggests: "The strategic implication is that a company should strive to dominate the market. . . ." P. Conley, *Experience Curves as a Planning Tool* (Boston: Boston Consulting Group, 1970), p. 11.
30. R. E. Caves and M. E. Porter, "From Entry Barriers to Mobility Barriers," *Quarterly Journal of Economics* 91 (May 1977): 241–61; D. J. Teece, "Technology Transfer by Multinational Firms: The Resource Cost of Transferring Technological Know-How," *Economic Journal* 87 (June 1977): 242–61; D. J. Teece, "Economies of Scope and the Scope of the Enterprise: The Diversification of Petroleum Companies," *Journal of Economic Behavior and Organization* 1, no. 3 (1980): 223–47.
31. F. H. Hahn, "Proportionality, Divisibility and Economies of Scale: Comment," *Quarterly Journal of Economics* 63 (February 1949): 131–37.
32. Arrow and Hahn, *General Competitive Analysis*, p. 61. *Cf.* Debreu, *Theory of Value*, p. 41.
33. Debreu, *Theory of Value*, p. 32.
34. Ibid., p. 29.
35. Ricardo's phrase characterizing land as a factor of production was "the original and indestructible powers of the soil." This is clearly much too narrow to cover the range of examples of production circumstances set forth above. Marshall, in the *Principles*, came much closer to the required concept, though his discussion was still overly focused on ordinary agriculture as an example. In particular he was clear that it is not just the soil but the whole bundle of physical aspects of the location that is involved: ". . . the space relations of the plot in question, and the annuity that nature has given it of sunlight and air and rain." (A. Marshall, *Principles of Economics*, 8th ed. [New York: Macmillan Co., 1948], p. 147.)
36. The book by Scherer et al. on multiplant operation is very illuminating on the relationships of scale economies, transportation costs, and industrial structure. F. M. Scherer et al., *The Economics of Multi-Plant Operation: An International Comparisons Study* (Cambridge, Mass.: Harvard University Press, 1975).
37. J N. Wilford, "A 'Traffic Jam' in Outer Space," *New York Times*, March 24, 1980.
38. See R. C. Levin, "Technical Change and Optimal Scale: Some Evidence

and Implications," *Southern Economic Journal* 2 (October 1977): 208–21, for a discussion of the phenomenon and some dramatic empirical examples.

Comments by GLENN C. LOURY

Professor Winter's fine essay develops two central points. The first is the critical observation that the treatment of the activity of production in modern economic theory must be judged unsatisfactory. The second point is the suggestion that an improved theory of production can be fruitfully sought through the development of what Winter calls the "knowledge perspective." In these remarks I comment briefly on each of these points.

The failings of modern production theory (i.e., the neoclassical theory of the firm) identified by Winter are threefold: (1) it is unrealistic as a description of what firms do, (2) the phenomenon of technical change is inadequately explained by the theory, and (3) the theory does not come to grips with the nature of the firm as an economic institution. I find the first of these criticisms considerably less telling than the last two. The claim that a theory is "unrealistic" can mean one of two things. Either the theory in question fails to explain experience, or its basic constructs and inner logic do not correspond to one's intuitive perception of the phenomenon with which the theory deals. In the former instance, the critic does well to specify those aspects of experience which the theory does not explain, as Winter has done in points (2) and (3) above. However, it is in that latter "intuitive" sense that I believe the "lack of realism" comment is intended. Firms simply do not (seem to) act as we posit they do in the theory. Yet science is replete with instances in which intuitively "unrealistic" assumptions have proven to be the key to important advancement. (Einstein's rejection of Newton's "realistic" notions of absolute space and time provide one example.) Indeed, our very perception of what is realistic is continually being altered as science advances. Thus, I think Winter errs when he claims "the attempt to explicate the basic commitments of a theory in concrete terms can reveal the sense and circumstances in which those commitments might be strained, and thus help to demarcate its valid claims to predictive and explanatory strength." Translating an abstract logical system from mathematics into English does not reveal whether the implications of that system are refuted by experience. By this I do not mean to free the economist of his need to consider actual institutions when developing his theories. I am merely suggesting that he need not be confined to some consensus perception of what those institutions "really" do.

The second and third criticisms are, however, much more telling in my view. Regarding the second, as Winter convincingly documents, the modern theory of the firm says almost nothing of interest about the process of technological advance. Either it is regarded as an exogenous phenomenon whose consequences are studied, or it is thought to respond in some mechanical fashion to expenditures on research and development. The former treatment is obviously unsatisfactory, while the latter involves a kind of infinite regress. That is, if some "production function" relates technical change to research and development (R&D) expenditures, then how does one represent advancement which makes a given level of R&D financing more effective?

Regarding the third criticism, one of the oldest puzzles in economics is the problem of explaining why certain economic transactions occur within a firm, and others between firms. What, in other words, determines the extent of a single productive enterprise? Winter correctly notes that the neoclassical theory of production does not even consider this problem, since it regards the set of firms and their production possibilities as exogenous. I agree with his judgment that future development of the theory ought to be directed in large part at this issue. Indeed, much current work on market failures under conditions of imperfect information has direct bearing on the question of the internal organization of the firm.

The "knowledge perspective" is Professor Winter's answer to these difficulties. He suggests that considerable light may be shed on the issues of technical change and the internal organization of the firm by "theoriz[ing] usefully about the phenomena associated with the fact that individuals and organizations 'know how to do things.' " He identifies several important consequences of this approach. First, it seems clear that the set of things which a person or organization "knows how to do" is not sharply and unambiguously defined. While there are many problems that a given individual definitely can or cannot solve, there are also problems whose tractability can only be known after one has tried to solve them. A second point is that much of what individuals know is not how to perform a specific task, but rather how to figure out how that task is to be performed, once they are confronted with it. Thus, Winter introduces the important distinction between "planning knowledge" and "performance knowledge." The latter is know-how relevant to the performance of specific tasks, developed within (and therefore dependent upon) a particular environment. The former is knowledge of certain problem-solving heuristics—methods of adapting old solutions to new problems as the environment changes. Received theory speaks only of "performance knowledge," and presumes it possible to delineate such know-how precisely.

Professor Winter's idea seems to me both interesting and conducive to elaboration. It provides a way of thinking about phenomena important in practice but not treated in conventional theory. For example, Winter show us that problems of technology transfer, the social cost of bankruptcy, antitrust policy regarding mergers or the breakup of dominant firms, the nature of arbitrage and the role of potential firms in defining a competitive industry, all appear in a different light when viewed from the knowledge perspective. It seems to me therefore that the knowledge perspective represents a potentially fruitful avenue of investigation. The difficult problem which its adherents must tackle is to develop their ideas in a way which is compatible with "the wealth of useful concepts, techniques, and insights represented by the traditional theory of production." That is, I regard as crucial the requirement that progress in economic theory proceed through stages of successive generalization, with each stage adding to the set of phenomena explained at the previous stage. While this does not rule out radical revision of a theory, it disciplines the revisionist in a scientifically useful manner.

Stabilization Policy in a Quandary

JAMES S. DUESENBERRY

The record of post–World War II stabilization theory and policy is full of contrast and paradox. In terms of real output growth, the postwar period looks like a huge success for stabilization policy. In spite of two subsequent wars, less than global, and an energy crisis, the growth of real output has been more stable than in any other period of comparable length. But in terms of inflation the record has been terrible. When we look to causation, we find that government has been a major force for stability and at the same time a major source of instability.

Macroeconomic theory shows the same contrasts. When I first taught economics 51 at the University of Michigan, Shorey Peterson's syllabus labeled the Keynesian approach as unorthodox. In 1939 I thought he was behind the times. Now it appears that he was way ahead. Macroeconomic theory has made great progress, but not enough to keep up with events. The econometric models, which once seemed to represent scientific economics, are now in head-to-head competition with single-equation panacea producers. Rational expectations theorists tell us that by controlling the money supply, we can painlessly control inflation. It used to be thought that one fought inflation by raising taxes; now Arthur Laffer tells us that we can do it by lowering them.

These gimmicky ideas reflect the fact that our present situation is a difficult one. They also reflect the belief that our present difficulties result mainly from fundamental errors in policy making rather than from the characteristics of our economy. I shall argue that in fact both our successes and our failures regarding economic stabilization reflect not only wars and oil crises, but fundamental changes in the structure of our economy. Economic policy has played an important role, as well, but it has to be understood to involve an uneasy compromise

James S. Duesenberry is professor of economics at Harvard University and received his A.B. and Ph.D. degrees from Michigan, the latter in 1948.

between the goals of full employment and price stability in a world in which those goals have been in conflict. We now need to make major changes in our policy stance, not because it was always wrong, but because events have overtaken it.

Structural Changes

The performance of the postwar economy reflects important structural changes, resulting from the Great Depression and World War II. The very large increase in the scale of government between 1929 and 1951 is primarily responsible for the relative stability of real gross national product (GNP) in the postwar period. High marginal tax and transfer rates have reduced the mutiplier to half its 1929 value. Moreover, total government outlays substantially exceed the sum of gross private domestic investment and exports, and these expenditures have grown continuously. The automatic stabilization resulting from the large scale of government has been reinforced by changes in the financial system. Thus far, deposit insurance and changes in the operation of the private banking system have reduced the economy's vulnerability to financial panic. In view of recent events, one might not wish to describe monetary policy as a stabilizing force, but the fact is that while the Federal Reserve can turn on a monetary crunch, it can also turn it off again. In earlier periods when money supply was not controllable, the credit crunch often produced a financial panic. Of course, financial institutions and corporations have responded to a more stable financial climate by taking greater risks. Thus far, however, although all sorts of unexpected movements in consumer demand and investment expenditures have made life difficult for forecasters, we have not had the financial panic which some authors have been predicting for the past twenty years. "Autonomous" fluctuations in consumer and investment demand not explained by the prior history of the economy have not, on the whole, appeared terribly important. The combined consumer durable and investment boom of 1955 seems to be the outstanding exception.

But while government action has been in one sense a source of stability, in another it, rather than the erratic behavior of the private sector, has been the most important source of instability, with the oil and food shocks of 1973–74 taking second place. In my judgment, the expansion of defense expenditures during the Korean War and the ensuing decline, like the expansion and decline associated with the

Vietnam war, have played a central role in causing fluctuations in demand. Swings in monetary policy, especially the credit crunches of 1966, 1969, 1974, and, I suppose, 1979–80, have played an important role. Many economists would give fiscal and monetary policy a good deal of the credit for bringing on the recessions of 1958 and 1960–61, and would extend the same credit to the excessively rapid expansion of 1972–73. Those changes in turn reflected shifts in attitude toward inflation and recession. From some points of view, the slumps during 1956–61 are the most important examples of the destabilizing aspects of the conflict between high employment and price stability. Several years of monetary and fiscal constraint offset strong private demand and brought on two recessions which in turn cured the inflation which had started in the mid-1950s. Structural changes in our economy have increased its vulnerability to inflation.

In my view, unionization has played a major role in the inflationary process. It has become fashionable for economists to deprecate the role of unions. They are almost completely neglected in the theoretical literature on inflation. There is general agreement that trade unions can raise the relative wages of their members and in fact trade union wages and fringe benefits have risen relative to others in most of the past twenty-five years. They have more than made up for the ground lost due to contract lag in the late sixties. At the same time there is general agreement that the potential relative wage gain for unions is limited. In some cases the relative wage gain of unions may be held down or, as in the case of coal in the 1950s and construction in the 1970s, may even be reversed by market forces. However, the widespread use of the comparability doctrine by all large nonunion employers, and the attachment of the minimum wage to the average level of wages, will pull up the whole wage structure so that union relative wage gains raise the rate of increase of money wage levels throughout the system. (I have, of course, assumed that monetary and fiscal policy are adjusted in nominal terms, so as to accommodate the implied rise in money wages to maintain full employment.)

The second aspect of structural change in our economy is the increased inertia of wages and prices. Employers, nonunion as well as union, generally tend to pursue long-run policies in price and wage making. On the down side, employers do not attempt to reduce money wages when unemployment is high, and, indeed, appear to be willing to raise money wages when the cost of living is rising, even though they have no current problems recruiting. They are willing to forego the opportunity for short-run gains in the interest of a stable, high quality labor force in the long run. Unions, of course, reinforce that tendency. In the same way, producers tend to follow long-run pricing policy. They do not extract all the traffic will bear in periods of high capacity utilization, and they are reluctant to reduce prices during periods of slack. For a given degree of instability in demand, the inertia of prices and wages should serve to make the price level more stable and need not contribute to an inflationary trend. In fact, however, there seems to be some asymmetry. When prices fail to adjust to changes in nominal aggregate demand, there must be a corresponding shift in employment and real output. On the down side, any amount of shift is possible; one simply observes unemployment and unused capacity. On the up side, quantity adjustments are limited, and the failure of prices to adjust upward in response to nominal demand increases shows up in shortages of labor or capacity. The inertia of prices and wages appears to give way to the pressure of shortages more readily than to the downward pressure of surpluses. Here a change in the structure of economic policy responses enters the picture. During slumps, monetary and fiscal policy react to the appearance of unemployment and excess capacity in ways which raise nominal aggregate demand and thereby reduce unemployment, excess capacity, and downward pressure on prices. Moreover, the fact that fiscal and monetary policy are expected to react in that way increases the inertia of wages and prices to downward pressures. On the up side, monetary and fiscal policy have often accommodated the pressures producing rising prices, rather than acting to reduce those pressures, though the record in that respect is very mixed.

Issues in the Theory of Aggregate Demand and Inflation
Active stabilization policy depends for its success on knowledge of the structure of the economy. In recent years we have tried to give quantitative expression to our views about economic structure by the use of large-scale econometric models. With all due respect to Klein, Hymans, and their colleagues in the model-building industry, those models do have some very serious problems. Even so, our profession has made tremendous progress in theoretical and empirical macroeconomic analysis. At the end of World War II, about all we had was

the "Keynes for Kiddies" multiplier model. Monetary theory was in a state of disarray. Price theory consisted only of an elementary excess demand theory of inflation, while the theory of investment demand emphasized either an oversimplified acceleration principle, or relied on vague expectational theories. The Klein-Goldberger model, which laid the foundations for the Research Seminar in Quantitative Economics at the University of Michigan and then for much other work in econometric model building, had, as I recall it, only about thirteen equations. Today's models are tremendously complex, and run at times to four or five hundred equations. They represent an enormous amount of research on all aspects of demand theory, on monetary theory, and on price and wage theory. Nonetheless, major issues remain unresolved. Recent comparisons of alternative theories of investment demand show all of them to have limitations in forecasting, and it is hard to choose any of them as a consistently better performer than another. Yet they may have quite different implications. The same thing may be said for the theories of consumption and saving, inventory investment, and housing demand. When simulation studies take account of all the interactions in the system, the results are even more divergent. One recent study of the impact of hypothetical open-market operations using six different models produced estimates of nominal GNP change ranging from 4 to 40 billion dollars. To a considerable extent, the weaknesses of econometric models result from the application of regression-related statistical analysis to nonexperimental data. At least some questions could be resolved by greater use of microdata and fieldwork interviews. Single equation monetarist models are even weaker on that account, and simple monetarist models have an exceedingly poor forecasting record. They treat monetary policy as though it were exogenous. In fact, postwar monetary policy can be characterized as accommodation punctuated by occasional panic. Money appears to exert its most powerful influence through credit crunches, which in the nineteenth century led to bankruptcies and financial panic, and in more recent years have caused major swings in residential construction. Those swings have played a major role in several postwar recessions.

Our ability to understand and forecast the course of inflation is even more limited than our ability to forecast changes in output. There is a certain measure of agreement about the general nature of the

ELMER E. RASMUSON LIBRARY
UNIVERSITY OF ALASKA

inflationary process. The most common type of inflation model is based on four propositions:

1. Most prices behave as though they were set by a simple markup over cyclically adjusted unit labor costs, with minor cyclical variations in the markup.

2. Cyclically adjusted unit labor costs depend on wage and fringe benefit costs and the productivity trend.

3. Changes in wage rates are responsive to the level and change of the unemployment rate but are also strongly influenced by the past history of wages and prices and by expectations about their future changes.

4. While wage costs dominate the movement of most prices, the price level can at times be strongly influenced by food, raw material, and energy prices which are not closely related to wage costs.

In a crude way, the inflation model derived from these propositions does serve to explain some major features of the recent history of inflation. It helps explain how the rapid expansion of demand in the last half of the 1960s caused an acceleration in the rate of price increase. It also shows in a general way how increases in energy and food prices feed through into wage increases and then lead to further price increases. It shows why the rate of inflation shows so much inertia in periods of balance in labor markets, or even in times of slack in a mild recession. But it has not enabled us, even in the absence of surprises from such elements as oil and food prices, to predict the rate of inflation very accurately. Moreover, within the general framework that I have described, there is room for a great deal of disagreement. The relationship between the level of unemployment and the rate of wage increase appears to be fairly loose. Much of our evidence about it comes from a few major episodes in inflation history. Indeed, the sequence dealt with in most of the statistical studies focuses upon the shift from relatively low unemployment in the mid-1950s to the higher rates of the early 1960s, and the return to low unemployment in the late 1960s.

The role of unions in the process is a major source of disagreement. The pattern of wage movements is certainly complicated by the lags which result from multi-year contracts and from variations in the cost-of-living adjustment built into different contracts. There is fundamental disagreement about the extent to which the apparent power of unions to raise wages in relatively weak labor markets is an important factor in the process. Despite the general tendency for economists to minimize the role of unions in the inflation process, I find it hard to explain the wage movements in many industries without recognition of union power.

There is also a great deal of disagreement as to the nature of the linkage between current wage movements and past wage and price movements. Some economists propose that current wage movements are influenced by workers' and employers' expectations regarding the future movements of prices—expectations which in turn have been influenced by the *past* history of prices. Within this expectational framework, some economists emphasize employers' expectations regarding future product prices, while others emphasize the importance of workers' expectations regarding future changes in the cost of living. Others propose that the cost of living is involved because workers demand wage increases to "catchup" with its changes. Still others use a wage/wage spiral approach, arguing that both unions and personnel administrators are strongly influenced by "comparability" considerations in making wage decisions. Since wages and prices show a strong correlation, it has proven difficult to sort out the relative importance of the different considerations involved. I think that there is plenty of evidence to show that all of them play a role. I also think it unlikely that the structure of these interactions has remained constant over the past twenty-five or thirty years.

Finally, there are grounds for great uncertainty regarding the role of productivity behavior in the inflation process. We expect that a given movement of money wages will cause a greater increase in prices when productivity growth is low than when it is high. The resulting step-up in the rate of price increase associated with poor productivity performance leads to further wage increases. We should expect the inflation rate to accelerate, unless the unemployment rate rises enough to offset it. On the other hand, we have to recognize that some increases in wages are directly connected with the kind of productivity increase associated with an upgrading of the work force as we adopt more complex technology. Moreover, poor productivity performance may affect employers' willingness to give wage increases.

In spite of all of the disputes over important details, the most widely accepted inflation model may be summarized as follows:

1. With a balanced labor market (at perhaps 6 percent measured unemployment), an established inflation rate tends to persist.

2. The rate will be accelerated by a positive demand shock; it will be decelerated by a negative demand shock.

3. Supply shocks such as oil price increases or a falling rate of productivity gain will accelerate the inflation rate. Negative supply shocks may, of course, also occur and decelerate the inflation rate.

The actual course of inflation since 1965 may be explained in terms of interactions among the model I have sketched and (a) the positive demand shock set off by expansion of the Vietnam war, (b) the oil shock of 1974 (partially offset by the recession of 1975), (c) more oil shocks in 1979, and (d) a declining productivity trend since at least 1973. In that explanation, excess demand plays an important role in 1965–69, and a supporting role in 1973. But the model implies that since 1970 excess demand did not cause inflation. On the other hand, neither was aggregate demand constrained enough to break the inertia of the demand-induced inflation of the late 1960s, to offset the impact of oil shocks, or to compensate for the adverse effect of poor productivity performance.

Many may feel that I have not given enough attention to government spending, deficits, and money supply growth as causes of inflation. One way to describe their role is to say that the growth of government expenditures and of the money supply help to explain both the excessive real demand growth of the late 1960s, and its continued growth in line with potential output through the 1970s. With the exception of the credit crunches of 1966, 1969, and 1974, money supply has been accommodative. Government expenditures surged during the late 1960s, then moved ahead unevenly. In the 1970s the trend of government expenditures kept pace with high employment revenues. Because revenues were swollen by the effect of "bracket-creep", government increased its share of GNP. From this point of view, neither fiscal nor monetary policy can be seen to have done much in the 1970s to offset the aftereffects of the Vietnam expansion or the effects of the oil shocks (though they were expansive in some years and restrictive in others). On the other hand, they were not powerful causes of unusually rapid real demand expansion, and we did not have unusually rapid real demand expansion. Federal deficits entered the picture in two ways. During periods of slack, especially 1975–77, there were large passive deficits. But there were also, at times, quite large high employment deficits. Given a basic policy of aiming at full employment, it can be argued that federal deficits were required to offset state and local surpluses, and part of the oil deficit. That justification does not, however, apply convincingly to 1978 or 1972–73, when demand expanded too rapidly.

On the whole, it would seem that deficits—like monetary growth—are a reflection of our unwillingness to use monetary and fiscal restraint to generate negative demand shocks in order to offset the positive shocks described earlier. A policy of accommodating a one-time inflationary shock such as an oil price increase makes a good deal of sense. The cost of offsetting the supply shock by demand restraint is very high. That argument can be extended to justify accommodation of the aftermath of the Vietnam expansion and two big oil price shocks. One might hope that, in the absence of any further shocks, the inflation rate thus accommodated would eventually decline. Even if it did not, we might be able to live with a continuing 10 percent inflation rate.

The Current Policy Setting

Most of the current forecasts predict that after a relatively mild recession (in 1980 or 1980–81) we can move back to a 6 percent unemployment rate while the inflation rate levels off at around 10 percent. On the whole, I fear that those forecasts are distinctly optimistic about the outlook for inflation. The decline in productivity growth increases the inflationary bias in our economy. So does the continuing rise in energy prices. For the short run the forecasts assume that the prospective recession curbs the tendency for wages to rise in response to the high rates of inflation during the past year. That may be so, but it must be admitted that if it becomes apparent that the long-awaited recession is in fact a very mild one, there is a significant risk that the acceleration of wage increases will be substantially larger than the one projected by the forecasts. Even if we get past that danger, there remains a substantial risk of another sharp step-up in inflation from other sources. As I have already indicated, the reaction of consumers and investors through a period of sustained inflation at a high level is difficult to predict. Moderation of interest rates in the face of inflation rates approaching 10 percent implies that the investment decisions of consumers and investors will be based on negative aftertax interest rates. Gradualist policy and the control of demand may again be upset by declining personal saving rates and by investment oriented toward cashing in on the negative interest rates. An unexpected surge of demand, coupled with a change in inflationary expectations regarding wage and price making, during the course of gradualist recovery, cannot be ruled out. Indeed, that kind of reaction accounts for much of the economy's strength in the past year, despite the adverse effects of rising gasoline prices on automobile sales, and the decline in housing starts induced by the change in monetary policy. Moreover, a couple of years of bad weather or disruption in oil supplies could easily produce more supply shocks which would again step up the rate of inflation. We could, of course, have good luck instead. But in our present situation, it seems more important to emphasize the risks of accelerated inflation implied by the gradualist policies underlying the forecasts I have sketched.

Another step-up in the inflation rate would in all likelihood provoke another round of fiscal and monetary restraint and another recession. A continuation of policies aimed at realization of the forecasts I have outlined is likely to lead to an era of stop-and-go policy, with increasing uncertainty as to the inflationary consequences of each *go* period, and increasing uncertainty as to the impact of each restrictive or *stop* period. That scenario implies a significant risk of a major recession which will be serious and prolonged—more severe and less readily controlled than the others we have experienced since World War II. The danger arises from the instabilities of both the international and domestic financial systems, and from the potential instability of consumer and investment demand in a world in which so many decisions are based on inflation expectations. And conceivably, the fiscal and monetary policy adjustments which might be appropriate may be inhibited by a political climate which blames all our troubles on deficits and monetary expansion.

I cannot give a precise scenario for the possible disaster that I envisage, but I will mention some of the elements which could contribute. First, another sharp rise in the United States inflation rate would generate renewed speculation against the dollar and almost inevitably force the Federal Reserve Bank to move interest rates up. The required adjustment of interest rates in an adverse, speculative climate would, in all probability, exceed the observed rise in inflation rates since it would have to offset expectations of still further increases in the inflation rate and a desire on the part of dollar holders to further diversify their portfolios to limit the risk of loss through dollar depreciation. The Federal Reserve Bank would, of course, also be motivated to raise interest rates on purely domestic grounds. In our present circumstances, with many borrowers heavily dependent on short-term credit and with thrift institutions already in difficulty, rising interest rates would not only have their usual adverse impact on residential construction, but could also trip off bankruptcies in other firms. Banks with losses on the books would curtail credit to weak borrowers. Given the initially low saving rates, any decline in income might have a greater than usual adverse effect on durable goods purchases. An additional source of vulnerability in the foreign sector arises from the fact that many, if not most, non-OPEC countries have serious balance of payments problems, and many less developed countries (LDCs) are already having trouble servicing their debts. A United States recession of major proportions can lead to a general contraction in world trade and debt-service problems for LDCs. Although these might not cause any failures among American banks, the banks might be forced to attempt to improve their liquidity and raise the quality of their domestic loan portfolios. Finally, as I have already noted, the political climate might inhibit a timely action to stem the tide of recession.

We find ourselves in a situation in which any policy choice is a gamble. An attempt to live with inflation and avoid severe and prolonged unemployment has some chance of success. But it entails substantial risk of a period of high average unemployment together with higher inflation rates. And it entails some risk of producing first more inflation and then a deep recession.

On the other hand, the costs of fighting inflation by demand restraint alone are very high and the results uncertain. The analogy of the 1957–61 episode usefully illustrates the costs of controlling inflation by demand measures alone. By all accounts that episode did bring the inflation of the mid-1950s to a halt; however, our present situation is far more difficult. The inflation rate is much higher, inflation has gone on for a much longer time, the rate of productivity growth is very low, and we face continuing increases in energy prices. In the four years 1958 through 1961, the unemployment rate averaged 6.1 percent (about two percentage points higher than in the 1955–57 period). To replicate that experience from our current base would required four years with unemployment averaging 8 percent. After 1961, we had a relatively gradual recovery in which the unemployment rate was reduced a little each year. I think it unlikely that a repetition of that episode would make inflation disappear today, although it might be reduced substantially if it were known early in the game that a quick recovery was unlikely. But, as I have indicated, there is some reason to fear that the inflation process has acquired greater inertia now than it had in 1957. Even if we are willing to pay the enormous costs involved in repeating that episode, we should be taking other measures to insure that the desired result is achieved, and to minimize the costs we may have to pay in the form of reduced output, unemployment, and social disruption.

The Hobson's choice between the dangers and costs of continuing and probably accelerating inflation, and the costs of a severe recession as a remedy for inflation, is not new to us. For many years economists have been arguing that there is a middle ground between accepting inflation and fighting it by demand control alone. The 1980 economic report of the Council of Economic Advisers (CEA) contains a long list of actions which the government can take to reduce the costs of regulation, to make labor markets more efficient, and to strengthen the forces of competition. It also takes a sanguine view of the prospects for the current version of incomes policy. Very similiar observations are to be found in the 1967 and 1968 economic reports. As I have already suggested, price control was chosen as an alternative to deep recession in 1971, and a gradualist recovery involving incomes policy was the choice of the Carter administration from the start. One cannot disagree with the proposition that improving the efficiency of labor markets, encouraging investment to increase productivity, reducing the cost of regulation, creating grain reserves to limit the risk of a sharp rise in food prices, and adopting measures to solve our energy problems are all desirable on their own merits and would also help to contain inflation. But complete success in *all* these areas would still not solve the problem, and our experience shows that we can expect only modest success due to the many political conflicts involved.

The logical case for some form of incomes policy thus seems overwhelming. After all, the inflation process involves large changes in absolute price levels that produce relatively small changes in relative prices. It should be possible to make the relative price changes which are economically or politically necessary without raising the whole price level at a rapid and accelerating rate. Unfortunately, our experience shows that it is extremely difficult to operate formal price controls for long periods without great loss of efficiency and without generating political resistance which eventually destroys them. Our experience shows that a system of price controls which meets legal requirements of equal treatment under law is impossible to realize. The relatively simple set of regulations is soon found to create various inequities, or to be inconsistent with market forces. The result is a proliferation and complication of the regulations to allow for all sorts of special cases, and those adjustments create new sets of problems which lead to further proliferation and complication of the regulation. It is for that reason that many of us have preferred a voluntary or semivoluntary program, which allows more flexibility while still imposing some constraint on wage and price increases. We have learned, however, that voluntary incomes policy will not work unless some way can be found to reach an agreement with trade unions regarding wage restraint. The Carter administration's program recognizes that, but, as far as I can tell, it allows so much leeway that it will impose very little effective restraint on the collective bargaining process.

Conclusion
In principle, a consistent policy of control of nominal demand growth using both fiscal and monetary policy will sooner or later defeat inflation. But if it works only through the brute force of unemployment and excess capacity, the cost will prove too high and it will not be applied consistently. It could work if sufficiently supported by incomes policy and supply-side actions. Obviously, effective incomes policy and effective supply-side actions require the support of a political consensus strong enough to override the special interest and distributional conflicts involved in incomes policy and supply-side measures. That kind of consensus is also required to maintain a consistent demand policy. It seems to me that economists could do with a little consensus. We ought to be able to recognize the need for more supply-side actions without indulging in Lafferism or pretending that

it is easy to turn on a lot of productivity-creating investment. We ought to be able to recognize the expectational effects of government policy without accepting oversimplified rational expectations models. We ought to be able to recognize that wages and prices are not made in auction markets and that intervention in those processes can make a difference. We ought to be able to recognize now, if not before, that monetary policy works through imperfect and sometimes fragile markets. Finally, we ought to be telling the public that resources are always limited and that if there is no productivity gain, no one's income can grow except at the expense of someone else's.

Comments by GARDNER ACKLEY

Like Professor Duesenberry, I have been rethinking my views on stabilization policy in the past few years. Reading his paper, I was pleased to find so many points on which our rethinking has gone in parallel directions. Indeed, we agree so fully, and he has said most of it so well, that I can limit myself to a very few observations.

I agree that there have been, since the decade of the 1930s, major structural changes which have made our aggregate output more stable, but our price level more prone to inflation. Duesenberry refers to growth in the relative size of government, the strengthening of the financial system, and the institution of collective bargaining in basic industries. I would add a couple of other structural changes that I think are also relevant to our stabilization problems.

One is the bureaucratization or, if you prefer, the professionalization of business. I suggest that professionally trained management, improved and expanded management information systems, and growth in the absolute size and complexity of business firms have increasingly led to most industrial prices being set on the basis of measured direct costs, plus allocations of various large "overheads," topped off by a "reasonable" profit, rather than at levels that reflect current marginal costs and marginal revenues in the markets for the firms' products.

Changes in the practices and the results of wage setting, I suggest, have emerged as much from the development of "scientific" personnel management, and the acceptance of employer responsibility for employee welfare, as from the increased role of unions. Wage rates are now set for considerably longer periods; they are also set at levels that reflect important considerations of long-term "strategy," both of corporations and unions. But less than ever do they reflect the short-run supply and demand for labor. Wage rates have thus become far less sensitive to immediate market conditions, and far more sensitive to changes in employee living costs and in employers' longer-term profitability. Moreover, effective wage costs contain increasingly large and inflexible "overhead" elements of employee benefits: the costs of pensions, life insurance, worker's compensation, medical, dental, legal, vacation, and other plans. Thus, whatever variation does occur in the "market wage rate" has considerably less influence than it used to have on unit labor costs.

A further structural change (that the author did not list but which may be implicit in some of his comments) has been the new politics of redress—the increased willingness of every group that feels itself badly treated by our economy, society, or politics to demand government protection and restitution; and, equally important, the ability and willingness of political leaders to capitalize on such issues for electoral purposes. This development is not all bad, but special-interest politics has contributed to the destruction of political parties, and thereby reduced the effectiveness of government (including government's ability to manage stabilization policy). Moreover, it has substantially increased the inflationary bias of public policy.

I also agree with the view that inflation must be dealt with by a combination of continuing fairly restrictive demand management, and attempting to mount a truly effective incomes policy. These are necessary *complements;* not *alternatives.* (And restrictive demand management does not necessarily preclude some tax cuts later on.)

I have long preached that an effective incomes policy must rest on the consent of those supposed to be governed by it—in short, it presupposes an at least implicit "social compact" among the major economic interest groups. The legislation establishing the Council on Wage and Price Stability provides an element of legitimacy for the current incomes policy that was not available to support the incomes policy that Duesenberry and I tried to run in the 1960s when we served together on the Council of Economic Advisers. But Duesenberry believes—as I do—that there must also be an explicit direct involvement of labor and management in the program; indeed, he has said that he would advocate wage and price controls only if a workable incomes policy "cannot be negotiated." However, the recent involvement of labor and management negotiated by the author's Harvard colleague, John Dunlop, seems to me to have given away far too much, which is what one of Duesenberry's careful comments also seems to imply.

I must add that I disagree fundamentally with one point in the paper. Even if a social compact cannot be negotiated, I do not advocate wage and price controls. One basic reason is that effective wage and price controls require the same kind of social consensus that is needed to support a noncompulsory incomes policy. Proponents of controls frequently ignore the fact that our inflation reflects deepseated problems and characteristics of our society and of our economy, national and international, that would not disappear just because we imposed controls. Our bias toward inflation also reflects weaknesses of the institutions through which we attempt to achieve social and political consensus, and that weakness would not disappear just because we imposed controls. Rather, it would be exacerbated by controls.

Even relatively loose wage controls could well lead to strikes—essentially, strikes against the government. This happened during the Korean War controls, and even during World War II. I urge those advocating controls to think hard about what would be done in that circumstance—remembering that it would occur in a nation threatened only by an internal quarrel over income distribution, not by foreign aggression.

The kind of inflation that we now face reflects not an excessive demand for goods and services, but basically the effort, the practice, the habit of every group or sector of our society struggling to pass along to others the price increases that its members must pay. Controls won't alter this. Controls would merely transfer this struggle from the market place into the political and administrative arena. I very much doubt that, in the absence of a war emergency, our political and administrative processes can successfully resolve such conflicts.

The Scholarly Foundations of the Econometrics Industry

LAWRENCE R. KLEIN

It is often claimed that social science research does not lead to practical developments in the real world. Reductions in the constant dollar value of research support from the National Science Foundation—the largest source of funding for social science research—have been accompanied by charges of impractical research, of the "golden fleece" variety. This prevailing view of general social science research has sometimes focused on economics, in particular. Some economists do meet a regular payroll, and numbering among those, I feel that I do know what it means to survive in the world of practical affairs.

In order to justify a continuing flow of research support from the National Science Foundation (NSF), I shall try to outline the course of development of the present econometrics industry and to show how this practical application of our subject is rooted in deep research carried out in the world of academia.

Today, the business of forecasting, policy analysis, and general applications of econometric models enjoys a commercial market of more than $100 million annually. The noncommercial market accounts for a great deal more; so we are talking about a very significant activity. In addition to forecasting the gross national product (GNP), we account for some small part of it as well.

The work of Tinbergen, Frisch, Kalecki, and Clark make up the prehistory of the present development, and the breaking point of World War II serves as a convenient start for the present analysis.

During the 1940s, a new generation of American models was developed at the Cowles Commission (now Foundation) of the University of Chicago. This academic research group, of which I was a member, concentrated on application of the methods of modern statistical inference to the estimation and testing of models. Considerable

Lawrence R. Klein is Benjamin Franklin Professor of Economics at the University of Pennsylvania and was a member of the Michigan faculty during 1950–54.

111

emphasis was devoted as well to problems of identification and specification. At this time, the rooting of model specification in received economic doctrine was firmly established.

The Cowles Commission effort was only a beginning. It gave rise to an enormous degree of understanding of the subject. It spawned textbooks, research monographs, and some models. The principal model was actually applied to a significant forecast situation for the Committee for Economic Development. An attempt was made, in 1946, to look into the prospects for postwar development of the United States economy in the short run. In contrast to many dire predictions that we would return to the severely depressed state of the economy of the 1930s, the Cowles Commission model gave a very cheerful forecast. The impact of that forecast on public policy was not great because the econometric approach had not yet achieved national recognition.

There is no doubt that the research group at the Cowles Commission got postwar econometrics on its way, but Cowles's central emphasis on estimation methods and sophisticated statistical inference was not the critical factor in establishing the discipline in its present position of prominence. Research along these lines continues, and makes contributions to scholarly knowledge, but does not have striking effects on applications. Of all the methods of inference that were actively discussed then, the issues of random (or variable) parameters and errors of observation (together with equation disturbances) are the lines of development that have the greatest potential for leading to a breakthrough now, in power of application.

The principal model built in Chicago during the 1940s has been, of course, discarded and is of no more than historical interest, but a small three-equation model, known as Klein Model I, that was built only for methodological experiments, is used even today for numerous sampling experiments and other prototype cases.

Two factors limiting further development of macro model building at the Cowles Commission were computational bottlenecks and lack of availability of data. Enormous progress on both those fronts did not take place until the 1960s, but the beginnings occurred in Ann Arbor, in connection with the founding of the Research Seminar in Quantitative Economics (RSQE), together with some work on the saving function done at the Survey Research Center.

The RSQE was established on the basis of the original distribution of Ford Foundation funds to the University of Michigan (among other institutions). With a tiny budget of $20,000 per year (for three years) which looked quite big then, we put together the Klein-Goldberger model of the United States economy.

That particular piece of work stands out in the story that I am telling because it initiated the whole idea of regular, replicated forecasts and policy exercises using an econometric model. Data were becoming better all the time, and we drew on the improved renditions of the national income accounts provided by the United States Department of Commerce, but we supplemented them with important tabulations from the Survey Research Center and with some of our own work on social accounting. All these sources are evident in the Klein-Goldberger model, in the parts dealing with income distribution, differential marginal propensities to spend, and liquid asset effects.

The first uses of high-speed computers in macroeconometrics took place in Ann Arbor. The heavy computation involved in application of the Cowles Commission methods was always forbidding, but some of the most arduous chores were done on the Card Programmed Electronic Sequence Computer, then housed in the university's administration building.

The Michigan Digital Electronic Computer (MIDEC) being operational at Willow Run, research was started on dynamic simulation of the Klein-Goldberger model. Unfortunately, that work was halted in midstream and never brought to fruition in Ann Arbor, although it was independently restarted and very successfully concluded by Irma Adelman at the University of California a few years later.

Arthur Goldberger was considering building a model of the United States money market as a thesis topic, for we realized then that the monetary aspects of the Klein-Goldberger model were in urgent need of development. It was undoubtedly a good thing that he changed subjects and looked into the dynamic and multiplier properties of the model instead, for he achieved a breakthrough in implementing a system for use in this way. Again, the early use of the computer was important in deriving explicit reduced form equations and dynamic multipliers, for the first time on a significant scale from a live model.

A parallel development was Stefan Valavanis's production of a statistical growth model for the United States, based on Kuznets's decade data from the late nineteenth century, carried forward to the

1940s. His was a forerunner of a present generation of macroeconometric growth models.

Daniel Suits carried on forecast and other applications of what became known as the Michigan model for several years. This was the oldest and most widely used model in repeated application of this sort in the United States. The tradition was maintained and expanded by Harold Shapiro and Saul Hymans, first with the older Michigan model, then with the Dernburg-Hymans-Lusher (DHL) model that Saul Hymans brought back from a Washington stint, then with a new generation of the Michigan model.

The Social Science Research Council-Brookings econometric model project that shaped the course of much macroeconometric research in the United States had some Ann Arbor origins. The SSRC meeting that gave rise to the Committee on Economic Stability took place in Ann Arbor in 1959. After the committee was established it designed the model-building project that set the standards for large-scale model management on such matters as

1. simulation algorithms for dynamic nonlinear systems
2. data bank construction and maintenance
3. integration of input-output with final demand (NIA) models
4. integration of monetary and real sectors
5. balance of payments modeling

These thrusts were not, by any means, final steps in the direction of model management by computer, input-output modeling, or monetary-financial modeling, but they were all first steps, implemented in the tradition of the RSQE and Michigan economics.

The next phase, from my own perspective, was the building and using of various generations of Wharton models. These were quarterly, and used anticipatory data in the spirit of the Survey Research Center's investigations; they were later influenced by the econometric studies of Saul Hymans, Harold Shapiro, and Thomas Juster. Other studies by George Katona and James Morgan were equally influential.

The founding of the econometrics industry itself grew out of the attempt to fund the research program in econometrics at the Wharton School of the University of Pennsylvania. In this respect, we took a lesson from the University of Michigan's annual Economic Outlook Conference (started in 1953) which involved the private sector in forecast applications of quantitative economics. The Wharton approach was different from Michigan's, in that the Wharton group held quarterly meetings with subscribers and discussed the forecasts, thus placing the model in a feedback relationship between forecaster and user. The Michigan Economic Outlook Conference was more an annual gathering in an auditorium than a frequent working meeting.

Two major developments occurred in the 1960s. The computer was harnessed to the needs of econometrics, and this covered all aspects—data management, model estimation, model testing, and model application. Centers throughout the country participated in this development but MIT, Brookings, the University of Pennsylvania, the University of Michigan, Princeton, and UCLA were particularly active in making contributions, and one might say that the TROLL software package produced at MIT is the best example of a good outcome of this research activity.

The other major development was in the continuing provision of good data bases for macroeconometric research. The major breakthroughs occurred in the 1930s and 1940s, partly in academic institutions, partly in research organizations, and partly in public offices. With good data, efficient computer programs, increasingly available hardware, and a growing collection of useful models it has been possible to provide applications, in the form of forecasts, multipliers, policy scenarios, and growth scenarios, to a rapidly growing user group consisting of industrial corporations, financial firms, government offices (federal, state, local, and international), and foreign companies.

The theory of system design, the methods of estimation, the methods of testing, the techniques of simulation, and the management of data—all essential to this new growth industry—emanate from the scholarly research development of macroeconometrics, and the University of Michigan has played a significant role in that process. Not only the various generations of Michigan models but also Michigan's active participation in two NSF-sponsored seminars of the Committee on Econometrics and Mathematical Economics—one on model testing and one on model comparison—has helped push the development of the industry forward. There can be no doubt that the academic research underpinnings of this kind of commercial development were absolutely necessary and that a great deal of the original thinking came from Ann Arbor.

Now that an industry has been launched, how might we expect to see it grow, not from a sales perspective, but in terms of substantive content? As macroeconometric forecasting and applications get more commercialized, the industry will drift from its academic ties, and the monitoring of its professional content will drift away from objective academic appraisals to votes from the marketplace.

There can be no doubt that econometrics has already met the test of the market. With enough advertising, a professionally poor piece of forecasting can be sold in a short burst, but it cannot be sold quarter after quarter over a period of almost twenty years unless it has real merit. There are numerous complaints and charges about the inaccuracy of econometric forecasts, but they could not be sold on the scale that they are now, over such a long time period, unless they had real merit. The issue is, what are the alternatives? Is there another method of forecasting that shows better promise on a repetitive, replicated basis? No challenger appears on the horizon.

The tests that have been made do not show superior performance of other methods. They do not show a better ability to call turning points, or even perform better in the revival/recessionary phases. What is more important, other methods do not have simulation capability for dealing with "what if" issues in a way that is meaningful to a wide variety of users. At the present time, it is inconceivable that a major economic program will be assessed in Washington, D.C., without running the issues through many model simulations. The final decisions may not be a straightforward adaptation of a particular simulation, but they will be significantly influenced by the model simulations.

An entire generation of youthful graduates who have entered public service and private enterprise are trained in the computer-based modeling techniques of modern quantitative economics. Their first reaction to questions posed by their superiors (from an older generation) is to turn to econometric model analysis, and this is surely evidence that the approach is here to stay.

Forecasts have to be good in order to keep selling, and a badly flawed forecasting group will realize its just desserts in today's marketplace. In this respect we need not feel disheartened by the drift toward commercialism and away from a sound academic base, but when it comes to the matter of policy simulation, answers to questions regarding standards are more dubious.

It is entirely possible that special interest groups will use models, even if they are not up to standard, in order to establish points in support of their own special interests. It is at this stage of the process that a wholly independent modeling group, such as the RSQE team at Michigan, must always be at the ready to monitor econometric simulations. During 1977 and 1978 some commercial models were used to simulate effects of reductions in capital gains taxes. These changes in the statutes (the Steiger Amendments) may have been favorable for the economy, but the econometric claims that justified them were not soundly established in terms of reliable simulation applications. It is important, in this respect, that econometric findings be presented in professional forums with qualified discussants, or be submitted to refereed journals where analytical flaws in the arguments can be isolated and commented upon. There are real dangers in having all or most of the practical econometric work done in the commercial sphere.

A large model, in today's environment, consists of several hundred, or in some cases a few thousand, equations. These dynamic systems of simultaneous equations are solved on high-speed computers by the methods already referred to. In this respect, the model becomes a "black box." It is understandable only in a general way to the casual user or observer. It requires many weeks or months of training and experience in use to gain deep and full understanding. It is relatively easy, therefore, for a particular model proprietor to operate a system in a highly sheltered environment. Short of replication by outsiders on critical occasions, it is important to have academically based outside operators with their own "black boxes" to perform a monitoring function. To some extent, the publicly supported models in the Federal Reserve and Commerce Department can participate in the monitoring exercises, but their use also involves some special interests. Academia gave birth to this new industry, and it is becoming increasingly difficult for academia to continue to find funding for it because the costs have become substantial, but it is important that academics continue to play a prominent role.

Models of national economies, the United States being a prime example, will continue to become more elaborate. They will grow in size; they will have more supply-side characteristics; they will have more monetary detail, more demographic detail, and more international detail.

As for the commercial centers of econometrics, they will go where the money is, and that means toward model building more for individual companies, markets, or industries. That will be relatively straightforward work and probably not on the frontiers of the discipline, although significant developments in microeconometrics could come from this effort. For supply-side economics, most of the breakthroughs have already been made. It is mainly a question of implementation.

There are, however, two research directions that call for much more scholarly input, and which will only gradually be commercialized. These are the construction and interrelating of regional models of a national economy, and of national models of the world economy.

Many if not most of the states, and even some metropolitan areas, in the United States have macroeconometric models. It is a challenging problem to build up the whole from the parts, not in order to get a better estimate of the whole, but to get some estimates of distributions of economic magnitudes among the parts. There are formidable data problems confronting this research, but they are gradually being overcome. There is hardly a major national economic issue that does not have regional impact. It remains for scholarly researchers to work out usable techniques for effectively covering the nation with regional models. A great potential for commercialization exists, once suitable regional network systems have been designed and constructed.

At the world level, project LINK, sponsored by the same committee of the SSRC that initiated the SSRC-Brookings model project and the Federal Reserve model project, has had a decade of experience in modeling the world trade system by integrating macroeconometric models of individual countries or regions. Just as national model investigations sprang up at several United States academic centers (University of Michigan, University of Pennsylvania, MIT, UCLA) they also appeared at the University of Toronto, Kyoto University, London Business School, Cambridge University, University of Bologna, Institute for Advanced Studies in Vienna, Free University of Brussels, Stockholm School of Economics, Bonn University, Hamburg University, University of Madrid, Melbourne University, and others. In several cases, these universities have developed centers that are supported by private users of forecasts along the lines of the Wharton group.

The LINK project effectively brings these different models together for consistent world trade solutions. They are also mutually consistent with respect to production, inflation, and other variables. The LINK technology, developed in research centers throughout the world, is now being used by the Wharton group and other econometric companies for commercial distribution.

Work on the frontiers with respect to international modeling will procede in many directions. More countries or areas will be added to the system, and this requires the construction of national models for leading developing countries and centrally planned economies. More comprehensive balance of payments modeling, especially for international linkage, will also occur. The full endogenization of exchange rates is a present target. This became important once the floating system was introduced, and is still in need of further development. Given the pressures on world balance of payments adjustments as a result of OPEC pricing, work along the lines indicated is urgent. This is an area where deep research is likely to pay off handsomely.

The modeling of developing countries has flourished in the American academic system because the building and application of their own national models became a favorite doctoral thesis topic for hundreds of foreign students. A great deal has been learned about the model structure of the developing world, and ongoing commercial applications for Mexico, Brazil, and Venezuela, to mention only some leading cases, have grown from dissertations.

In the same way, model building has taken hold in the centrally planned economies, as evidenced by Harold Shapiro's investigations into this subject. A model of the USSR was developed at Pennsylvania and is now actively used, but in the public policy and research sector, not on a commercial basis.

A China model project is presently underway at Stanford, and there are active centers in Poland, Hungary, Czechoslovakia, and Yugoslavia in Eastern Europe. In Poland and Yugoslavia work takes place at the Universities of Lodz and Lubljana, respectively; in the other countries, and in the USSR, the research is being done in centers of the Academy of Sciences.

International econometric modeling, and model building for many countries outside the United States, is a ripe field for expansion. The commercialization has begun, but is not as far along as national modeling in this country. It promises, however, to be an area of expansion for the econometrics industry. In the process, we shall undoubtedly learn much about the structure of the world economy, which is less appreciated or understood than the structure of many national economies.

Economists have stuck pretty well to their lasts, leaving demography, resources, environment, and other aspects of social life to sister fields of specialization. It is only natural that we should begin to look further afield, inspired in no small degree by our feeling of dissatisfaction with the early efforts of systems engineers. Because of supply-side considerations and general inquisitiveness, economists are adding demographic content to models; they are building in complete energy sectors, and gradually becoming concerned with quantification of factors dealing with environment, other natural resources besides fuels, food, social relations, and other components of global models. The energy predicament, among other reasons, has induced econometricians to try to take a longer view, focusing on extrapolations of models to the year 2000 and beyond. There is great commercial interest in long-term scenarios and their production will continue, but relatively little is known, in any deep sense, about the properties of long-term macro models. Extensions of the kind of system initiated by Valavanis at Michigan, and of the Leontief-type interindustry system, are now being worked on in great detail, and this is likely to be another area in which good economic research in the academic establishment pays off in the marketplace for econometric information.

Many of the same engineers who are goading economists into taking a more global view are also pushing for the use of engineering methods of automatic control in the regulation of economic systems. Control theory applications are commonplace in the scholarly literature of econometrics, but they are not being used to any great extent in the econometrics industry. They constitute a powerful set of tools and may come to have their day (more likely in public policy analysis than in strict commercial application), but will be a field of significant research activity in the coming years.

Econometricians in the commercial sector have gone far in packaging the product. In order to sell econometrics it has to be extremely "user oriented." That means that software packages must be easy to use, even by the nonsophisticated quantitative economist. Also, the output must be in neat tables and graphs, easily assimilated by executives or policy makers, as well as by professional econometricians. The econometrics industry has made a genuine contribution in this respect. Its practitioners took an initial lead from the academic community, when the solutions to mathematical equation systems were first tabulated in neat social accounting statements, but the commercial sector has gone much further in the production of booklets with highly informative tables and graphs. This part of the development was a feedback to academia, for it greatly enhanced the exposition of the subject and contributed significantly to pedagogy. It did not make deep contributions to knowledge, nor did it make econometric systems any better in terms of accuracy or detail, but it did make the results more understandable and usable.

A new development in connection with the fast-growing field of microelectronics lies on the horizon. Minicomputers with mini components, now in the form of "chips," may replace, at least in part, the large main frame computer with giant data banks available by time-sharing systems at remote terminals.

The next generation of delivery systems is likely to bring econometric information to users in more modest (smaller) establishments, on more of a mass distribution scale. It is hard to see that this will, in itself, improve the inherent nature of the product, but it should make it more attractive. It will be a base on which the now-thriving econometrics industry may expand in a new burst during the 1980s.

REFERENCES

Adelman, I., and Adelman, F. "The Dynamic Properties of the Klein-Goldberger Model." *Econometrica* 27 (October, 1959): 596–625.
Ball, R. J., ed. *The International Linkage of National Economic Models.* Amsterdam: North-Holland, 1973.
———. *Committee on Policy Optimisation, Report.* London: HMSO, 1978.
Duesenberry, J.; Fromm, G.; Klein, L. R.; and Kuh, E., eds. *The Brookings Quarterly Econometric Model of the United States.* Chicago: Rand-McNally, 1965.
———. *The Brookings Model: Some Further Results.* Chicago: Rand-McNally, 1969.
Fromm, G., and Klein, L. R., *The Brookings Model: Perspective and Recent Developments.* Amsterdam: North-Holland, 1975.
Goldberger, A. S. *Impact Multipliers and Dynamic Properties of the Klein-Goldberger Model.* Amsterdam: North-Holland, 1959.
Green, D., and Higgins, C., *SOVMOD I.* New York: Academic Press, 1977.
Hickman, B., and Klein, L. R., "A Decade of Research by Project LINK," *Items,* (Social Science Research Council) 33 (December 1979):49–56.
Klein, L. R. *Economic Fluctuations in the United States, 1921–1941.* New York: Wiley, 1950.

Klein, L. R., and Burmeister, E., eds. *Econometric Model Performance.* Philadelphia: University of Pennsylvania Press, 1976.

Klein, L. R., and Evans, M. K., *The Wharton Econometric Forecasting Model.* Philadelphia: Economic Research Unit, University of Pennsylvania, 1968.

Klein, L. R., and Goldberger, A. S., *An Econometric Model of the United States 1929–1952.* Amsterdam: North-Holland, 1955.

Klein, L. R., and Young, R. M., *An Introduction to Econometric Forecasting and Forecasting Models.* Lexington: Lexington Books, 1980.

Koopmans, T. C., ed. *Statistical Inference in Dynamic Economic Models.* New York: Wiley, 1950.

Sawyer, J., ed. *Modeling the International Transmission Mechanism.* Amsterdam: North-Holland, 1979.

Shapiro, H. T., and Halabuk, L., "Macro-Econometric Model Building in Socialist and Non-Socialist Countries: A Comparative Study," *International Economic Review* 17 (October, 1976):529–65.

Waelbroeck, J., ed. *The Models of Project LINK.* Amsterdam: North-Holland, 1976.

Comments by F. THOMAS JUSTER

Professor Klein's interesting, informative, and provocative paper is basically concerned with the question, what has been the role of econometrics in producing practical knowledge about the functioning of society and the economy? Implicitly, the paper contains a knowledge production function—practical knowledge is related to the state of theoretical knowledge, the state of statistical knowledge, the size and appropriateness of the relative data base, and the capacity to manipulate data by way of computing software and hardware. The paper focuses primarily on the contribution of econometric theory and practice to practical knowledge, and provides an overall assessment of the contribution of econometrics plus some judgments about priorities for future work. Overall, Klein's assessment of the contribution of econometrics to present knowledge is highly positive, and his priorities relate both to aggregation and disaggregation—the former toward linking national econometric models into an international model of the world economy, the latter toward the generation of regional or other local modeling efforts.

Besides demonstrating the contribution of econometrics to the production of useful societal knowledge, Klein's paper is full of fascinating footnotes relating to the historical development of the econometrics industry. Klein is ideally suited to present such a case, for he is indeed the father of what has come to be a genuine industry with a measurable fraction of the gross national product (GNP)—the econometrics business. Few people can lay claim to having invented an industry. Hence there is much to be learned that is of both historical interest and current relevance, in terms of how one takes an abstraction—the idea of an econometric model—and helps it to grow into an important and measurable activity with an enormous influence on both public and private decision making.

I also find Klein's description of the early role of the Survey Research Center in providing model elements relating to distribution, and in providing important inputs into specification of some of the model functions, a fascinating piece of social science history. It is worth noting that the Survey Research Center appears to have played a more important role in the econometrics business during its origins than it has during recent years, a situation that seems to me both undesirable and unfortunate. Everyone seems to have gotten more specialized in recent years. The econometricians stick to their time-series modeling, the survey researchers stick to their cross-section behavioral modeling, and there is little interaction between the two.

The third piece of relevant history is the parallel that Klein's paper suggests between the early days of macroeconomic models and what now seems to be a burgeoning industry in sociology and political science. What appears to be happening is that sociologists and political scientists have discovered time-series models, and are busy constructing models to explain divorce, crime, party preference, voting behavior, and so forth. It is not at all clear to me that they have learned either from economists' successes or failures, and I would not be surprised to see our fellow social scientists both reinventing the wheel and discovering that some of its spokes are a little on the weak side.

The main thrust of Professor Klein's paper is that econometrics, by which I think he means modeling of complete system, has moved from a solid base of academic and scholarly development to a central role in the making of both public and private policy. The paper expresses an optimism regarding the present scholarly state of macroeconometrics models that I think needs leavening with a few cautions, but I will turn to that later. On Klein's agenda of important econometric work yet to be done, he focuses (I think properly) on estimation methods relating to variable coefficients and on work on the statistical properties of error structures. The frontiers yet to be developed, in Klein's view, are those dealing with disaggregation—downward from national to regional models—and aggregation—linkages relating national models to the world economy.

Thus the basic message is that econometrics is firmly established as a key decision-making technique in both the public and the private sectors, that there are a few important estimation problems that need to be explored, and that the proper direction in which to proceed is to spread the influence of national econometric models across both regions and other geographic subdivisions of nations and to global models that link the entire set of national models through trade linkages and resulting disturbances.

The reader is left in no doubt as to where Klein stands concerning the role and importance of econometrics and in particular, large-scale econometric models: a new industry has been born, it has stood the test of scientific usefulness, and it needs to be refined around a couple of its rough edges and spread to a set of related uses. One could, I think, find support for alternative views of where the econometrics industry presently is, and where it ought to go. As a discussant and skeptic, let me point to a few places where I find the argument unpersuasive and the evidence unconvincing.

Is there a Solid Scientific Foundation for the Econometric Modeling Industry?

The argument in Klein's paper is an interesting way to approach this question. He does not here recount the evidence of scientific accomplishments that can be attributed to the econometric modeling fraternity. Rather, he uses a market argument—models have met the market test in that they are acquired and used by both private and public decision makers; they must have genuine scholarly merit or people would not be so interested in paying for the service.

The fragile nature of that argument is recognized in a revealing sentence in Klein's paper, where he notes that other methods of forecasting "do not show superior performance. . . . They do not show a better ability to call turning points. . . ." Such praise of modeling thus seems weak indeed—the alternatives are no better.

While the market-test argument is interesting, I find it only partially persuasive as a demonstration of scientific merit. The trouble is that the argument assumes that buyers are purchasing scientific structure as reflected by the model, and it is not at all clear to me that either business or government buyers are purchasing a scientific product. There are, obviously, alternative reasons why people might wish to acquire econometric models—credibility at the monthly or quarterly meeting of the directors of the corporation or at meetings of the Senate Budget Committee, a security blanket in the face of a highly uncertain world, or even simple bragging rights at the local watering hole. Both corporations and government bodies buy all kinds of things for all kinds of purposes, and better decision making is sometimes only the excuse for the purchase, rather than the basic reason.

It cannot really be true that people are buying econometric models in the market because they need to know what the model says about the future path of the national economy. If that is all buyers want, they can get it as a free good, or as a virtually free good—every quarter the American Statistical Association, in conjunction with the National Bureau of Economic Research, publishes a freely distributed release outlining the views of some forty professional business and government forecasters, many of whom use full-scale econometric models as their prime forecasting ingredient. And if people don't trust what comes for free, they can always turn to one of a number of commercially available services which summarize what all the models in the world have been saying recently about the economy (Mr. Eggert's Blue Chip Indicators in the commercial sector, or the Federal Reserve Bank of Richmond's Digest of Forecasts in the public sector).

However, the free availability of model forecasts does not really damage Klein's argument, since what people are really buying is their capacity to manipulate the model for their own particular industrial or public program needs, as he points out in the paper.

Most importantly, from my point of view, neither the public nor the private purchasers of econometric services can really be buying understanding of the economy as the main output, simply because the models don't understand important parts of the economy that well. That may seem a bit unjust if not unfair. But consider that all functioning econometric models are really a combination of a theoretical and statistical structure, which is the scientific part, combined with a myriad of ad hoc adjustments that model builders call constant-term adjustments and critics call fiddle factors. The forecasting accuracy of large-scale models is largely a function of the expertise of model builders in constructing appropriate ad hoc adjustments, which are always needed to make the model resemble the most recent version of the real world. Those procedures are of course sensible, but it is stretching the use of the term to call them scientific.

To be evenhanded about model performance, we should of course recognize that Klein is entirely correct in his assessment of the scientific achievement of the econometrics industry if one is comparing models of the 1960s and 1970s with the simpler and cruder instruments available during the 1940s, to say nothing of the guesses and hopes that must have formed the basis for economic forecasts in earlier decades. Models are clearly, by those standards, major engines of scientific advancement. It is only when one asks how well they perform according to relatively high standards, or perhaps more to the point, whether the 1970s have seen much scientific gain in modeling structures, that judgments would be much less favorable.

The proposition that models don't really understand important dimensions of the way the economy works can be documented simply by looking at the performance of econometric models during the 1973–75 recession. To paraphrase one distinguished critic, "Never has the profession been so uniformly wrong" in failing to understand the depth of the slide from fall 1974 through spring 1975. After all, President Ford, presumably guided at least in part by his modelers, was on record as favoring a tax increase to fight inflation in the fall of 1974, just before we began to get concrete evidence of the dimensions of the air pocket that showed up in consumer demand during that same period. And the persistent failure of models to understand what makes prices move the way that they do is further testimony to the weaknesses of existing econometric modeling structures.

During recent years, much of the weaknesses in econometric models have been in the price sector, where extrapolation of recent price performance would probably have given systematically better results than forecasts produced out of the models. In part, this is likely to reflect the difficulty macro models have in comprehending the macro effects of micro phenomena—explosions in oil or food prices, for example.

A fair summary of the views of the critics of econometric modeling performance would be that we are not in such good scientific shape as the Klein paper suggests, and perhaps more importantly, we do not seem to have made much progress during the past decade, after having made very considerable progress during the preceding several decades.

Estimation Methods and Error Structures

The paper's comment concerning frontier developments needed in statistical estimation methods deals with errors in macro structures. One could argue that a significant number of the problems associated with parameter estimation in macro models is precisely that they are entirely macro and deal uncomfortably with insights that might be gleaned from analysis of microdata.

One way to see the problem as I do is to note that all macro variables are essentially mean values, and that while mean values have some merits (modest measurement error) they also have severe drawbacks (extreme sensitivity to minor changes in relationships, especially in the estimation of partial relationships). Although all of us are fundamentally interested in the behavior of the macro system, the dynamics of any economic or social system must come out of an aggregation of individual behavioral responses. It is arguable that such responses are not, and cannot be, adequately modeled at the macro level, and that the full complexity which is needed to comprehend what is really going on in the world cannot be captured without at least some serious effort at disaggregating the estimation of behavioral relationships.

Of course one problem with that general philosophy is that micro parameters have their own problems—they may be better able to specify the linkages between one variable and another, but they are clearly subject to very large measurement errors for which easy remedies are not in sight. Recent developments in estimation of the random and correlated error components of observable variables offers one direction that could be fruitfully pursued in the estimation of better macro parameters.

Disaggregation and Aggregation

Although Klein is clearly right, in my view, in suggesting that an important frontier for econometric modeling is to disaggregate in the direction of subnational components like regions or states, it is interesting that he makes that case on the argument that such disaggregation will illuminate distributions of relevant variables in the economy as a whole. While one would certainly expect to get a better feel for how cyclical movements affect various parts of the society if one had different models for the Southwest and the Northeast, one would also hope that disaggregation would produce a more accurate picture of the whole, as well as illuminating some of its distributional characteristics.

The proposition has often been made in the investment literature that an investment function relating to output as a whole does not characterize investment behavior in an economy with a number of expanding areas and a number of declining areas. Assuming that the accelerator works, there should be more net investment in rapidly rising regions that there is negative net investment in declining regions, hence there will be a different amount of net investment than in an economy where all sectors have a zero growth rate. One would hope that regional models would get that picture more accurately, not only for the regions in question, but also for the economy as a whole.

One problem with regional modeling is the absence of an appropriate data base. Many of the existing regional models are not genuine models based on real data at all. Rather, they represent models based on a few genuinely regional series, plus a number of other series interpolated from the combination of national estimates for the series (industrial production, for example), and information about the state's industrial structure from which differences in industrial production between the state or region and the national economy can be inferred. But that kind of synthetic data base is not likely to be satisfactory given all the specification problems present even when the data are genuine.

While one might have some doubts about the future of regional models unless the appropriate data bases can be developed, it should be kept in mind that development of the models is bound to encourage development of the data bases. After all, much of what we now point to with proper pride as a highly sophisticated national economic data base clearly grew out of the demands associated with development of full-scale national econometric models. The best way to remedy a data deficiency is to demonstrate the role played by a particular variable in development of a particular model.

Finally, I am in complete agreement with the thrust of Klein's paper regarding the potential for linking national econometric models into an overview of the world market economy. In past decades, many economists, including myself, took a rather cavalier view of the importance of developments outside the United States on our country's economic development. But that view can no longer be sustained, and it has become increasingly clear during the past decade that the United States economy is strongly and continually affected by events that cannot be predicted from behavior within the country, but which depend on an adequate understanding of developments elsewhere in the world. No one underestimates the difficulty of achieving that kind of grandiose conception of a world economic model with consistent and linked parts, but one can hope that the same rate of rapid progress that characterized the development of national models during past decades may be on the verge of occurring in systems that encompass the world economy as a whole. Clearly, one would have been better able to model the behavior of the United States economy during the 1972–73 period if one had a model which linked the demands for raw materials in the United States with similar models of raw material demands elsewhere in the developed and developing world. Needless to say, the data base problems here are formidable, although perhaps not so far from solution as may be true for disaggregated regional or other subnational models.

PART TWO

Perspective on a Department

The Economics Department of the University of Michigan: A Centennial Retrospective

MARJORIE C. BRAZER

An academic department is a unique institution. It provides a structure for the association of scholars concerned with a defined body of knowledge and the setting in which they transmit their discipline to students. Yet each member functions autonomously in his teaching and in his research. The department is, in principle, merely an administrative convenience. In practice it is much more than that. Participation in the group itself generates an atmosphere of intellectual and social interchange that, with the passage of time, stamps a university department with a distinctive personality.

This centennial history seeks to identify the shared experiences and the themes of collegial life that have created the traditions and special sense of entity of the economics department of the University of Michigan. It is a social history, which includes portrayal of influential faculty members but does not trace their intellectual development in detail, nor analyze their research and scholarship. Rather the emphasis is on their interactions with their students and with one another, as economists at Michigan have led or responded to changes in their social and intellectual environment over the past one hundred years. Of individual faculty achievements, only a few of the highest honors and positions can be mentioned. Similarly, with respect to the accomplishments of alumni, space allows for only a few to be identified as representatives of many others; more than 8,000 people have been awarded degrees in economics at Michigan.

As much as possible the story is told in the words of those who have shaped it. In addition to review of departmental archives, tape-recorded interviews with several dozen current and former faculty members and students were obtained for the anecdotal recollections that breathe life into the narrative. All of those interviewed were of inestimable help, but I am especially indebted to Shorey Peterson's rich memory and his unfailingly cheerful response to my mid-paragraph telephone calls during the writing phase. The resources and assistance of the Michigan Historical Collections were indispensable to the task, and Mary Jo Pugh, associate archivist, was especially helpful in tracking down sources and photographs. My thanks, as well, to Deanna Johnson, who persevered in the tedious task of transcribing the interviews and typing the manuscript with care and good cheer.

The Launching of a Tradition, 1880–92

It was a quiet Wednesday morning in the world at large. The king of Sweden requested Count Arvid to form a new cabinet; St. Petersburg reported that Prince Gortschakoff passed a sleepless night as his heart weakened; the Burmese Ambassador declared unequivocally "that there is not a word of truth in the reports of massacres in Mandalay"; the Apaches were marauding in sections of New Mexico where no troops were stationed; General Grant was received warmly in Memphis on the same day that the Massachusetts State Convention rejected him and Blaine; New York merchants petitioned Congress to do something about the manufacture and sale of oleomargarine under the name of butter; New York Central closed at 132—and in the dignified President's Room at the University of Michigan eight men launched a tradition.

The date was April 14, 1880. The march of world affairs had reached the remote village of Ann Arbor when the United States Senate confirmed James Burrell Angell as minister to China. The regents must now appoint someone to teach President Angell's classes. At a university whose total faculty numbered fifty-two, half or more in medicine, it was not surprising that some professors taught several subjects. Indeed, according to one wag a professor might be said to occupy a settee rather than a chair. Thus it was necessary to replace President Angell, during his leave of absence, with three men. The regental subcommittee charged with the task recommended that "to provide for the instruction heretofore given by President Angell" Herbert Tuttle, A.M., be hired for one semester at $600 to teach international law, Theodore H. Johnson to teach Latin, and "Henry C. Adams, A.M., be and is hereby appointed Lecturer upon Political Economy for one semester, at a salary of $800."[1]

Henry Carter Adams was representative of a new breed of young scholars, and his appointment signaled a significant departure in academic organization of the social sciences. Although *The Wealth of Nations* had been published a hundred years previously, the discipline of economics remained at most universities approximately where Adam Smith had found it, as a branch of moral philosophy. One by one over the next couple of decades, however, the several social sciences would peel off into individual identity. At Michigan, economics led the way.

Adams was a good choice to take those first steps. He had come to the field himself by the moral philosophy route, and had given considerable thought to its definition and role as he moved beyond the traditional view. Born to a clergyman father and a literary-minded mother in 1851 at Davenport, Iowa, young Henry expected to follow his father's profession. While a student at Grinnell College, which his father had helped found, he suffered distressing doubts about the call of the clerical life. Nevertheless, he dutifully went on to the seminary at Andover in 1875. During the year he spent there he strove to understand Christianity from a historical perspective, but "I studied as far as inspiration. Then I broke down," he confided to his diary. "Philosophical abstraction I do not care anything about—I only want common sense."[2] This succinct statement of the cast of Adams's intellect was prophetic of both his personal career and of his impact upon economics at the University of Michigan. He would resist orthodoxy in economics, as he did in theology, and he would see the noblest meaning of political economy in its concern for social problems.

Adams left Andover intending to become a political journalist, but made a detour to Johns Hopkins on a $500 fellowship. There he came under the influence of Francis A. Walker, who steered him into public finance, and in 1878 his place in the alphabet conferred upon him the privilege of receiving the first Ph.D. to be awarded by that university (there were three others in his class). A year's postdoctoral study in Europe not only convinced him that he wanted to teach, but also exposed him to the German historical school under men like Adolph Wagner, which would exert a strong influence on his own thinking. On his return his first published essay, in *Penn Monthly* for April, 1879, was entitled "The Position of Socialism in the Historical Development of Political Economy." He recognized that this inflammatory topic might be damaging to his career prospects, but he chose to establish at the outset his claim to academic freedom and to "write what I believe."[3] This stance, while evoking admiration in some, would arouse the enmity of others, but it would become part of the economics tradition at Michigan.

By a curious coincidence of mistaken identity Adams landed his first job while he was still in Europe. Andrew D. White, on leave from the presidency of Cornell University to be ambassador to Germany, was looking for a substitute to teach his classes and mistook Henry Carter Adams for Johns Hopkins historian Herbert Baxter Adams. Gentleman enough not to reveal the error in his negotiations with economist Adams, White hired him to teach one semester a year. The social sciences were still sufficiently undifferentiated that discrepancies in training could apparently be overlooked. Adams did, in fact, teach money, banking, and finance at Cornell, however, and he rounded out his academic year with a half-time appointment at Hopkins.

By the spring of 1880, when he received the appointment at Michigan, he was operating in a three-part circuit. This gave him the opportunity to make comparisons among three leading universities. Although he may have been disappointed that his hopes for a permanent appointment at Hopkins were fading, he recognized that at Michigan "they treat a man decently . . . and not as though he were an everlasting experiment as they do at Baltimore."[4] Later he scored Michigan higher than Cornell because "the poverty of Ann Arbor . . . gives it for me a certain quality of charm, for I feel that the institution is living up to its capacity [while Cornell] is a brilliant prison rather than a charming home."[5]

Nevertheless, Adams would have been happy to accept a permanent, full-time job at Cornell, had his outspokenness not got him into trouble. By 1886 political economy was worthy of recognition by a full-scale professorship. President Angell of Michigan had, in fact, proposed this step to the regents as early as 1883. Budget stringency aside, however, Adams's publicized free trade views were in conflict with the regents' unanimous protectionist position, and they took no action to upgrade his status; neither did they consider nonrenewal of his appointment on this ground.

Cornell was another story. Its autocratic board chairman, Henry Sage, who was contemptuous of what a later period would call egghead college professors, found the right pretext to demand Adams's dismissal in 1886. In April of that year Adams made an impromptu speech, as a fill-in for a speaker who canceled, in which he expressed sympathy for the goals of the Knights of Labor, while deploring their methods. Conservative opinion was already inflamed by strikes against the Gould railroads during the previous year, and the Haymarket riot would follow Adams's speech by a few days. His philosophic position, that responsible labor unions were a natural development in industrial society, was overlooked as Sage demanded his head.

Charles Kendall Adams had by now come from Michigan to replace White as president of Cornell. (White had originally made the same journey in a game of musical presidents between the two universities that would continue until 1977.) Despite Sage, one Adams would have retained the other on the same part-time basis as before, but this arrangement was no longer acceptable. Even before the unfortunate speech, Henry Adams had written President Angell inquiring about his chances for promotion at Michigan, since it appeared that at Cornell he would never be considered more than an "apprentice." Angell, sensitive to the political pressures on a public university, questioned Adams in correspondence of 1886 and 1887 about his social views. This exchange culminated in Adams's observation that

> if you make a man's opinions the basis of his election to a professorship, you do, whether you intend it or not, place bonds upon the free movement of his intellect. It seems that a Board has two things to hold in view. First, is a man a scholar? Second, is he intellectually honest?[6]

Angell was convinced, and put through appointment of the man whose experience at Cornell was already a cause celebre in the annals of academic freedom.

Time would, of course, demonstrate the wisdom of Angell's decision, as Henry Carter Adams became one of America's leading economists. He had already published a good deal, and with Richard T. Ely and others had helped to found the American Economic Association in 1885. But for the thirty-six-year-old Adams that appointment as full professor at $2200 per year meant that he could finally settle down in one place, and perhaps even think about marriage.

The university at which Henry Carter Adams was appointed professor of political economy and finance in June of 1887 had by then been fifty years on the leafy Ann Arbor campus. Its growth had ac-

celerated steadily to a total student body that year of 1,572, half of
them from out of state, in six departments as follows:

	Total Enrollment	Women
Department of Literature, Science, and the Arts	693	175
Department of Law	338	6
Department of Medicine and Surgery	321	51
College of Dental Surgery	91	4
School of Pharmacy	67	2
Homeopathic Medical College	62	27

The Department of Literature, Science, and the Arts (LSA) was the
fastest growing unit, having almost doubled since Adams's first appointment in 1880. In 1881 it was subdivided into four faculties: philosophy, science, engineering, and political science. The last named
was organized as a school under the deanship of Charles Kendall
Adams, to which only students of junior standing were eligible for
admission. The "political" sciences encompassed history, political
economy, finance, statistics, political, social and sanitary science, forestry, political ethics, constitutional and administrative law, and international law. This unwieldy organization was short-lived, however,
and the school concept was abandoned in 1887 after its second dean,
Thomas M. Cooley, became chairman of the new Interstate Commerce Commission (ICC).

Most of the political science courses were elective, as the requirements for a Bachelor of Arts degree retained a neoclassical look:
English, geography, history, mathematics, Latin, and Greek. Concentration in a single discipline at the junior level lay fifty years into the
future, although there were a few students then taking degrees under
"The University System," as distinguished from the credit system. A
university system student, after two credit years, was expected to pre-
pare himself for special examination in one major and two minor
fields.

When Henry Carter Adams began teaching at Michigan he was
allotted space in University Hall, an imposing structure fronting on
State Street. There he would remain for thirteen years. During his
first semester's residence he offered Course 1, "Elements of Political
Economy," in two sections, each meeting twice a week from 2:00 to
3:00 and using Mill for a text, and Course 2, "Advanced Political
Economy," also meeting two hours per week. The pair covered a great

deal of territory. Within a couple of years he introduced Course 3, "Principles and Methods of Finance," and a financial seminary. In 1885 a more descriptive title was conferred upon Course 2, "Unsettled Questions in Political Economy," and a seminary in the history of industrial society was added. There were also listed under political economy during the early 1880s courses with the intriguing titles "Public Scientific Surveys," "Economic Development of Mineral Resources," and "Science of Forestry." They were not taught by Mr. Adams.

The first year that Adams devoted all his time to Michigan he added Course 4, "Principles of the Science of Statistics;" Course 5, a one semester general course using Marshall's *Economics of Industry,* for students who would not take more economics; Course 6, "Development of Economic Thought"; and Course 7, a seminary in financial history in the United States. By 1888 he had graduate students under his tutelage, and Frederick C. Hicks, who in 1890 would earn the first Ph.D. conferred in economics at Michigan, began to assist in the recitation sections of the principles course. That gave Adams time to introduce a two-semester seminary in economics for graduate students, and a new Course 3, "Social and Industrial Reforms." Course 7 was changed to "Tariff Legislation in the United States," using Taussig's *Tariff History* as text. In 1889 Hicks introduced two semesters of foreign commercial relations of the United States. In short, the curriculum reflected Adams's interest in empiricism and the pragmatic relations of economic principles to social and financial (essentially public financial) questions. The first economics tradition at Michigan was established.

The appointment of Judge Thomas Cooley as first chairman of the ICC was important to the career of Henry Carter Adams, and thereby signaled the establishment of a second economics tradition at Michigan—public service. Cooley promptly appointed Adams to the post of chief statistician of the commission. In this position, which Adams held on a part-time basis until 1911, he put into practice his strong belief in the applicability of economic science to the conduct of public affairs. He saw the collection of statistical data and the rationalization of railroad accounting as not only a means to enforce the Interstate Commerce Act, but as an instrument of public control for "the betterment of mankind." In the policies and practices he established he set the pattern for later public utility accounting and, indeed, has been called the "philosophical parent of much of the political-economic legislation of the next fifty years."[7] He also started the march of Michigan economists to Washington.

During the first semester of 1890–91 Adams went on leave to get the ICC statistical system off to a good start, and a professor of history and belles lettres at Albion College was hired temporarily to teach his courses. His name was Fred Taylor. When Adams returned in the spring semester he taught the unsettled questions course as a team effort with guest lecturers Carroll D. Wright and E. R. A. Seligman. The following year, 1891–92, the curriculum was expanded further, with Hicks's courses in "Socialism and Communism" and "Current Economic Literature and Legislation." Adams introduced "The Railroad Problem," a course which was offered in the law curriculum as well, and an advanced "Critical Analysis of Economic Theories."

A Second String to the Bow, 1892–1901

By 1892 the University's enrollment had grown 70 percent in five years, to 2,692. Enrollment in LSA, however, had doubled to 1,330, of whom 437 were women. Unfortunately, there are no data available for enrollments in economics classes, but these were undoubtedly growing at a commensurate rate. More help was needed. Two graduate assistants were hired that year, Charles H. Cooley and Frank H. Dixon. More significant for the sweep of department history, at its May meeting the regents appointed Fred Manville Taylor assistant professor of political economy for three years. With two professors and two assistants (Hicks departed for the University of Missouri, later to become president of the University of Cincinnati) political economy was now a sizable unit.

Like Henry Carter Adams, Fred M. Taylor was the son of a clergyman and grew up in the Midwest. There the resemblance ended. It would be hard to find two more dissimilar men to share a thirty-year collegial relationship. Whereas Adams valued the study of political economy for what it could reveal about solutions to social problems, Taylor sought to elucidate the harmony of a logical body of theory and system of analysis. For him the deductive reasoning of the neoclassicists, the Austrian school in particular, lit the path toward economic understanding. Adams found more promise in the historical tool of analysis. In policy terms Taylor was led to support of laissez-faire and the gold standard. Adams was a free trader, who believed in the legitimacy of trade unionism. While Adams put into practice the outcome of his studies through public service in the world of affairs, Taylor saw his mission fulfilled entirely within the walls of academe and never took a leave of absence.

Thus the intellectual tension between the theoretician and the empiricist, the cloistered academician and the worldly public servant, stimulated and enriched the intellectual life of the department, and established an equilibrium between the two major streams of the discipline. Whether the two men liked each other is hard to say. The one living department member who knew them both reports that they did not, but that judgment may reflect his own opinion more than theirs. The fact is that for twenty years of their thirty-year association they towered together and undisputedly over the comings and goings of (with one exception) a succession of short-term faculty members.

When Fred Taylor took up residence at 17 Church Street (later 527 Church Street and now a parking structure) in the fall of 1892 he was thirty-seven years old and well established in life, married twelve years and the father of two sons and two daughters. He had grown up in various small towns in Michigan, acquired his A.B. from Northwestern University in 1876 and earned his M.A. degree there in 1879, beginning that year his thirteen-year career at Albion College. Political economy didn't intrude much into his life until the term he spent at Johns Hopkins in the fall of 1884, where he was exposed to Richard T. Ely, and where he perhaps read the book that "really sold him on Economics,"[8] J. B. Clark's *Philosophy of Wealth*. At Hopkins he also studied political philosophy with George Sylvester Morris, who the following year returned to Ann Arbor to teach philosophy. It was under his tutelage that Taylor wrote his dissertation, "The Right of the State to Be," and earned the doctorate in philosophy at Michigan in 1888. As an accredited philosopher Taylor may have hoped for appointment at Michigan upon Morris's death in 1890, but that professorship went to another aspiring philosopher, John Dewey.

Meanwhile Taylor's interest in political economy had grown. He had attended some of Adams's lectures when in Ann Arbor, and had incorporated more and more on the subject into his own courses at Albion. The semester during which he substituted for Adams in 1890 and institutional schools and in the use of statistics as an empirical undoubtedly confirmed the shift. His teaching load the first year, 1892–93, consisted entirely of courses using the historical and philosophical approaches and materials in which he was most qualified. As the decade wore on his interests became more theoretical, and by the turn of the century he had carved out his role as the expositor of economic theory and the standard bearer of analytic rigor. His life work would be devoted to the teaching of principles and theory as a means of training the student's mind.

The catalog of 1892–93 offered the first narrative description of the program in political economy. It identified three levels of courses—undergraduate, courses 1 to 3 and 5; intermediate, courses 4 and 6 to 13; and graduate, courses 15 to 18, and 20 to 22—and described their content. Requirements for the bachelor's degree still identified the classic assortment: English, history, mathematics, Latin, and Greek, with physics and botany added in recognition of the growing importance of the sciences. Economics remained elective. But it was a growing field for graduate study, as were others in the university, and this was the year that the Graduate School was established within the Department of Literature, Science, and the Arts.

Frederick Hicks, with the first Ph.D. in 1890, was followed by Fred Converse Clark in 1891, and four more doctorates were awarded in 1894. Among these was Charles H. Cooley. A son of Judge Thomas M. Cooley, he had started his professional life as an engineer, decided on his first job that he didn't like it, then went to work for Adams as a statistician at the ICC. Here was a field more congenial to his taste. He returned to the university for a Ph.D. and began his teaching career with "Elements of Economics" (the short course for students who would be exposed only once), "Statistics," and "History of Political Economy."

With degree in hand in 1894, Cooley turned to an even newer interest and introduced the first sociology courses, entitled respectively, and not unexpectedly, "Principles of Sociology" and "Problems of Sociology." Legend has it that Adams suggested to Taylor that a course in sociology should be added, and when Taylor didn't pick it up Cooley happily volunteered. A Sociology Club of instructors and graduate students was also announced in that year, meeting on Saturday mornings for discussion of the literature. Cooley continued to teach statistics, and published in the economics journals, while his offerings in sociology grew gradually in number and variety. But he carried the entire load by himself for fifteen years. In 1909 new Ph.D. Carl Eugene Parry was appointed instructor in economics and sociology. Nevertheless, the field was recognized by 1895 when the catalog listed the department's courses under the heading "Political Economy and Sociology." Cooley's switch in field was also recognized that year when the regents appointed him instructor in sociology for one year. The following year they gave him an instructorship for three years, upgraded to assistant professor in 1899 and junior professor in 1904.

The course offering of 1892, beyond "Principles," could be grouped under three major headings: economic history (6 courses); analysis of economic problems, literature, and thought (6 courses); and money and finance (3 courses), with additional individual courses in statistics, transportation, and a seminar in economics. Supplementary course meetings were introduced over the decade to serve the growing body of graduate students.

Just after the turn of the century a third theme was entered into the curriculum beside the theoretical and empirical, one that might be termed the pragmatic. While Adams and Taylor had been building an economics department at Michigan, the nation had been building an industrial capability that needed a new class of managers to run it. America had come of age as an industrial power, and the department responded to its needs with a program quaintly described in the 1901–2 catalog as "Higher Commercial Education."

A Growing Adolescent, 1901–12
A new title in the university catalog for 1902–3 signified the new era. The courses were now listed under "Political Economy," "Industry and Commerce," and "Sociology." The arrival of Edward David Jones in 1901 inaugurated the offering in commercial subjects. Jones, a thirty-one-year-old Wisconsin Ph.D. (the first non-Michigan Ph.D. appointed since Adams) was named assistant professor of commerce and industry for a three-year term and promoted to junior professor with tenure three years later. He introduced two courses on the extractive industries, two courses on manufacturing industries, two courses in foreign trade (one focusing on the Far East) and a course in European economic geography. Supplementing Jones's basic curriculum were two courses each (one per semester) in accounting, commercial law, and annuities and insurance. The latter two were taught by visitors from law and mathematics, respectively. Accounting would

be taught for a number of years by junior instructors and teaching assistants. There were also courses listed that year in the history of industrial physics and history of industrial chemistry, both "presupposing" a knowledge of these sciences.

The 1902–3 curriculum was not entirely historical and institutional in its approach, although Adams and Smalley taught the history of the development of industrial society from the twelfth century to date, and Taylor's money course was still titled "Theory and History of Money." Taylor now offered two advanced theory courses. And in line with the contemporary societal emphasis on business, Adams introduced a new course in administration of corporate and public industries. A balanced outlook was retained with his long-standing courses in problems and in reform. Three courses in finance and one in transportation rounded out the economics curriculum. Of sociology courses there were eight, including such pertinent topics as "Social Development of the Church," "Rural Sociology," and "Psychological Sociology."

This broadening of the curriculum undoubtedly attracted many more students to the department in succeeding years, although there are no separate enrollment data available for that period. During the decade of 1892 to 1902 the university's growth rate had slowed to 30 percent, most of it in the professional schools and colleges. The Department of Literature, Science, and the Arts had barely grown at all, from 1,330 to 1,400. Almost half of that group, 688, were women and 105 of them were graduate students. It is quite possible that a larger proportion of students were taking courses in economics, as requirements for the Bachelor of Arts degree were gradually being relaxed. One hundred twenty credit hours were now established as the minimum to be accumulated and, while first year students were still limited to the traditional subjects, upperclassmen were permitted to select any courses for which they were qualified.

One of those students was Harrison Standish Smalley, who received his Bachelor of Arts degree in 1900. By the fall of 1902 he was assisting Adams. His Ph.D. was awarded in 1903, and the regents appointed him instructor in political economy for one year, subsequently reappointed him several times and promoted him to assistant professor in 1907. His fields were transportation, corporations, and public control, which enabled him to take over Adams's work during the senior man's increasingly frequent absences.

In 1907 the Interstate Commerce Commission reorganized under its growing burden of work to include a section on accounts and statistics headed by Adams. By the time he retired from the post in 1911, the statistical staff had grown from one person (himself) to 250. Not only did the ICC job take him away on leaves and short-term absences from the university, but as one of the nation's most prominent economists Adams was called upon for many other functions. During 1895–97 he served as president of the American Economic Association, succeeding John Bates Clark. In 1913 he took leave to spend a year in China, setting up a system of railroad accounting for the Chinese government which he continued to work on intensively for the next four years.

The Michigan economics department's connection with the Far East had begun over a decade earlier, however, when the first Ph.D. degree in economics ever to be attained by a Japanese national was awarded to Riotaro Kodama in 1898. He had written his dissertation under Adams on railway transportation in Japan, and it became the first journal article published in English on the Japanese economy. Kodama was followed here by three more of his countrymen between 1901 and 1903. Indeed, during the fifteen years between 1898 and 1913, these four Japanese accounted for a considerable proportion of the ten Ph.D.'s awarded.

Two of the perennial problems of the university entered as a theme in the President's Reports beginning around the turn of the century. These were faculty salaries and space. As early as 1892 President Angell had requested the regents to think about raising salaries, not only because eastern and even some western schools were paying more, but "whereas formerly it was rather rare that a professor was called from one institution to another, now the custom is very general."[9] In 1902 he was still pointing out that the university was constantly threatened with faculty losses because its salary scale was lower than other leading institutions. Henry Carter Adams was paid $2,200 in 1887, the first year of his full professorship. Twenty years later, in 1907, his salary stood at $2,700. Fred Taylor, promoted to full professor of political economy and finance in 1904, was raised to the same $2,700 in 1907.

Angell began the appeal for more space for the literary department in 1901, pointing out that Tappan Hall, built for it in 1894, was already becoming overcrowded. By 1907 he was more forceful: "We need sorely larger and better accommodations for the work in history and political economy. The old Chemical Laboratory is both worn out and outgrown."[10] Chemistry's problem was about to become political economy's solution. In 1909 Angell reported that with the opening of the new Chemistry Building the old Chemical Laboratory would soon be renovated for physiology and materia medica (later to be known as pharmacology) and "with some additions to furnish ample quarters for a portion of the work in Political Economy and History."[11]

When the old Chemical Laboratory opened in 1856 it enjoyed the distinction of being one of the first buildings in the world devoted exclusively to chemistry. Its three rooms, built for $6,000, were soon inadequate, however, and additions dating from 1861, 1866, 1868, 1874, 1880, 1888, 1901, and 1909 ultimately submerged both the core and each other. There is no certainty as to which parts were built when, except that some part of the second story was added in 1880, and the tower housed a water tank until 1897. When the new tenants began to move in in 1909 the neighborhood looked entirely different from its appearance today. To the north, space for a cemetery had been set aside by the regents in 1845 (apparently never used for that purpose); to the east were a medical building, 1850–1911, and a small building for geology and surveying, 1907–19; southeast was the boiler house, demolished in 1914 to make way for West Engineering; and on the southwest the old library, third on the site, that would come down in 1918. Only the present School of Natural Resources, built for medicine in 1904, remains from that time. The Chemical Laboratory was the most imposing building on that part of the campus. The large north wing, demolished in 1958, housed physiology and materia medica, while the remainder of the building was shared not with history, as it turned out, but with political science. Nevertheless, it was the name ECONOMICS which went up in cast iron on the portico, probably about 1910. No doubt someone was economizing on space and iron, considering that the major occupant was the Department of Political Economy, Sociology, and Business Administration.

The move was a gradual one. During the 1909–10 year only Fred Taylor and Harrison Smalley were in the old Chemical Laboratory, occupying room 205 together. Adams, Jones, and Cooley were still in room 8A at Tappan Hall. By the following year they had all moved over, the most senior people enjoying for the first time the luxury of private offices. Adams established the chairman's office in room 105, where it remained until 1975. Taylor settled down in room 206, where he remained until his retirement. Jones occupied room 209, though a few years later he would move down to room 107, which was at first shared by Cooley and Smalley. A large room on the second floor housed the department library until 1924, when it was moved to the third floor of the new Angell Hall. During the 1960s it became but another section of the general library.

The five men who comprised the senior staff of the Department of Political Economy, Sociology, and Business Administration in 1910 were a diverse lot. Probably no more than any two of them had much affinity for one another. Henry Carter Adams, at fifty-nine, was a cool, sophisticated public figure, who was away almost as much as he was in residence. Fred M. Taylor, younger by four years, a small man, quick in his movements, may have had little fondness for his more prominent colleague, but by this time Taylor's place in the sun as a teacher was firmly established. Charles H. Cooley was a gentle scholar and gentle man, whose talent for reflection and writing far transcended his performance in the classroom. Forty-year-old Edward Jones didn't get on well with any of the other three. He felt that Adams neglected the department for his outside commitments and that Taylor taught the elementary course, now his personal fiefdom, as an exercise in logic rather than instruction in the use of scientific method. Harrison S. Smalley, at thirty-two, was a young man of great promise, who worked closely with Adams. The following year he would be the first, among the economists at any rate, to use an offer from another university (Stanford) to elicit from the regents a double promotion from assistant to full professor, with a commensurate leap in salary to $2,500.

In 1908 two graduate students were given the title of instructor in political economy, Carl Eugene Parry and David Friday.[12] Parry earned his doctorate in 1909, and remained in the department four years, teaching sociology as well as economics courses. Friday would never complete the degree, but the quality of his mind and his teaching abilities were sufficiently noteworthy for promotion in 1913. While some ascribed to him only a superficial cleverness, Taylor was reported to say "He was a brilliant fellow, you know."[13] And, according to William Paton, "He had a knack as a teacher." It is Professor Paton's view that "Friday really launched accounting" at Michigan,[14] although he wasn't especially trained in it. Paton reports that Adams said he put Friday in charge of the course "even though he doesn't know a thing about it, but that doesn't matter." The implication in Paton's quotation of Adams was that Friday had both the intellectual and teaching capacity to make a success of it, and apparently he did.

Two Hamiltons were appointed instructor in 1910–11, Walton Hale Hamilton in political economy and Stuart McCune Hamilton in commerce and industry. They each stayed four years, long enough to be promoted to assistant professor. Walton earned his Ph.D. in 1913 and went on to become the first economist to teach in a law school, at Yale. With a couple of additional instructorships the department settled comfortably into its new home and stabilized during these years at a faculty of ten to twelve members.

The Links of Continuity, 1912–21
In the early fall of 1912 a personal tragedy became the occasion for a portentious event in the life of the economics department. Harrison Smalley, age thirty-four and diabetic, died suddenly at his summer home in Charlevoix, missing the salvation of insulin by a mere decade. The following June his widow presented to the university his collection of portraits of prominent European and American political economists and 200 books from his library. The photographic collection seems to have evaporated; the books may be found in the Hatcher Graduate Library. There was no compensation for the widow in those days, however, and in February of 1913 the regents used the appropriation for Smalley's salary to reassign his course work. Isaiah Leo Sharfman was appointed lecturer in political economy, at $1,000 for the semester. The following fall he became junior professor of political economy, and in 1914 full professor.

Sharfman's unobtrusive entrance into the faculty of political economy, as a substitute in a crisis, was an altogether misleading hint of the future, for Leo Sharfman would create and personify yet another unique economics tradition at Michigan. If Henry Carter Adams established the department's national reputation, and Fred M. Taylor set the pattern for ten generations of American economics students and teachers, I. Leo Sharfman, by the remarkable force of his personality, molded an assortment of faculty into a collegium of legendary esprit de corps. And his long years of service from Adams's day onward would forge the link of continuity for seventy-five of the department's hundred year history.

Nor was his internal influence the greatest of his achievements,

for Sharfman, like Adams and Taylor, gave luster to the department
in the world at large. He had earned his baccalaureate degree at Harvard in 1907, specializing in economics, and went on to a Harvard law
degree in 1910. He then accepted a teaching post at Imperial Pei-Yang
University in Tientsin, China, but the Boxer Rebellion forced his
return earlier than planned. It was law that first brought Sharfman to
Michigan. He was scheduled for a visiting lectureship in the Law
School when Smalley died, and, in fact, he continued as a lecturer
there for some years. His research and publishing were in transportation and public control, especially railroad regulation, the fields he
taught at Michigan along with business law.

In 1914 the Department of Literature, Science, and the Arts
adopted new requirements for the Bachelor's degree, which allowed
a latitude that would continue for the next twenty years. After completing the freshman requirements in rhetoric (later called English)
a student chose at least twelve hours in each of the three discipline
groups, but not more than forty hours in any one department. In the
Department of Economics, however (and this is the first time economics is called a department), sixty hours could be elected, but no more
than forty in any one of the subdivisions. Two years before, in 1912,
the traditional pass/fail assessment had been replaced with a letter
grading system.

There was little change in the economics curriculum over the
decade of the 1910s. Its three major themes—the empirical, the theoretical, and the practical—were now well established and would continue in approximately the same balance until the mid-twenties. The
expansion in size and complexity of American business enterprise
was, perhaps, the dominant feature of the society at large during this
period, and the Michigan curriculum reflected this preoccupation.
Half of the senior faculty were entirely or largely devoted to the teaching of business subjects. The 1913–14 catalog listed twenty-nine
courses under "Business Administration," contrasted to twenty-two
under the parent "Political Economy," and eight under "Sociology."
(These totals include courses that were offered in both semesters.)

The greatest change over the previous decade occurred in the
business sequence. Where in 1902–3 two courses in accounting had
been offered, now there were seven under Friday's direction, including
a special course each for engineering and for pharmacy students. Similarly the three courses in annuities and insurance had doubled to six,

still taught by Professor Glover of the mathematics department. In the latter year his courses in the mathematical theory of statistics were also cross-listed under business administration. Except for the law sequence, taught by Sharfman, the rest of the business curriculum appears to be quite transformed from the offering a decade earlier. Jones's earlier courses in commercial geography and other courses whose names had implied description of the various kinds of economic activity now assumed more generalized titles, such as "Principles of Industry," "Problems of Production," and "Industrial History of the United States." Furthermore, some very important additions were made, like marketing, management, and administration under Jones, and corporation finance taught by Sharfman. In short, the business curriculum had shed its quaintness and looked much like a basic business administration curriculum looks today.

In 1909 a special interdisciplinary program, leading to a Certificate in Business Administration, was introduced under Professor Jones, later Friday, as secretary. Designed for students preparing for "either a general business career or for particular lines of business, such as railway administration, insurance, accounting, and banking,"[15] it required courses in both law and engineering, in addition to the business subjects.

The political economy offering continued, as it would to the present, to support both the theoretical and the empirical approaches to the discipline. Nor did it look very different from its appearance in 1902–3. During these years, when the discipline focused so heavily on what is today called microeconomics, there was often little beyond nuance of approach to distinguish institutional and empirical political economy from the professional business courses. Thus Adams's courses in corporations and in railroads were part of the economics curriculum, as was statistics. But statistics, as essentially an enumerative rather than an analytical technique, at that time had a close relationship to accounting. Indeed, the two terms were often used interchangeably. Accounting, under William A. Paton, a Michigan Ph.D. who joined the staff in 1917 upon completing his degree, and whose original work in accounting theory gave Michigan a national reputation in this field, remained an important component of the economics curriculum for decades to come. Yet Adams's social emphasis in his courses on public finance, reform, and historical development was reinforced by Sharfman's interests and his courses in corporation problems and transportation problems. Transportation, with particular emphasis on railroads, continued for the next twenty years, as it had for the past twenty, to loom large in the curriculum and in student-faculty research. Fifteen out of forty-six doctoral dissertations completed between 1891 and 1931 were devoted to issues in this field.

In terms of student numbers the seven principles courses (three offered both semesters) far outweighed all the other twelve political economy courses taught in 1913–14, by 1,109 to 387. In the principles courses, reinforced by the later sequence in theory, Fred M. Taylor reigned in undisputed command. And Alfred Marshall was his prime minister. In Taylor's view the neoclassical system, exemplified in equilibrium theory and marginal analysis, revealed to the careful student all that he needed to know for an understanding of the economy in which he lived. But Taylor's five-hour principles course was designed to give the student more than mere acquaintance with the workings of the economic system. It was directed to the training of his mind, to the fine tuning of his intellect, to inculcating the ability to think with the tools of an impeccable logic. With this immutable goal before him Taylor would brook no dalliance, no slippage from the hard tightrope of logical rigor, no fuzzy threads left unwoven.

> My fundamental demand in this course is to get *definite results.*
> I have no patience with the notion of some teachers of our subject that they have done enough if they have aroused interest in this subject and left the student with some suggestive ideas.
> ... I expect the student to come out with a *body of sharply defined doctrines.* Nothing else goes ... *they must master the stuff given in the text* whether true or false. Nothing is so inconsistent with real scholarship, real scientific attainments, as vagueness.
> ... The very definiteness is a blessing even when the doctrines are wrong or overstated: for definiteness enables one to realize just what is the issue in controversy and makes fruitful criticism possible.[16]

That is how Taylor described his own pedagogical values. And he did get his message across.

> To his teaching ... [he] brought much of the flavor and methodology of mathematics and the "exact" sciences. It was his belief that the essentials of economics were subject to formula-

tion and presentation in terms of fundamental assumptions, orderly processes of reasoning, and clear-cut conclusions.[17]

According to Fred Taylor

there was only one proper way of saying anything in the field of
economics. He insisted upon precision in statement, and accuracy, and straight thinking. . . . The Taylorian method . . . required that one be extremely accurate in answering questions,
that he not stray away from the main argument.[18]

He was a very clear, able, and extremely demanding teacher. I
think everyone . . . came away with a sense of rigor that very few
teachers are able to convey. . . . His idea of making a principle
real was not to put it in a real setting, which . . . related to some
current problem. . . , but it was to take a situation in which an
economic fallacy developed. He used the fallacy method of teaching to break the area down . . . which was fascinating intellectually, but not the kind that made the student feel that this was
. . . explaining the real world.[19]

Such are the recollections of three men who came under his influence.

Fred Taylor's influence spread far and wide, not only through
the thousands of undergraduates and graduates he taught, but through
the textbook that was his major publication. The book evolved over
the course of many years, published in bits and pieces on a nonprofit
basis by George Wahr in Ann Arbor for the use of Taylor's own students before it became a complete volume in 1911.[20] One of Taylor's
objectives in publishing the book was to abridge Marshall, as Marshall
had undertaken to abridge Mill, to restate and elaborate the enduring
principles in light of refinements in the discipline since the master
had written. Taylor wrote as he lectured. Paton, in describing the
book, again uses the analogy to mathematics.

In its precision and clarity of statement, and in its array of definite
"principles" and "corollaries," his "Principles of Economics" is
suggestive of a typical treatise on geometry.[21]

It went through nine editions between 1911 and 1925.

Taylor's method of running the principles course was almost as
important in its impact on students as the content was. He lectured
for one of the course's five hours. The other four were spent in quiz

sections of no more than twenty students each, conducted by able young graduate students with the official title of instructor, but known in common parlance as "section hands." These people were hand picked by Taylor for the job, and they learned as much as their charges did. All of them were required to attend every lecture, and the group met in conference with Taylor once a week, where the several tests to be given throughout the term were handed out. Nor did Taylor leave the sections entirely to his assistants. He took each one himself once or twice a term and was "suspected of occasionally listening through an open transom to check on what was going on.[22] In addition to hour-long tests, students were required to turn in, weekly or more often, written answers to assigned problems. These were corrected by nonteaching graduate students as well as the section hands, so that many could benefit from the teaching-as-learning experience.

Although teaching assistants might propose questions for the examinations, it was Taylor who made them up, without consultation. When they were passed out in the sections each student received a number with which to code his blue books, instead of using his name. Thus grading was totally anonymous. Each teaching assistant graded one or two questions for all the students taking the course, then Taylor put it all together, computing separately the performance of each quiz section so that the accomplishments of the teaching assistants might be fairly judged.

"Each of the . . . instructors who participate in the teaching of the course is rated according to his success in 'putting the stuff over,' turning out students who can pass written tests set for the class as a whole by myself," he explained to a new recruit. All sections have

> a common lesson assigned by myself. At first you may find the rigidity of the procedure a little trying; but in the end most of the men like it, and all agree that they have found it to be the most useful part of their own economic training. I may add that, while I insist on definite results, I do not indulge in any dictation as to specific methods of teaching.[23]

Thus the principles course served a double teaching function, for graduates and undergraduates alike. Taylor's teaching on the graduate level was quite different from his style with undergraduates. With the beginners he tended to be rigid and doctrinaire, something less than spellbinding from the podium. But in his graduate theory course he was said to be spectacular. He encouraged questioning and probing. He also taught a Saturday morning seminar, which focused on a particular concept or issue or a new book each term, so that graduate students, particularly the section hands, took it every term they were in residence. While examination and exposition of neoclassical theory was central to the course, in this advanced work Taylor explored its relation to the real world of issues and problems. Nor did he neglect the socialist and the American institutionalist schools, although he disapproved of both. For Taylor, laissez-faire and the free market were enduring principles not to be tampered with.

Although the graduate courses were more open than the undergraduate, Taylor still did almost all the talking. "He would turn to a member of the seminar occasionally to get verification of the truth of something that he had said, but you seldom had any chance to expand upon any ideas that you may have had of your own.[24] When Clark Dickinson was writing his biography of Taylor he obtained from Bruce Knight, an instructor from 1921 to 1923, a graphic description of Taylor's teaching style:

(1) Reaching a certain stage of his exposition, he would suddenly stop to demand: "And now, what am I about to say?" (2) He would describe somebody's proposition in such words as, "What he meant—or, at any rate, what he should have meant. . . ." (3) He would pull off his glasses, nibble at the end of one of the bows, walk up and down in a sort of dance-step. . . . Then about the time you thought he had sunk into a brown abstraction never to rise again, he would suddenly stop, pierce you with his blue eyes, and pounce on you with the question, *"How about that, Mr. . . ?"* (4) He seemed to remember unerringly just what he had said to precisely whom, no matter if it had been weeks before. Once, on getting from one of my colleagues an answer almost irrelevant enough to be mine, he transfixed the culprit in mock horror and squeaked out, "Damn you, how many times do I have to teach you that?" (5) He was pretty stubborn about admitting it when any of us caught him in a slip, as of course we were constantly conspiring to do. Once another section hand and I were delighted to note that, after explaining the difference between demand as cause of price and as effect of price, he himself had confused the two in a problem on foreign exchange. . . .

When we went up to him about it, he gave us quite a battle. But in his next edition he changed the problem.[25]

Despite the eccentricities and dogmatism of "Freddy" Taylor, as he was known, he was loved as well as revered by many of the thousands of students he sent forth to the world, whether they continued to hold his doctrine or not. Indeed, his following formed a kind of cult that could be likened flatteringly to Socrates and the original Academy or more irreverently to the "groupies" of a later time. While he could be a rather forbidding person he exuded warmth and sociability to his intimates and those who shared his views and interests. Judging from the output of doggerel about him he appears to have had a sense of humor. Of interests there were many, and his hobbies became legendary. He took these up in succession with the same perfectionism he displayed in the classroom—bicycling (the whole family was required to participate), sailing, roses, golf (he was a charter member of Ann Arbor's first golf club), wild flowers (though he suffered acutely from hay fever), whist, ornithology, chess, and dancing. Many of them he gave up after a few years of mastery, but "he never abandoned his roses."[26]

If we have dwelt longer on Fred Taylor's teaching and his personality than on others it is because more information about him is available. That, in itself, is a measure of his personal influence. It is rather ironic to note the contrasts between him and Adams in these respects. If Adams is identified as the liberal and Taylor the conservative in their professional positions, their social behavior was just the reverse. Adams, whose influence was worldly rather than personal, tended to be stiff and formal, impeccably dressed, cool, and socially correct. Taylor, whose influence was direct and intimate, who shunned titles and offices, was casual and informal outside the classroom, an enthusiastic outdoorsman. The Adamses entertained at stiff dinners; the Taylors gave candlelit dancing parties.

Of the other senior faculty members during the decade of the 1910s, David Friday was perhaps the most colorful. He had returned to graduate school rather late in life, and when he joined the staff in 1908 he was thirty-two years old, married, and a father. "Friday was a person of strong personality with a big expressive voice and real speaking ability to a large audience. . . . He had broad interests, some intellectual and some not so much so." His courses tended to consist of Friday 1 and Friday 2.

> You didn't know at all what you'd get. I had a course called Statistics, but one never learned any systematic statistics at all in the course. And in another course we were to do some reading, and incidentally get prepared for our German examinations, because he spoke German. I don't know that we did any of that. But he was always interesting.[27]

Friday did a lot of outside consulting work, engaging graduate student assistants he could rely upon so that he could keep many balls in the air simultaneously. Florence Middaugh was one of those, a thoroughly competent young woman who was a teaching assistant in the department from 1919–21. It was rumored that a good deal of Friday's output was more hers than his. And what probably started as a relationship of mutual admiration culminated in Friday's divorce and remarriage to her. That occurred some years later, however, after Friday left the University of Michigan to assume the presidency of Michigan State College in 1921.

The most noticeable effect of World War I on the economics department was a one-year drop in enrollments. The earliest enrollment data available are for 1913–14, when in the first semester 1,424 students were registered for twenty-one courses (2,943 in forty courses for the full year). These numbers climbed in the fall of 1916 to 2,013 and twenty-seven, fell off a bit the following year, then plummeted to 884 students in twenty-three courses in the fall of 1918, half of whom were women. But after the war the economics department, like the university, took a great leap upward: 3,216 students (650 were women) were enrolled in the twenty-eight courses in the first semester of 1919–20 (7,217 total, 1,259 women, in sixty-two courses for the year). Everything would be bigger, and some things better, in the decade to follow.

A Time of Change, 1921–30
When the new decade opened it revealed a drastically changed world. The wrenching of world war had so transformed modern life that there would be little return to the old ways. The pace of life quickened, institutional changes followed one another rapidly, the aspirations of masses of people rose to previously undreamed levels. All of these

developments were reflected in the University of Michigan and its economics department.

Students were coming to college in droves. In the eight years from 1912–13 to 1920–21 university enrollments almost doubled, from 5,805 to 10,623. Literature, Science, and the Arts jumped from 2,378 to 6,242, and the administrative structure was elaborated to take care of them. Economics elections, as they were called, stayed up around the 7,000–8,000 mark, 18 to 20 percent of them women, through the first half of the 1920s. A third of these students were in the introductory courses, including the one-semester course for those who would not take any additional economics, and the special course for engineers which ran to three sections. Course 1, Taylor's five-hour "Elements of Economics," in which he lectured to 807 students in the Natural Science Auditorium, required thirty sections in the fall of 1920 to keep size down to 20 students each. His stable of section hands, which had averaged eight during the previous decade, doubled to sixteen that year. The next most populous course was number 38, "Principles of Accounting," which, under William Paton's direction, enrolled 381 students that fall in eighteen sections conducted by seven junior faculty. "Money and Banking" (Wilbur Calhoun), "Corporations" (Leo Sharfman), and "Business Law" (Earl Wolaver) all followed close behind with enrollments at around 300 in five to ten sections. Then came "Marketing" (Clare Griffin) at 167 and "Corporation Finance" (Sharfman) at 123. Clearly the popularity of the "practical" business focus of the curriculum had carried over from the previous decade and indeed, increased.

Although there were few fundamental changes in economics during the first couple of decades of the century, an important addition to the curriculum by 1920 pointed to future directions. One course and one seminar in labor problems were offered by Isador Lubin, who came in 1919 as a predoctoral instructor, was promoted to assistant professor in 1921, and left in 1923 to join the new Brookings Institution in Washington. In later years Lubin would become an important figure in Roosevelt's "brain trust" and commissioner of the highly respected Bureau of Labor Statistics.

"Statistics," taught by David Friday for graduate students only, was defined as a course "devoted to a study of economic problems whose solution depends upon statistical investigation." As such it reflected Adams's traditional interest. For statistical theory and training in statistics as a tool of analysis the student must still depend upon the mathematics courses cross-listed in the "Economics" section of the catalog.

Two other interests of Adams do not show up at all in the offering for 1920–21; history of economic thought, and his long-standing course in reform. But the department's preoccupation with transportation and railroads was still much in evidence, and Adams himself still taught the seminar in public finance. The latter field had expanded to include a course in the income tax, taught by Paton, and one in municipal and institutional accounting, taught by Ross Walker, a young instructor on the staff from 1919–22. Again, both these courses had an accounting emphasis, but they nevertheless reflected new interests in subject matter.

In short, such shifts as occurred in the curriculum immediately after World War I were topical, rather than theoretical or methodological. The department had been an early leader, under Adams, in development of the empirical aspects of the discipline, and it would jump to the forefront again in this area a few decades later. William Paton, as a leading figure in the theory of accounting, gave luster to Michigan in that field, but business administration was becoming a freestanding discipline itself and this work was not in the mainstream of economics, as such. Fred Taylor was an important interpreter and synthesizer of economic theory, but he was not an innovator. Thus in the 1920s Michigan presented a sound, fairly traditional, highly respected, but perhaps unexciting, economics department. The most important changes that would take place there over the decade were organizational and personal. Indeed, these were profound, and the department would look quite different at the end of the decade than it did at the beginning.

The first of these changes was the departure of Henry Carter Adams. He retired at the end of the 1920–21 year, expecting to return to China for further work on their railroad accounts. He never did, although a grateful Chinese government erected a special memorial tablet at his grave. Adams was awarded the title of professor emeritus, but lived only a few months to enjoy it. On August 11, 1921, his death broke the continuity of forty years.

A nomenclature that defined "department" as we have come to use it does not seem to have been officially adopted by the university. When the "Department" of Literature, Science, and the Arts became a "College" in 1915 the designation of its component units as departments was already in use. An appendix to the Regents Proceedings of 1913 refers to "Political Economy" as a subdepartment, but a year later there was a reference to the Department of Economics. In 1916 the overall title "Economics" appeared in the catalog, with the three subdivisions included under that. The name "Political Economy" in the subdivision would not be dropped until 1927, although the last professorial appointment with that title was George Dowrie in 1917. By that time all the instructors were in "Economics," however. A title once conferred is never rescinded, of course, so that Adams and Taylor remained professors of political economy and finance until the end.

Just as the officiality of the designation "department" was vague, so was that of "chairman." Custom apparently considered the most senior faculty member in terms of rank and service to be the chairman, and he held that position for life. Thus Adams was acknowledged chairman of the department, though an official appointment as such does not appear in the record. Shortly before his retirement, however, the University of Michigan began moving to the department "committee system," with rotating chairmen, that a number of other universities, notably Harvard, were adopting. In 1921 "after the retirement of Professor Henry C. Adams the Department of Economics was placed upon the committee basis, and Professor F. M. Taylor was appointed Chairman."[28] There is no evidence in the record, however, that a committee ever functioned at this time (or for the next thirty-five years) and the chairmanship certainly didn't rotate. Nor does it appear that Taylor ever took this administrative responsibility very seriously. The fact is that the department had been run for the past five years by the very able man appointed secretary in 1916, I. Leo Sharfman. Adams may have reserved major decisions for himself, but the day-to-day conduct of the department's affairs, including the counseling of students, was handled by Sharfman, and the archival record of the department dates from his appearance in 1913.

Thus a change in the table of organization signified little change in fact, until the winter of 1923. That was when the commanding figure of Edmund Ezra Day appeared on the scene. The thirty-eight-year-old professor of economics and chairman of the department at Harvard was appointed by the regents in March of 1922 to replace Henry Carter Adams as professor of economics, chairman of the Department of Economics, and director of curricula in business administration.

As we have noted, the curriculum in business administration had expanded to look like the tail wagging the economics department. It was also becoming more professionalized. Edward Jones had not been the strongest of scholars and, according to one report, Adams took the first opportunity to replace him in 1919. Clare Elmer Griffin, with a Ph.D. from Johns Hopkins, a specialist in marketing, was appointed associate professor of commerce and industry in 1919. Griffin had some definite ideas on the teaching of economics and business administration and communicated them to Adams in a memorandum, which bears no date but must have been sent during the 1920–21 year. He identified two general purposes in teaching economics: (1) the cultural, which involves explanation of principles, development of a critical attitude and analytic skill, and appreciation for public problems; (2) the professional includes these but goes beyond in that "the professional student has to be constantly shifting his vantage point from that of citizen to that of the individual business man in search for profit [sic]." He, therefore, favored establishment of a separate school of commerce and cited, among several advantages in separating cultural economics from professional the "tendency for economics which should be studied from a purely scientific point of view to become 'commercialized'."[29] He did not advocate total disassociation, however, and urged that some of the faculty have joint appointments.

The rationale presented by Griffin in this memorandum reflected a widely held view, and Day was brought in for the express purpose of establishing a school of business administration. In 1924 the School of Business Administration became official, with a separate listing in the catalog that described its curriculum, although the courses remained in the political economy and business administration listing under "Economics" until 1927. Even after that some of the courses, most notably accounting, continued under "Economics" for more than thirty years. And, as Griffin had recommended, many of the faculty appointments remained joint. Added to William Paton's title of professor of economics, which he retained to retirement, was that of professor of accounting.

Edmund Day served the University of Michigan a scant four years, but his vibrant personality left its mark. He was a handsome man of great energy who did not relinquish prior responsibilities as he acquired new ones. When he left in 1927 to head the Social Science Research Council (he became fifth president of Cornell in 1937, in good Michigan tradition) he held four titles: professor of economics, chairman of the economics department, dean of the School of Business Administration, and university dean of administration. He was also a good teacher.

> He was the kind of speaker whose lectures made the first draft of a book on statistics. . . . His fluency, his orderliness, his ability to put his thoughts into beautiful sentences, were all extraordinary. He had a nice sense of humor. And he was a very cultivated man. He was a purist in his use of language, more so than most educated people are, and so he noticed if words were not used right, and he would find occasion to mention their misuse, gently.[30]

As new administrators of new organizations are wont to do, Day brought a number of people with him from Harvard to teach at Michigan. It is difficult to sort out, during the four transitional Day years, just who should be classified as a member of the economics department and who belongs in business administration. There was considerable overlap for some time. The distinction is made here, and in the appendix list of faculty, according to which word was used in the title. Thus, of the people who came here with Day or shortly thereafter, three can be considered economics faculty: John Van Sickle, who remained only four years; Margaret Elliott, who came in 1924 as assistant professor of personnel management, but when promoted to associate professor in 1929 "economics" was added to her title; and Z. Clark Dickinson, a Harvard Ph.D. who was teaching at Minnesota when Day invited him to join the Michigan faculty, and who came in at the rank of associate professor.

Dickinson had shown great promise at Harvard, where he was a University Scholar and Edward Austin Fellow, and his doctoral thesis, "Economics Motives," won the David A. Wells prize for 1919–20. There was a dissenter from the Harvard judgment of Dickinson's work, however. Charles Cooley appraised it in a memo to Day, in which he described the book as careful and well written, revealing "a keen and cultured mind . . . but somewhat lacking into intellectual initiative." He found rather sterile "the marriage of a remote and abstract psychology to a remote and abstract economic theory."[31] Psychological economics had not yet arrived. Dickinson taught in a number of fields over the years, including labor, theory, comparative systems, and history of thought. He performed best in the small, advanced classes where his erudition was displayed to advantage and his gentle personality came across. A tall, rangy man, "Zeke," as he was known, was much loved in the department. He was a slow talker but had an infallible memory for "episodes, anecdotes, and words. . . . He always amazed me when I would be feeling for a word (especially a name) that it would come to him first."[32]

Margaret Elliott was the other member of the "Day group," who continued in the department for the remainder of her career. She was the first woman to teach economics at Michigan. (The first woman to earn a Ph.D., Dorothy Miles Brown, did so a few years earlier in 1922, and a few years later, 1928–30, Ruth Marion Engle would be the first female graduate student–instructor.) As something of a pioneer, Miss Elliott in a letter to I. Leo Sharfman years later recalled her trepidation upon arrival in Ann Arbor, clutching her brand-new Radcliffe Ph.D.

> It was just thirteen years ago today—J-Hop Friday—that I arrived in Ann Arbor to begin work on the following Monday. I stepped off the train in the semi-darkness at 6:30 in the morning, and saw the hospital looming up huge and grey in the distance. I was scared to death, as I very well remember.
>
> That was the beginning of what has been for me a long stretch of happy years.[33]

Her tenure was a happy one for the university as well, in that "she was one of the people that was just universally loved."[34] After her marriage in 1933 to John Tracy, professor of law, she continued to teach industrial relations and personnel management courses under her joint appointment until her husband's retirement in 1949. She then retired along with him so that they might travel and enjoy life together, but attended department social functions almost until her death in 1978.

The other major appointment made by Day was Carter Goodrich, a 1921 Chicago Ph.D., who was described in a letter of recommendation as "about the keenest young fellow I have come across."[35] Goodrich came in 1924 as an assistant professor at $3,000, and was an instant success in teaching, scholarship, and the liveliness of his personality. The university's appreciation of his talents was expressed in conferring upon him the first Henry Russel Award in 1926, and in promotion to associate professor in 1927 and to full professor at $5,000 in 1929. But despite the happy association and an active role in department affairs while he was here, Goodrich left in 1931 to take an appointment at Columbia, where he remained until retirement. Goodrich's teaching assignments were in economic history and in labor. Thus three almost simultaneous appointments in labor and industrial relations—Goodrich, Elliott, and Dickinson—attest to the rapidly growing importance of this field of economics, which for three previous years had been handled by one predoctoral instructor.

At the new School of Business Administration, Day established the Bureau of Business Research, which over the years published a number of economics studies authored by members of both units. In the department he started the Economics Club, which gathered in the evening from time to time during the next forty years to hear presentations by colleagues or visiting faculty. But perhaps "Rufus" Day's most enduring legacy to the University of Michigan was a sporting one. He was nicknamed Rufus during his student days after Rufus Choate, the only other Dartmouth graduate to have achieved an all-A record. In addition to being brilliant Day was also athletic. He introduced squash to the Michigan campus. From his authoritative position it was no problem to get a handball court at Waterman Gym converted to his favorite sport. He also inaugurated team softball in the economics department, the married men against the single men. When business administration split off the school played the department, Day pitching for one, Sharfman for the other. Such athletic tradition as remains in the department may be fairly attributed to Edmund Ezra Day.

While Day was taking the business curriculum out of the economics department the more anomalous sociology was destined to remain legally under the aegis of economics until 1931, and an occupant of the building until 1933. For all practical purposes, however, it was a separate unit, recognized as such in the catalog of 1927–28 which finally alphabetized department course listings and placed sociology in its rightful location. Through the decade of the 1910s it had been a two- or three-man unit: Charles Cooley; Warren Thompson, later replaced by Roy Holmes; and Arthur Wood, all of whom occupied rooms 107 and 108. Lowell Carr came on in 1921 and Robert C. Angell in 1922, both predoctoral instructors, who would earn their degrees in 1925, Angell being the first Michigan Ph.D. in sociology. There were two additional instructorships until 1925, then three, with a variety of occupants. This number jumped to six in 1929. In addition there were a number of part-time, or "nonresident" lecturers, particularly for the social work part of the curriculum which operated largely in Detroit. In short, by 1929 sociology had sufficient teaching faculty to comprise a substantial unit. In May of that year, however, it lost its sixty-five-year-old founder and leader to cancer.

Charles Cooley had never wanted to have

a separate department because he didn't want to be bothered with administration. . . . He didn't neglect what he had to do, but he was pretty bored with it and wanted to get back to his front room in 706 Forest [his home] where he spent most of his time thinking. He really sat down and thought. He had little 4 x 6 . . . slips of paper and he kept a great stack of them. He would go in there every morning after breakfast and begin to think on whatever he was thinking about, and when he got a good idea he would write it down. He collected these for long periods until he felt he had maybe enough for an article or maybe enough for a book . . . and then . . . he took these and he rearranged them to see how they kind of fitted nicely. And then he wrote transitions between. . . . The excellence of his literary quality largely, I think, comes from the fact that he didn't bother to read much of the ordinary sociology. . . . He read people like Goethe, . . . Emerson, . . . Bryce, and . . . Montesquieu . . . because he had a very broad approach to things. . . . [As a teacher] he was a poor lecturer. He was partially deaf. He didn't speak loud enough. . . . It was really too bad. [But] he was good, he was very good in one situation.[36]

That was in the graduate seminars, which one enterprising young senior took in 1928, along with the graduate seminar offered by Taylor.

Each, in his own way, I remember as a superlative teacher, and yet they were as different as black and white. Taylor did 99 percent of the talking in his seminar, Cooley about one percent in his seminar. Cooley succeeded through a number of devices that I've employed ever since in bringing out the student in the seminar. . . . We had read in the books that Cooley had written what his ideas were on the subject, but he didn't want us simply to restate his thinking. He wanted us to look at the problem that he was analyzing and see what we could add.[37]

Cooley's long-time senior associate, Fred Taylor, also taught until 1929, and over the course of the decade of the 1920s more than thirty instructors were brought in to assist him. Most of them eventually earned their doctorates at Michigan, but it took quite a while as predoctoral instructors customarily carried a teaching load of twelve hours. The names of those who were on the staff three years or more are listed in the appendix, but four who did not stay to complete their degrees here should be mentioned. In 1920 Taylor hired two bright new baccalaureates from the State University of Iowa—Edward Chamberlin and Howard Ellis. Friends and roommates, they both went on to Harvard for their doctorates two years later. Chamberlin remained there; Ellis returned to Michigan in 1925. Both men had been students of Frank Knight at Iowa, and Knight's younger brother, Bruce, was an instructor here from 1921–23. Willard Thorp was another of that short-term crop of the 1920–23 period, who went on to the Ph.D. and later prominence in the East.

Another of Taylor's 1920 hires was an unusual man. Carroll May was then thirty-seven years old, a Harvard Ph.D. in classics. Teaching Greek and Latin in high schools and tiny colleges had not satisfied him, and he came to Michigan as both an instructor in economics and a special student. The dissertation he never completed was to deal with mathematical treatment of economic questions. May was Taylor's second in command, selected perhaps because of his maturity, to help supervise the large and growing crop of section hands. He fell victim to a serious heart condition, however, in the spring of 1929. Although he still hoped to make progress on his dissertation from his bed, he was never able to return to work, and the end came for him in the fall of 1930. His widow, ironically, lived to ninety-nine years of age; she died in 1978.

Two section hands who came on in the early twenties would remain in the department until their retirement, both exerting a strong and benevolent influence. Shorey Peterson was an Albion College graduate, who came in 1920 for graduate study. After one year and a master's degree Taylor invited him to teach in the principles course. Peterson had the good fortune to be assigned only three sections, rather than the customary four, because that year's student total was not evenly divisible by four. Taylor clearly took a shine to the tall, amiable young scholar because after three years as a section hand he was assigned the one-semester course for his own. Shortly after Peterson started teaching, Taylor "asked me if I'd like to hang my hat in his office . . . in those later years he would just come over, hang his hat in his office, teach a class and go home."[38] So Shorey Peterson became the permanent tenant of room 206, sharing it first with the great man himself, then with Carroll May and Howard Ellis. In the fullness of senior faculty status, he succeeded to private occupancy rights, but continued to share with younger colleagues, as Taylor had with him.

Leonard Watkins, born in Tantley, Alabama, was a University of Texas graduate who, after military service in 1917–18, returned to Austin. In 1922 he wrote the chairman of the economics department at Michigan that he wanted to take a Ph.D. at a university that had an adequate job available (he was married and a father). Fortunately, there happened to be an instructorship available, and on the strength of his one year's teaching experience at Texas, Taylor decided to "nominate you for the place without further investigation."[39] Such was the power of a department chairman in those days. Watkins was expected to teach twelve hours for $1,500 and also keep up with his graduate work. He did so, and then went off to Cincinnati for two years while finishing his dissertation, which won a national prize, as did those of two other students from Michigan during these years, Lawrence S. Seltzer and Nelson Lee Smith. When Watkins returned in 1926 as an assistant professor he settled into a career as one of the most popular teachers the department ever had.

"He taught money and banking, and I took all of the courses that he taught in this area," recollects one of his many admirers.

Leonard was a southerner. He still had a bit of the southern accent and he had all the characteristics of a Southern gentleman. He would always smile when he asked you a question. He would smile even if you did not answer it quite properly. He would point out that you hadn't, but there was never any malice in any of his interaction with students. This leads to an anecdote [about another] graduate student . . . from Alabama. . . . He came into my office (I was then an instructor) and said "I don't know when I've been more annoyed and irritated than I have just been. I was in a class that Professor Watkins was teaching and one of the students . . . was just outright rude to Professor Watkins. This is something I just cannot tolerate, how anyone can treat a gentleman like Professor Watkins in the way in which this student did. . . . If I had had that student I would have picked him up by both ears and peeled him like a banana."[40]

Watkins's easygoing ways were recollected in a different vein by another former student.

One of the things that I remember about Leonard was that he always lectured overtime. He never got through on time. And I thought at first that this was just an accident, that he really couldn't keep track of time—until somebody pointed out to me . . . that every day at five minutes to the hour Leonard would walk over and close the door to the classroom, so that the noise of . . . students passing by and changing classes wouldn't disrupt him.

Watkins wasn't all leisurely drawl, however. When he gave an assignment, he would then

ask some questions in class about the assignment. And if it appeared that not enough of us had read the assignment he would give us a lecture in which he almost wept, in which he would say now he knew that this was not the most important thing we had to do, and we had many other things that needed doing, but after all. . . . He would very nearly break down, and we would all rush out to the library and frantically read the next two weeks' assignments.[41]

In 1925 occurred the first gala occasion of which there is a record in the department, although there may have been others before then. On the evening of August 1 almost 150 people sat down to a banquet in the Michigan Union to honor Fred M. Taylor on the occasion of his seventieth birthday. In addition to the usual toasts and speeches he was presented with two munificent gifts. One hundred nine of his ardent admirers had raised over $3,000 to purchase a new Buick sedan to replace his aging Willys-Knight, and there was enough left over to commission a portrait from Alexander Mastro Valerio, who later came to Michigan to teach art.

An interesting footnote to the story of the portrait is told by William Paton. It hung, of course, in the Economics Building. In 1943 the business school faculty wanted to designate Clare Griffin Fred M. Taylor Professor of Business Economics upon his stepping down from the deanship of the school. They needed Economics Chairman Leo Sharfman's acquiescence, but he was on leave in Washington at the time. Paton telephoned him there. At first Sharfman demurred, but Paton argued forcefully that, while Griffin had been a disappointment as a dean, he was an excellent teacher and the most honorable way to ease him out of the dean's office and back into the classroom was to award this named professorship. Sharfman finally yielded with reluctance, whereupon Paton "made a beeline for [President] Ruthven's office to make the recommendation to the regents."[42] As Paton feared, Sharfman was soon back on the phone to rescind the agreement made under pressure. Paton, with no little Machiavellian glee, told him it was too late. It was a rare occasion on which one could outwit Leo Sharfman. In fact, that may be the only instance in department history. But that is why the professorship named for a theorist who never taught business subjects, and his portrait as well, have remained in the business school from that day to this. After Griffin's retirement in 1962 the professorship remained vacant until awarded to Dick Leabo in 1978.

Although Taylor was honored in 1925, he did not retire until 1929, at the age of seventy-four. He and his wife then moved to California, where he took up the culture of ferns and could cultivate his flowers in relative freedom from hay fever. He died there in August 1932.

Upon Taylor's retirement Harcourt Caverly took over management of the principles course. Caverly was a Michigan baccalaureate, class of 1919, whom Taylor had taken on immediately as a section hand. Consequently he didn't complete his doctorate until 1929. His major fields were public finance and public control. He wrote his dissertation in the former, and assisted Sharfman in the latter. To assume the mantle of Freddy Taylor might earlier have required an act of courage, but by the time Taylor finally retired he had rather wound down, and the world of economic ideas was rapidly passing him by. His theory courses went to others and it was there that his popularity had centered. Undergraduates were less enamored. Caverly, on the other hand, was as demanding a teacher as Taylor had been, and a better lecturer.

By the closing years of the decade the original ferment of this period of transition was beginning to subside. Edmund Ezra Day's whirlwind years at Michigan ended officially in the spring of 1928 when he decided to stay on at the Laura Spelman Rockefeller Memorial where he had been for the year, on leave. The way was now clear for justice finally to be done to the department and to the man who had, in fact, maintained the continuity of steady guidance for most of the previous twelve years. I. Leo Sharfman was named by the regents as chairman of the economics department on October 26, 1928. One of the many letters of congratulation that poured in expressed a widely held view. It was addressed "Dear Sharf" from Paul D. Cahow "of our old department." Cahow, who had been an instructor from 1920 to 1924, noted with pleasure that the honor had finally come to "where most of us felt it should go [after] floating around all these years."[43]

Leo Sharfman was well suited to carry on the established traditions of economics at Michigan, and to establish a few of his own. In his research and teaching he stood with Adams in bringing the discipline of economics to bear on the problems of society. As a government advisor and arbitrator he rendered the public service that forged links between the "real world" and the academy. As a teacher he functioned in harmony with the Taylor tradition, although he was a far better lecturer, something of a spellbinder in fact. To him rigor and logic in argument were essential to performance as an economist. Just as Taylor has been described as mathematical, Sharfman exemplified what might be called the economics version of the legal mind.

> Leo [had] an organized mind, orderly, very committed to the truth and the facts. Impatient with dull students, [but] every student was precious. . . . You wouldn't walk down that hall without hearing Leo hold forth. And you would stop, get away from the door so he won't see your shadow there, but listen. . . . He was a brilliant teacher. You did not have to lean against the door . . . to hear him . . . for whether the class was eight or eighty the voice never changed. He'd stand in front of that class and argue the history of regulation of railroads, or public utilities in the United States, with a vigor and [with] the organization and the oratory he [would use if] addressing a crowd in Hill Auditorium,

[making] certain that the person in the last row of Hill Auditorium heard him.[44]

Such was a colleague's view. Now hear his students.

I took his course in railroad regulation and was enormously impressed by his classroom presence and his great oratorical skills. Leo was a man of . . . very strong personality and, in a sense, a very elegant person. . . . He couldn't say "good morning" without making a speech, and in nice long rounded sentences and paragraphs and nondangling clauses.[45]

His complicated sentences were legendary. "He plunges into a forest of dependent clauses and just when you think he's completely lost he comes out brandishing the independent clause."[46]

The students used to sit . . . on the edge of their benches . . . wondering whether he was going to end up with the right tense, the right type of conclusion, [whether] he would forget one of these phrases that he had introduced earlier, fail to bring it back. But he never did. He had this marvelous ability to articulate in most complicated fashion. But as a lawyer he insisted upon rigor in thinking. I remember being dressed down by him, when I answered a question that he raised in somewhat inelegant fashion grammatically, and he really laid in the bait. "Palmer, don't talk that way; it's inappropriate."[47]

Rigorous, strict, stentorian, Leo Sharfman had a sense of humor. Attending one of his classes was the typical student who persistently fell asleep. One day before class Sharfman secreted a pillow behind the lecture platform. Later, when the student was comfortably snoozing, he "quietly walked up to him and gently laid the pillow under his head."[48]

But it was as a leader that Leo Sharfman left his indelible mark on the economics department and the University of Michigan. Long chairmanships of indefinite duration can be disastrous to an academic department, but in economics Sharfman's twenty-six years forged a tradition of harmony, mutual respect, decency, and, indeed, love, that survives to this day. In these respects the department has been the envy of the university, for it has never been torn by internal dissension. This is not to say that there has not been disagreement and strenuous, even at times acrimonious, debate. But by wordlessly accepted custom those differences among faculty have never carried over into personal animosities. The custom is in no small measure the legacy of Leo Sharfman.

The department over which he finally assumed official leadership toward the close of the 1920s was almost entirely transformed from its character at the beginning of that decade. By 1929 death and retirement had removed the two men who had dominated its first half-century. Most of the business part of the curriculum, which had formed a major portion of the total offering since early in the century, was now removed to another unit. Sociology, which had been part of the department for twenty-five years, was soon to depart officially, in acknowledgement of its de facto independence.

Economics, no longer designated "Political Economy," now stood alone. Its staff, in fact, numbered the same at the end of the decade as it had at the beginning when the other two units were included, so large had been the growth in enrollments. But only five of the twenty faculty members of 1929 had been here in 1920, and only two of those, Sharfman and Paton, were senior people. Of the additional five senior faculty who came into the department during the 1920s four would remain until their retirement in the 1950s. Remarkably, or perhaps not so remarkably, all of them shared a common cast of character. They were all warm and profoundly humane people—gentle, quiet, competent folk, if not all world beaters, who exemplified the old-fashioned virtues of "gentlemen" and "ladies." Their character, and that of two assistant professors who shared their values and would shortly rise to senior status, was the stuff with which Leo Sharfman, as leader, would create a collegium of legendary harmony. They would all need it in the decades ahead.

The Hardship Years, 1930–45

If during the first couple of decades of the twentieth century the discipline enjoyed "equilibrium," by the early twenties the winds of change were blowing. The upheaval of World War I dispelled the earlier euphoric sense of socioeconomic progress and starkly exposed underlying dislocations in the social and economic structure. Neoclassical theory and its derivative social doctrine of laissez-faire were now questioned from the center as well as the left. Economic theorists, who more closely scrutinized the empirical evidence of economic behavior, developed new ways of explaining phonomena, ways which reflected spreading concern for the ill-fit of neoclassicism. And more attention was being given to the collection and analysis of the empirical evidence that would support and enlarge this theoretical work. A variety of private research organizations, established during the 1920s, devoted themselves to this purpose.

An indication of how the Michigan Department of Economics responded to these changes in the discipline can be gleaned from a comparison of the course offerings in the catalogs of 1920–21 and 1930–31. Under Adams's influence the department had always been strong in its emphasis on statistics as an instrument of both economic understanding and economic policy. But the study of statistical methods in 1920 was offered only as a cross-listing with mathematics, although there were four such courses listed. When Edmund Day came he took over the teaching of statistics to economists, introducing the two-course sequence which remained after both his departure and the departure of the mathematics cross-listings to the business administration curriculum. In addition, there was a one-semester "elements" course to accommodate students who wanted only that much background, a convenience offered in a number of fields besides principles.

Although David Friday had included the words "business cycles" in one of his course titles, the subject was really introduced to the curriculum by Day. When Day left the course in business cycles lapsed for a few years, while statistics was taken over by Carroll May, the classicist turned mathematician. The year of his untimely death, 1930, a joint instructorship in economics and business administration was given to Vladimir Timoshenko, a forty-five-year-old Russian émigré with an American Ph.D. He taught the one-semester statistics, regenerated business cycles, and also taught a course in European economic problems.

The major sequence in statistics was the province of another 1930 appointment, this one at the rank of full professor. Morris Copeland, a 1921 Chicago Ph.D., after several years of teaching at Cornell, was with the Federal Reserve Board when Sharfman invited him to lecture to, and be "looked over" by, the Michigan Economics Club in the spring of 1929—just a few days after Copeland had accepted reappointment at Cornell. Michigan appealed to him, however, particularly because it offered better career opportunities for his wife, and he reopened negotiations during the winter of 1929–30. After considerable correspondence with William Paton, who was acting chairman in Sharfman's absence that term, the bargain was struck for a $5,500 salary, hope for $750 worth of research assistance from the dean of the graduate school, and a few other perquisites.

Copeland was known as one of the "young Turks" in economics and brought a fresh outlook to the department. "He was trying to stir things up. . . . An original mind, and a somewhat aggressive person, [he was] quite willing to speak out."[49] He introduced a two-semester graduate course, entitled "The Price System," in which the first semester reviewed neoclassical theory and the second offered critique and variations, his own preference for the statistical/institutional approach, Veblen, Mitchell, and so on. In addition, he offered a new course in the distribution of income and wealth, again from the statistical perspective "to supplement theoretical analysis."[50]

He was a provocative teacher, as one of his former students recollects.

> I remember going into . . . a theory seminar. I had never met Professor Copeland. As far as I know he had never met me. But I sat down at the table and Professor Copeland looked at me and said, "Palmer, would the law of supply and demand apply to the *Pithecanthropus erectus?*" I must say I was somewhat taken aback. I wasn't quite sure that I recalled accurately what the *Pithecanthropus erectus* was. But this was characteristic of Morris, who was an institutional type economist who was very skeptical about many accepted axioms in the field. . . . This was his way of jolting the members of the seminar into thinking.[51]

Leo Sharfman, like every chairman since his time, believed that the hiring of top quality faculty members was one of his most important responsibilities. He was required to confront this task immediately upon his accession to the chairmanship, for he had to replace both his predecessor, Day, and John Van Sickle (public finance) who left at the same time. A letter to Frank Taussig at Harvard outlined the department's need to fill the gaps in statistics and public finance created by the two departures, but emphasized that a first rate senior man was desired, whatever his special field. Taussig had a ready recommendation, Charles (Carl) F. Remer, a thirty-nine-year-old Harvard Ph.D. then teaching at Williams College. In an interview setting characteristic of those years, Sharfman arranged to meet Remer during a stopover in Pittsfield a few days after Taussig's letter came, and the offer was made less than two weeks after that. Remer would be asked to pinch-hit in public finance for the first year or two, but his field was international economics, and his arrival at Michigan established international economics firmly in the curriculum. Whereas two courses had been offered by Clare Griffin in 1920, from the business perspective, by 1930 Remer was offering three courses and two seminars, along with Timoshenko's "European Economic Problems," and Watkins's "International Finance."

The strengthening of the international field at Michigan, albeit a little late in coming, was a response to the greatly increased involvement of the United States in world affairs. Remer's perspective was a more uncommon one than most professors of international economics, however, for his special field was China. His presence continued the thread of Michigan's connection to that nation, which had, coincidentally but independently, begun in the 1910–13 period with Adams's advisory role to the Chinese government and Sharfman's years of teaching in Tientsin. Carl Remer had spent eight predoctoral years teaching in China in two stints at St. John's University in Shanghai. He would return a number of times in future years in pursuit of his research and his compassionate devotion to the Chinese people. Remer's involvement in China also brought an interesting perspective to his courses in that the catalog description of "International Trade 2" notes that "Attention will be given to the relations between developed and undeveloped countries," a familiar phrase fifty years later.

Carl Remer was not known as an exciting teacher, but he was an exciting person and an outstanding scholar. He endeared himself to students by his warmth—he was the only one who invited students home, one admirer recalled—and by his talent as a storyteller. In his Chinese economy course

> we'd start out with a reading list . . . but, of course, his life was so filled with rich experiences and he'd always begin to talk about them, so by the end of the first term you barely got to the turn of the nineteenth century. Way behind schedule he swore the second term he was going to catch up, but we all were enthralled with the stories and we didn't urge him to speed it up any. . . . It was a wonderful course, in which he would relate experiences in China, and gave you a very good feel for the

economy. . . . His stories were filled with compassion for these
people. . . . I think until the day he died he kept asking . . . un-
answerable questions about the cleverness of the Chinese, the
hard work of the Chinese, and what a lovely people they were,
and how come they really were up against it all the time. Why
these people that have worked so hard and have tried so hard,
why are they so far behind in economic development?[52]

A man of many anecdotes . . . who not only could tell an awfully
good story but had the knack of remembering whether he had
told it already to someone in his audience. And he would turn
to that person and say, "I apologize; I've already told you this."
. . . Another real gentleman.[53]

Carl, personally, was the most unusual individual. He knew
everybody . . . particularly in connection with the Far East . . .
and was an extremely good reconteur when you'd get him started
talking about these people. . . . I remember he was sent as an
observer by the government of the United States to some kind
of a big international meeting in the Far East. . . . He came back
and gave a short report to the faculty. . . . He knew what everybody was thinking about and where he was coming from, and
what he meant when he said something, and what the background for it all was, and he . . . put it all together in a beautiful
way.[54]

The other economics offerings that appeared in the 1930 catalog,
which had not been present in 1920, consisted of the labor courses
taught by Elliott, Dickinson's course in the economics of consumption, Carter Goodrich's course in American economic history, Sharfman's two seminars in public control, and Howard Ellis's two-semester
sequence in the history of economic thought. Ellis also restored, in
title at least, Adams's old course in reform. Given the philosophic
content of the course description it probably resembled it in substance
as well.

But none of these courses seems especially innovative. They
represent enrichment and deepening of the Michigan curriculum, but
not an extension to the frontiers of the discipline. The Michigan department remained an essentially conventional, even conservative, one.
There was actually a diminution of the theory offering, from three

courses to two, and these remained essentially neoclassical, although some attention was given to dissenters like Veblen. In short, where new content was introduced into courses it tended to follow, as most of the faculty always had, the institutional path of economic thought.

And the institutions began to impinge heavily on the department as the first shock waves of the Great Depression reverberated. Oddly enough, the first casualty was the man who had taken charge of the principles course after Taylor's retirement. Harcourt Caverly was a good teacher, and Sharfman found himself recommending him to the University of Cincinnati in June of 1931 as "one of the very best men in Theory that ever worked under Professor Taylor [but] our financial stringency makes impossible the promotion which he is expecting."[55] He did get the promotion after all, but the salary situation was pretty dismal by the time he left the university in 1933 to spend the remainder of his career as a nonacademic economist with a Detroit law firm.

A brief resume of the university's salary history sheds light on a small corner of American economic history. (Furthermore, the history of an economics department should contain at least one table in the text.) 1907 appears to be the first year when a formal scale was adopted. Instructors began at $900 per year, with $100 annual increments until $1,400, at which time they were given three-year appointments. Assistant professors began at $1,600 for the first three years, then $1,800, "if advanced." Junior professorships (the title was changed to associate professor in 1915) were permanent appointments at $2,000 for the first three years, at $2,200 thereafter, "if advanced."[56] It would seem that full professors might be paid what the market required as the footnote doesn't mention them, but we do know that Adams and Taylor were paid $2,700 at the time.

In 1920–21 the following salary schedule was adopted:

	Minimum	Maximum	1920–21 Average
Instructor	$1,500	$3,000	$1,837
Assistant professor	2,500	5,000	2,897
Associate professor	3,500	5,000	3,679
Full professor	4,000	7,500	4,935

Source: President's Report, 1920–21.

Salaries were paid in ten installments, the first coming at the end of October and a double payment issued at the end of June to ease the difficult summer gap. A list of selected economics department salaries for 1922–23, and the teaching loads each represented, offers a clearer illustration of how the scale worked:

	Total Salary	Total Hours (No. of courses)	
		Fall Term	Spring Term
Edmund E. Day	$7,500	—	6 (2)
Fred M. Taylor	5,500	8 (4)	8 (4)
I. Leo Sharfman	5,000	8 (2)	5 (2)
William A. Paton	4,500	8 (3)	8 (3)
Charles H. Cooley	5,000	10 (4)	8 (4)
Clare E. Griffin (assoc.)	3,800	11 (2)	8 (2)
Wilbur P. Calhoun (asst.)	3,000	11 (1)	9 (2)
Harcourt L. Caverly (inst.)	2,400	11 (2)	11 (2)
Carroll May (inst.)	2,200	6 (1)	9 (2)
Francis E. Ross (inst.)	1,900	12 (2)	12 (2)
Paul D. Cahow (inst.)	1,700	10 (2)	10 (3)
10 additional instructors	1,650	12 (2)	12 (2)
5 instructors	1,500	8–12 (2)	8–12 (2)
2 instructors	750	6 (1)	6 (1)

Source: Michigan Historical Collections, Economics Department Collection, Box 4, Election Statistics file.

By the spring of 1933 the full impact of the Depression was felt at the department level. Leo Sharfman wrote of his budget troubles to Morris Copeland, who was on leave in Washington.

Under the circumstances which now prevail . . . [it] is a pretty nasty job. . . . We are first called upon to effect a substantial contraction of staff; the regents will then determine, in view of the savings thus realized, how much of a salary cut to impose.[57]

He went on to say that economics would save by dropping Caverly, granting leave to Ellis without replacement, and eliminating an instructor. One month later he reported to Copeland the salary reduction formula adopted by the regents. The first $1,500 of salary, or less, was exempted; the next $2,000 or less was to be reduced by 8 percent; the next $2,000 or less to be reduced by 12 percent; all salaries above $7,500 were to be reduced by 20 percent.

It was hard times all around, and Franklin Delano Roosevelt had entered the White House as the people's hope for doing something about it. But he needed a lot of help. One of the first things that needed doing was finding out just how bad things were, and where. Statistician Morris Copeland was part of that first group of young, eager academics who carried to the nation's capital their wit and learning to help work a new deal for the troubled people. At first it was just for the summer of 1933 that he took leave. But these were exciting years for economists in Washington, and Morris Copeland apparently found it difficult to decide whether he wanted to return to a more contemplative academic career or pursue one of direct action in government. After much vacillating, correspondence with Sharfman about his return, and even one abortive term in the fall of 1935, he finally made his choice. Government won. The department's old friend, Frank Knight, stepped into the breach as visiting professor for the spring term. In fact, 1935–36 was rather a banner year for visitors; Oscar Lange was also a "nonresident lecturer." But during the Depression the siren call of a new kind of public service in Washington lured several of the younger Michigan faculty to a variety of agencies.

Enrollments in economics remained remarkably steady at a first semester level of 1,700–1,800 during the first half of the 1930s. This actually represented an increase over the 1,500–1,600 level of the second half of the twenties, after business administration became a separated school. In the fall of 1934 a rising trend began, first at 1,900, then to the 2,300 level for a couple of years, and to 2,500 by the end of the decade. This trend no doubt reflected in part the change in requirements for a Bachelor of Arts degree that LSA introduced in 1932, a change Day had proposed during his tenure. But it took more than five years to overcome resistance among the [LSA] college faculty. The basic requirements of courses 1 and 2 in English (now called English rather than rhetoric) and the twelve hours of distribution in each of three discipline groups were retained. In addition, "each student upon becoming a candidate for a degree, must select either a department or a division of concentration," and must elect a minimum of thirty hours in that concentration.

Whether or not the introduction of concentration acted as a spur to registrations, declining or low-level financial resources were required to be spread over stable or rising enrollments, no mean, if painfully familiar, feat. Inevitably, average class size rose, from about twenty to thirty. Counting faculty at this time poses some difficulties because of the uncertainties in the instructor and teaching fellow ranks. Teaching fellows appeared on the scene for the first time in 1932–33 and they performed much as instructors had in previous years, though apparently with lighter teaching loads. If teaching fellows are not counted as faculty, however, it appears that the numbers occupying the ranks from instructor up actually fell during the 1930s, from twenty-five in the initial year to twenty in 1935–36 and to seventeen in 1939–40. Then, as now, a chairman's job required that a great deal of time and effort be devoted to juggling teaching assignments, class loads, and sizes, within budgetary constraints and requests for leaves of absence.

Leaves began to figure more prominently in the life of the department from about the mid-twenties on, as the research qualifications of a faculty member became more important to his career. Prior to that time only Adams took leaves for professional research purposes, and correspondence with prospective faculty members focused on the courses a man was competent to teach. When Day took over from Taylor the emphasis in this correspondence shifted subtly to a man's potential for scholarship and research, reflecting a change from Taylor's biases. Before then the undergraduate teaching responsibilities of the university were paramount, in other fields as well as in economics. But as the research activity of the faculty became more important to their training of the growing body of graduate students, initial hiring policy came to focus more on those qualifications. The decision to make an offer was still the prerogative of the chairman, but Sharfman began the practice of inviting a prospective new colleague to present a lecture before the Economics Club so that the group as a whole could "look him over." (There were not any "hers" in those days.)

And there began in the 1930s a trickle that became a flood of correspondence with and about economists who might come to teach at Michigan, ranging from the world's most renowned to promising new Ph.D.'s who were never heard of again. The volume of this correspondence fluctuated with the needs of the department, but right up to the present it comprises an interesting who's who of the discipline. For a long time the department had hired large numbers of its own Ph.D.'s. Of thirty-five long-term appointments prior to 1930, ten (exclusive of Taylor, the sociologists after Cooley, and the business administration appointments after 1924) were the department's own products. Day introduced more external recruiting, and Sharfman continued that practice through the 1930s.

Carter Goodrich's departure in 1931 required that an economic historian be found to replace him. Even before Goodrich decided to leave Max Handman had been suggested as a potential addition to the faculty, and Goodrich admired him so much that he wrote to Sharfman late in 1929 that "I should gladly give up economic history for the sake of gaining so stimulating a colleague."[58] Handman was a forty-four-year-old native of Romania, who had been educated in the United States, receiving his Ph.D. from Chicago in 1917. He then went to the University of Texas as a professor of sociology, but in 1926 became professor of economics there. He was a man of vast learning, who spoke many languages, and when Sharfman was reconsidering him for appointment in 1931 Frank Knight wrote,

> With regard to the thing which seems to me most needs doing in the entire field of social science at the moment, I know of no one to place on an equality with Handman. I mean the study of fundamental institutions and social forces, historically and comparatively, with primary reference to economic life but giving full place to other cultural manifestations, carried out on the basis of the widest scholarship and the profoundest insight and critical faculty.[59]

Handman came in the fall of 1931, at the top of the salary scale, $7,500, although, along with others, he would suffer a cut coupled with an increase in teaching load two years later. His impact on the department was strong and personal, though tragically brief. Fondly known as Uncle Max, he was admired by students and associates alike. In the fall of 1939 he suffered a coronary thrombosis, and on December 26 he died, at the age of fifty-four. His 13,000-volume library, including many rare works of philosophy and literature as well as economics, was purchased from his widow by the university.

During the early 1930s public finance was handed around in an unsatisfactory way, but the onset of the Depression prevented a good solution. Harcourt Caverly had taken it over from Remer, but when Caverly left in 1933 there was nobody on the staff trained primarily in that field. In the spring of 1934 Leo Sharfman met a young man at the Department of Argriculture in Washington, who had earned his Ph.D. the previous year at Columbia. Robert Ford had been hopeful of an appointment at Michigan as long before as 1925, when he wrote to Day from California, where he had earned the M.A. Despite very strong recommendations from Seligman and Haig at Columbia, Sharfman wrote to Ford on June 1 that there wasn't much hope for a job in those difficult times. Six weeks later he offered a part-time assistant professorship at $400, coupled with a part-time twelve-month appointment as a research investigator in the Rackham Bureau of Reference and Research in Government. For the first time a member of the economics department was brought in on a joint appointment with a nonteaching unit of the university. It was a fortuitous way of finding the money to staff needed courses without assuming a burden the department budget couldn't tolerate, a strategem that would be used more frequently in later years. Four years later Ford became director of the newly titled Bureau of Government at $3,100 and associate professor of economics at $1,500 (part-time). He was not a brilliant teacher or a highly original scholar, but he was a most amiable man, who did a solid job of administering the research of the bureau, and published a good deal of his own pragmatic work in state and local finance under the bureau's imprimatur.

When Morris Copeland finally made up his mind to leave the university he, too, had to be replaced. And Sharfman found a winner. Edgar M. Hoover, a 1932 Harvard Ph.D., was glowingly recommended for his widely read and cultivated mind, and his promise of becoming one of the nations' best economists. He addressed the Economics Club in April of 1936 and was signed on as an assistant professor for three years at $3,000. He would teach statistics and business cycles, and introduce a new course in his own special area of interest—location theory. Although a shy man, so successful was he as a teacher, so far had he excelled even the Harvard recommendations, that Sharfman nominated him for the coveted Russel Award after just two years at Michigan. In addition to his performance as a lucid and inspiring teacher, he had been productive of significant research publication during his two years, and had taken an active role in university affairs. The nomination didn't make it that year, nor again in 1939 when it was renewed. Finally, in 1940 Hoover received the award jointly with Frank H. Bethell of the medical school, the first time it had been granted that way.

Thus, despite the stringencies of the Depression, turnover afforded the department opportunity to bring in stimulating new people. Another 1936 addition came in by a rather unusual route, however. The dean of the graduate school, Clarence Yoakum, invited William Haber, associate professor of economics at Michigan State College, to join the faculty of the University of Michigan School of Social Work, still located in Detroit. The invitation was seconded by President Alexander Ruthven. But Haber was not a social worker. He was an economist, who had earned his Ph.D. at Wisconsin in 1926. He would accept the invitation only if it carried a joint appointment in the economics department. As there were already two professors on the faculty teaching labor,

> the department would not have gone out of its way to recruit me, if somehow I hadn't come in through other doors. . . . [But the others] could not formally present me [to the regents] because I had to be nominated by the department. And so I came to Leo in a sense an embarrassment. How does he deal with a *fait accompli*? I haven't any doubt he had some problems. . . . I complicated the life of the department by not coming in the regular way, and I'm sure that one man . . . must have raised holy terror about somebody coming into the department without the department's initiative. I later learned from the chairman that there was a problem, but he never told it to me. Five, six years later when there was no problem . . . we were all dear and close friends.[60]

Unorthodox as his entrance may have been, the thirty-seven-year-old Haber came with excellent credentials. His warmth and ebullient personality won him friends among the staff, while his teaching won him the affection and admiration of the students. John R. Commons had been Haber's mentor at Wisconsin, and the younger man deliberately modeled his teaching style and his relations with students on Commons's example. Essentially it involved bringing worldly problems directly to the classroom, using the classroom as a laboratory for original research. In this way the students could apply the resources of their newly acquired learning to live issues rather than hypothetical cases. "Haber impressed me very much by his down-to-earth knowledge of the labor movement and what was going on in the world outside the university.[61]

When Haber arrived at the university in the fall of 1936 he had been closely involved for several years in Michigan's efforts to deal with the Depression. At the time he was state emergency relief administrator. (Attesting to the relative simplicity of those years, it was a part-time job.) That fall the legislature was ready to adopt an unemployment insurance law and Professor Haber was appointed chairman of a drafting committee. He came into his first class at the

University of Michigan, Economics 123, titled "Social Insurance," and announced

> "You all have the same term paper. You are going to write a law. I'm going to spend the next three meetings talking about that law, and we'll break up into committees: committee on contributions; committee on benefits; committee on appeal; committee on administration." . . . And that class worked. . . . Those students wrote the Michigan Unemployment Insurance Law, and sat in the gallery of the legislature at 3 A.M., December 21, 1936, when the Speaker said "It is a law."[62]

Leo Sharfman, as chairman, believed that a faculty member should be free to teach whatever innovative courses his own research and interests motivated him to teach, once the basic requirements of the program were cared for. In his correspondence with new staff members he typically inquired of them as to their preferences and accommodated them if he could. Consequently, a good deal of his time was taken up with juggling course assignments and getting new course descriptions assembled for the annual announcement of the university and the college. While some faculty praised this policy as broad-minded and stimulating to creativity, others felt that courses were sometimes introduced that were not well thought out, or for which the instructor was insufficiently prepared. And even in the case of assigned courses, academic freedom was so construed that the content might or might not closely match the title.

> When a person was assigned a course to teach, it couldn't be assumed that the name of the course would mean that the content would be at all what the chairman had in mind when he assigned the course . . . Leo . . . gave great freedom to people, when they were assigned courses, to run their courses as they pleased.[63]

Although Sharfman interfered not at all in the teaching function of the staff, when it came to administration of the department as a unit he was in undisputed command—a benevolent despot. He would not have thought himself so. Indeed, he considered himself a democrat. But it was a unique sort of Sharfmanesque democracy that he ran. Day had established the weekly staff luncheon and Sharfman continued the practice. In addition, special departmental meetings might be called to address specific questions that arose. On all of these occasions any topic of department interest could be brought up, and Sharfman would listen to various viewpoints. More than likely, however, if a decision had to be made he would already have made it, having consulted in advance of the meeting with a few of his senior faculty associates.

> He had a way of . . . preparing everybody in advance of the meeting. He'd come up to my office in 209 and talk to me about what the agenda is about and what items there'd be difficulties in. [He'd] more or less indoctrinate you, and he was persuasive. He was a democratic man, but you'd be in deep trouble if you didn't agree with him.[64]

At department meetings

> the decisions were all Quaker-type decisions, unanimous decisions, arrived at after everyone had given up to Sharfman's arguments and accepted them. He was a delightful sort of a democratic despot. Put it that way. He always said he was democratic and that he always listened to everything. And he thought he did. But he still held his own views.[65]

When a decision had to be made,

> the initiative was his. But he had a way of making sure it was a departmental decision and not a Leo Sharfman decision. . . . Decisions must be made by the group. What I think our colleagues didn't realize [was] the extent to which the group was influenced by its chairman. But I think the chairman could in all conscience and all truth say, "I never imposed anything upon the department."[66]

Sharfman's benevolent despotism was tolerated, even strongly supported, because he was a superb chairman. He was never considered unfair or governed by petty considerations.

> He was admired by his colleagues outside the department, by the people in the dean's office. It was always said that if a memo goes out to various departments, economics will be the first one to respond. Leo said he never left his desk with anything undone. He'd finish it up before he went home. And it was literally true

that he devoted a good part of his life to running the department. ... People were perfectly happy ... to let him make the decisions as to how many five-cent stamps you could buy and how many one-cent stamps.[67]

The opportunity to test, or contest, Sharfman's style of leadership came in October of 1934. Back in 1920 the College of Literature, Science, and the Arts had adopted for itself a dean's advisory committee, analogous to the departmental executive committees it was recommending at that time. Four members of the dean's committee, later known as the executive committee, were elected by the faculty of the college and three appointed by the dean. Leo Sharfman was one of the latter group on that first committee; by 1934 he was no longer serving. The college executive committee undertook that year to strengthen its authority and presented to the faculty a set of recommendations on departmental organization, which said in part: "In the interests of bringing about a greater degree of participation by the teaching staff in the administration of departmental affairs," but allowing flexibility among departments as well, the whole teaching staff should be required to meet at least twice a semester to consider and discuss matters other than budget, salary, and promotion. A special meeting should be held in each department during the next thirty days to "determine by a written ballot of all staff members entitled to vote, (*a*) whether it deems its existing organization satisfactory and adequate, or (*b*) whether it desires to organize an executive committee to act for the department, or (*c*) whether it wishes to propose some other arrangement."[68] After the vote full details of the adopted policy were to be forwarded to the executive committee of the college. Furthermore, whatever scheme was adopted, subsequent changes in it would require approval of that committee.

Accordingly, the department met on Friday, October 5, in Room 104 at 4 P.M. All but two members, from instructor through full professor, were present. They voted unanimously, by written ballot, that the existing organization was satisfactory and adequate. Further, they adopted a statement, as presented by the chairman in the call to the meeting, which said that:

> The Chairman assumes responsibility for initiating and executing all major departmental policies, but ... seeks at all times the counsel and assistance of the ... teaching staff, and particularly

of those on permanent tenure, both through individual conferences and through group meetings.

The entire teaching staff has a regular weekly luncheon
meeting, at which anyone present is free to bring forward for
discussion any matter of interest or concern to the department. . . .

In connection with budgetary matters, appointments, salaries, promotions, curriculum adjustments and assignments, and
all other major policies, the chairman seeks the advice and consent of the upper staff.

[No minutes are kept and no formal votes are taken] but it
is the tradition of the department to continue discussion . . . until
virtually unanimous agreement is reached, and the policies involved are carried out only when such support for them is forthcoming.[69]

The chairman went on to explain in his report to the dean that "on
the executive side of the department's activities" he tries to distribute
tasks to ensure participation by all, without imposing undue burdens,
through assignments as freshman advisors, classification (registration)
assistants, advisors for the concentration program, advisors in combined curricula, graduate student advisors, members of doctoral committees, ordering of books for the general library, supervision of the
economics reading room, conduct of the Economics Club and the economics section of the Michigan Academy of Arts and Sciences. Finally, the services of the department secretary are available to all.

It is not known precisely when Avis Mabbs was hired as the
department secretary. Robert Angell recalls her presence when he
arrived in 1922 to start his graduate work in sociology. "She was . . .
a very studious type . . . self-effacing. Very efficient, though."[70] She
handled the department's entire volume of secretarial duties. Quiet
and unobtrusive about her work, Miss Mabbs expressed such sense of
adventure as she had in the enjoyment of driving her car. But her
hobby brought her to a tragic end in late 1943. Ironically, an essay
was found among her papers in which she articulated her feelings
about driving and its closeness to death.

Shorey Peterson was acting chairman that year, and hired Evelyn
Uhlendorf to fill the vacant post. During her eighteen years in the
department the literary Mrs. Uhlendorf became rather an institution
as unofficial department mother. "Graduate students would come in,

you know, and want some favor and maybe a privilege that she wouldn't have the slightest authority to pass on, but would. . . . She was just kindly and wanted to be nice to people."[71]

> She was sort of in charge of things in general and was a very motherly figure, and was concerned about the welfare of everyone, students and faculty alike. And . . . did many favors of all kinds for all of us. She really loved us all. She was not a great secretary. Neither her typing nor her filing was infallible. And one could easily get very impatient with her failures of organization. But she was such a lovely soul, and loved us all so much, that she was really an important part of the department.[72]

On the list of faculty assignments Sharfman supplied to the dean and the college Executive Committee that of graduate student advisor referred essentially to master's degree students. Sharfman, himself, was the advisor to all Ph.D. candidates. Because time-to-degree varies so widely among doctoral students, it is difficult to judge how many were active at any one time. The timing of degree awards gives some clues. During the early 1920s one Ph.D. per year was standard. This increased dramatically to an average of four in the second half of that decade and the first few years of the 1930s. Then it dropped back to one or none during the middle thirties, to rise again to two or three during the last few years of that decade. The same pattern showed up in the 1940s, three or four per year in the first few years, one or none between 1943 and 1946, and back up to about four during the last few years of the forties. In any event, Sharfman took great personal interest in each Ph.D. candidate.

The preliminary examination system had been introduced by Day in 1924, consisting of five three-hour examinations, at least one in theory and its history, the whole set concluding with an oral examination. They were taken all in one week, one each afternoon. After the exam results were in

> Leo had a certain way in which he addressed each student. He would say "Now you have passed the first hurdle. You have passed your preliminary examinations. Now I want you to roll up your sleeves and get to work on that dissertation and not let it lag. . . . Get right in there and get working on the dissertation. Talk to your committee. Get a topic. Get an outline. Get ahead."[73]

For most students this pep talk from the chairman may well have been inspiring. But for one it was rather puzzling.

We had a graduate student by the name of Hsin-Ying, who I think had a speech difficulty in Chinese which carried over to English. . . . I was about the only member of the department that could ever understand Hsin-Ying. . . . He worked by himself. I suppose he didn't talk to people because people didn't understand him . . . but he was reasonably bright and very, very energetic. Lots of great ideas. Hsin-Ying appeared for his preliminaries and passed them, and was ushered into Sharfman's office. Professor Sharfman said, "Hsin-Ying, I congratulate you on passing these. We've had a few Chinese who have gone on and gotten Ph.D.s in economics and you're to be congratulated. I want you to roll up your sleeves and get to work on that dissertation." and Hsin-Ying said, "Mr. Sharfman . . . I have finished the dissertation." I understood what he had said, but Sharfman just missed it completely. "What I said, Hsin-Ying, is that you roll up your sleeves, pick a topic, and get to work on that dissertation." And Hsin-Ying kept on, "But Professor Sharfman, I have already finished the dissertation." And the amazing thing is that he had. No one knew this. He had written a dissertation . . . while preparing for and passing his preliminary examinations, the only time in the history of the department that this has happened. Finally, this dawned upon Leo . . . but it took a long time.[74]

Sharfman's efficiency and his dedication made him appear as a formidable personality, especially to the younger members of the staff.

I'm sure that all the younger people were scared to death of him. And I'm also sure, in restrospect, that he didn't know this, and that he'd have been horrified to think this. But we really tiptoed around Sharfman. When he spoke the world trembled. He was really a very sweet guy, and an extremely democratic person, in his way. But he came across as dour and sharp and explosive, and he always scared us.[75]

Sharfman had habits in his manner that affected many . . . young members of the staff, making them feel that he was a real autocrat. You'd go into his office to ask something . . . and what you got was a lecture. Chances are he'd get up from his desk, start walking around the office, and do a spiel. He was a forceful man.[76]

Sharfman in his office was all business.... You didn't go in there to chit-chat. But in his home he was one of the most gracious hosts that I have ever known. He and Minnie [gave] dinner parties for members of the department at which this expression of the other Sharfman became evident.[77]

It was the "other" Sharfman that created and sustained the harmony of the economics department. "The department to Leo was a family. His devotion and commitment [were] a dedication. And nothing would sadden him more than discord among his colleagues."[78] When there were disagreements he would invest the time and effort to work them out painstakingly. His attention to the smallest details that kept the department running smoothly, his care in fully and promptly responding to all correspondence, his graciousness in recognizing the accomplishments of his colleagues and his promptness in bringing them to the attention of the dean for recognition when promotion and salary increase time came around, his noninterference in the academic and scholarly conduct of the faculty, the respect and stature that he commanded for the department in university circles, and the personal warmth he displayed to those who got past his official demeanor to the man underneath—all of these things interacted to create an atmosphere of fraternity and pride in the department.

The measure was returned to Leo Sharfman on February 12, 1938, when a testimonial dinner at the Michigan Union celebrated simultaneously his twenty-five years at the University of Michigan and the publication of his definitive five-volume study of the Interstate Commerce Commission. After the shrimp cocktail and filet mignon there were speeches by Carl Remer, chairman of the event, President Alexander Ruthven, Dean Edward H. Kraus of LSA and Dean Clare E. Griffin of Business Administration, and Professor Shorey Peterson. But perhaps a letter from Margaret Elliott expressed best the feelings of Sharfman's devoted colleagues (even as it revealed the position of a lady economist).

After a good bit of hesitation, I have come to the conclusion that your twenty-fifth anniversary dinner should really be a "stag" party. But I am unwilling to let the occasion pass without telling you what it has meant to me to work under your leadership during the last half of that quarter-century. . . . I feel more deeply than I think you can realize that you have had a very large share in my professional and personal happiness during those years. It is to you chiefly that I owe my advancement; and the assurance of your support has meant more than I can say.[79]

Sharfman's magnum opus on the ICC was begun in the late 1920s, taking about ten years to complete. He wrote as he talked, in long involved sentences, but they were carefully thought out in advance and always came out right in the end. He wrote by hand on yellow paper.

> From the yellow pages came the typescript for the publisher. Hardly a word crossed out, page after page by the hundreds, and legible. I [watched] him and I could understand why nothing had to be crossed out. He didn't put the word down until he was sure of it, until the whole sentence was clear, and the whole paragraph was clear, and the whole page was clear. He thought that way. He talked that way. He wrote that way.[80]

In the initial stages of the project a number of the graduate students assisted Sharfman in the research and reading for the study. The one who lasted all the way through to the end was Shorey Peterson. He learned how to deal with Sharfman in a working relationship. "If you wanted to make a suggestion or have him change something, you didn't do it orally. . . . You always wrote it. But you didn't write out a criticism. You wrote out a draft, doing the job as you would do it. And the chances are you'd get [it] incorporated."[81]

Shorey Peterson had come to Michigan after graduation from Albion College in 1920. He and his roommate, Herman Wyngarden, were the first to take the written prelims that Day initiated, in the spring of 1924. With a nine-to-twelve-hour teaching load, assumed immediately upon receipt of the master's degree in 1921, it took them a while to work up to prelims. Peterson's thesis and early postdoctoral research were in the exciting new area of the economics of highway transportation, where he made important contributions. But his teaching was more varied. Early on he ran the one-semester principles course, and in the late 1920s took over the big special sequence offered for engineers. In between he taught courses in labor and international trade (when there were temporary absences of specialists in those fields). He continued to teach the economics of transporation for many years, while Sharfman concentrated on railroads in his course. And Peterson also taught for most of his career a two-semester sequence in corporations and antitrust, the field now known as industrial organization.

> Professor Peterson was the "storybook" professor if there ever was one and while he was a task-master, he was also a fatherly kind of professor and the kind that no one ever forgets. I recall being in his Corporate Economics class. . . . Professor Peterson, who was usually dressed in black suits, would glance at his fob watch at about 8:00, perhaps give us a two minute leeway, and then turn the thumb lock on the lecture hall door, locking out any students who dared to be late. He would then begin with what really must be called the Socratic teaching method involving a series of conceptual questions about the material in the current assignment. If a student stalled with an appropriate answer and/or engaged in a fictitious response, the good professor would simply say, "I think that requires a more serious academic reflection on the issues, don't you?" . . . He was one of the few instructors who taught us how to think and the real value of deep-probing beyond a simplistic first response.[82]

In 1924 the course numbering system was changed to reflect the growing sophistication of the curriculum. The introductory courses were assigned two-digit numbers, advanced undergraduate courses were numbered in the one hundreds, those at the 200 level were open to graduates and advanced undergraduates, and 300 level courses were for graduate students only.

After Harcourt Caverly left in 1933, economics 51–52, the principles course, was taught for a year by Carl Remer, but that was not his forte, and in 1934 Shorey Peterson took charge. He was to remain in command for about twenty-five years. Although his course was broader and more modern in content, Peterson adopted the best of the Taylor tradition in the teaching of principles—the emphasis on rigor and precision, the careful training of the teaching fellows and predoctoral instructors under his tutelage. The rather inglorious sobriquet, section hand, fell into disuse under Peterson's warm and gentle, though firm, guidance. He drafted the common examinations, which continued to be graded anonymously, with one grader going through all the (numbered) blue books on a single question, after Peterson had spent up to an hour with him establishing the standard. They were all essay examinations, and the quality of the questions were a marvel to the teaching fellows, as well as a terror.

> There was a good deal of . . . competitive pressure on everybody to make damn sure that he covered all the material, because you never knew in advance what Shorey would come up with for the questions. . . . He would . . . ask you if the questions were O.K., but nobody had enough nerve to be able to say, "Well, you know Professor Peterson, on this question I really didn't get to cover it." . . . So you would . . . sort of say, "That's O.K.," and then pray if you didn't cover the material that your students would have read the book.[83]

Because economics enrollments were rising through the decade of the 1930s demand for people to staff sections was sustained despite the Depression. One new Ph.D. brought in in 1936, Edward C. Simmons, received his degree from Ohio State University that year, and came to share the money and banking load with Leonard Watkins. He was an effective and successful teacher. Several of the predoctoral instructors engaged during the 1927–30 period, including William Palmer, stayed on through the decade to assist in principles. But after the introduction of the teaching fellowship in 1932 there were few hired as instructors for this aspect of the teaching load.

One of the early teaching fellows who would stay on for a long career in the department was George Anderson. He took the M.A. in 1933 and became a teaching fellow in 1934 but, although he passed prelims in 1939, he did not go on to complete the dissertation. Sharfman, recognizing his skill in the classroom, however, appointed him lecturer in 1942, and for many years he ran the principles courses for nonconcentrators.

Accounting, like principles, had several instructors. Among the most outstanding of these was Robert P. Briggs, who was one of the first recipients of the Michigan M.B.A., in 1928. He had joined the department in 1927 and was a superb teacher. When the *Michigan Daily* asked 200 graduating seniors in March of 1934 to name the 5 instructors from whom they had learned the most, among the 10 receiving the highest number of votes (out of 205 faculty members named) was Robert Briggs. Second in rank order on the list was Leonard Watkins; Robert Angell was also included in the ten best. The economics department, even if it could not quite legitimately claim Angell any longer, had done quite well.

One of the earliest teaching fellows to appear on the scene was an unusual variant of the species. In the summer of 1934 there came to the attention of William Paton, and through him to Leo Sharfman, a young man who had just completed his Ph.D. at Harvard. Arthur Smithies was born in 1907 in Tasmania, took a law degree there and then went to Oxford on a Rhodes scholarship, culminating his academic progress with the Harvard Ph.D. after two years of a three-year Commonwealth Fund fellowship. He wanted to spend the third year in the United States, preferably in a teaching job. Sharfman offered him a lectureship, but to satisfy immigration authorities with respect to his student visa he could accept nothing higher than a teaching fellowship, under which he taught theory, business cycles, and European economic problems, as well as principles. Then, to satisfy the Commonwealth Fund, he returned to Australia for three years of "exile from America,"[84] during which he worked for the federal Department of Statistics in the raw, new capital of Canberra.

In 1938 Howard Ellis decided to accept an offer from the University of California, and Sharfman wrote to Smithies about replacing him. His three-year "sentence" was coming to a close and Smithies jumped at the opportunity. But the appointment encountered some difficulties in the department. While Smithies was acknowledged brilliant and intellectually exciting, "he was an independent fellow and wanted to do [things] his own way. . . . In the elementary course . . . [he] paid no attention to the course plan and his students couldn't pass the common examinations . . . we had to boost them."[85] Furthermore, Smithies was one of the earliest "mathematical types" and "he proceeded at the first meeting of [his] section of beginning students . . . to lay out on the blackboard equation after equation. . . . The students . . . came into my office . . . and demanded that they be shifted to some other section. They just couldn't take it. Well, Smithies learned."[86]

While problems with the principles course may have been one reason for reservations on the part of some of the senior staff, apparently others were concerned about the "dogmatic or doctrinaire character of his economic theorizing."[87] Sharfman in his usual fashion would not force the issue until he saw consensus emerging. Paton, however, was less patient. He had been most favorably impressed by this man, who was an admirer of Friedrich Hayek. "What is this damned foolishness on the part of some members of the department founded on!" Paton wrote from California. "Has someone discovered Smithies to be a drunkard, an ogre, a pervert, a thief, or what? Do our colleagues expect to find someone with no angles? . . . If there is something serious against Smithies on the personal side let's hear what it is and have the matter out in the open. . . ." He urged the chairman to "cut through all this fuzziness and settle the matter."[88] Apparently Sharfman's patient persuasion won over such opposition as there was, and on March 4 a firm offer went out by cable.

But the Arthur Smithies who returned happily to Michigan in the fall of 1938 was not the same economist who had left three years before. If Paton had known this, he doubtless would not have pushed the appointment, for in three years' time the devotee of Hayek had become a thorough Keynesian. As such, and also by the force of his exuberant personality, he exerted a strong influence on the students of the immediate prewar years, several of whom would subsequently join the Michigan faculty.

Gardner Ackley was a graduate student at the time, who recalls the first attempt at Keynesian analysis in a seminar conducted jointly by Howard Ellis and Leonard Watkins within a year or two of publication of the *General Theory*.

> And I can assure you that none of us understood it, including either Ellis or Watkins. I have still, I think, a copy of the *General Theory* that I used in those days, which is full of . . . marginal notes, some of which I thought up, but most were profound observations made by either Watkins or Ellis which . . . display absolutely complete misunderstanding of what it was Keynes was trying to say. None of us really understood it.[89]

Then Smithies appeared, who not only understood Keynes, elucidated the theory for his students, and established its relation to the real world by using for a text the "Report of the Temporary National Economic Commission," but introduced as well the powerful tools of mathematics. Ackley was one of the first to use these methods in his dissertation, with committee member Smithies's helpful guidance. Later on Ackley, himself, would replace Smithies as the Keynesian macroeconomist on the staff.

Daniel Suits was an undergraduate in 1938, majoring in philosophy, although he had started out in physics. Under Smithies's influence he switched to economics when he started graduate work in 1940. Smithies

> was quite a charismatic person. . . . He had a relationship with
> . . . those of us that hung around him that was quite different
> from . . . most faculty members. . . . Now, of course, he was a
> young person at that time . . . and related to us as a brash young
> assistant professor will do. . . . He had that Australian sort of
> outspokenness about him. . . . I remember, in particular, one
> time he came in and he . . . was erasing the board. He erased
> into [an] announcement, and then he realized what he had done.
> He said, "Oh dear, oh dear!" He started restoring the announce-
> ment . . . and he drew a line around it and then . . . he said, "It
> said something else down here. What did it say?" Somebody said,
> "It said save." So he starts to write down save and then he erases
> it and says, "Oh, hell no." and he writes down "Invest."[90]

Smithies's absorption in the problems of the real world and the search for an understanding of the Depression that was the predominant influence on a whole generation was infectious to his students.

> He used to get the blame for everything we did. I remember
> . . . I was taking Leo Sharfman's course in railroad regulation
> and had to write a term paper . . . on rate regulation of the In-
> terstate Commerce Commission. I read [his] volume 3A . . . but
> it didn't seem to me there was much challenge in that, so I wrote
> a paper instead advocating that the Interstate Commerce Com-
> mission set railroad rates on the basis of marginal cost. And the
> next I knew about it Smithies called me in and said that Sharf-
> man had been down in his office ranting and raving, saying that
> the Interstate Commerce Commission had been setting rates for
> more than fifty years and who the hell did he think he was.[91]

Another who owed his career to the influence of Arthur Smithies was Harold Levinson. He discovered, as had Bill Palmer ten years before, that he took to economics in his sophomore year "like a duck to water," and found his calling when he tutored his less cerebrally endowed fraternity brothers. But undergraduate Levinson was headed for a business career and in his senior year entered the combined program which doubled for the first year of the M.B.A. program. He still hankered after economics, however, and in the second year took Smithies's course in macroeconomics. He was "fascinated by this stuff." Shortly before finishing the M.B.A. he was

> walking across the campus . . . not bothering a soul, when I met Professor Smithies. . . . And he said to me "what are you doing these days?" Levinson told him and added "but I really like economics much better than business administration." At which point he said to me, "Well, have you ever considered applying for a teaching fellowship? . . . If you are interested I'll be glad to put in a word for you with Shorey Peterson."[92]

That suggestion was the final nudge that reinforced the pull, and in the fall of 1942 Harold Levinson joined the band of predoctoral teaching fellows.

It was the teaching fellowship that had pulled Gardner Ackley into the same orbit a few years earlier. Upon graduating into the 1936 world of unemployment from Western State Teachers College (now Western Michigan University) with a combined history and English major, Ackley was fortunate to be Western's nominee for the State College Scholarship for one year's graduate study at the University of Michigan. The question was which field to take it in. In the course of inquiry friends advised that he think beyond the one year toward the possibility of a teaching fellowship and the Ph.D. Economics, he was told, was the most promising department for that. Like most other children of the Depression he was certainly interested in economic questions, and once on campus he found his courses, particularly theory with Howard Ellis, "a really exciting experience." Toward the close of that first year the department nominated Ackley for a $1,000 Rackham Fellowship. Upon receipt of the appointment the fine print revealed the ineligibility of married students. But his wedding date had already been set! An expression of regret that he must decline the fellowship under that condition, coupled with a polite protest to the graduate school dean, backed up by the department faculty, secured an exception to the rule. In fact, the fellowship was renewed the following year, enabling Ackley to complete his Ph.D. work in the field he had chosen because of the availability of teaching fellowships, which he never used.

Those few years around the turn of the decade spawned an especially outstanding group of graduate students, as had the 1919–22 years. In addition to Ackley, Levinson, and Suits, there were Suits's roommates James Duesenberry and Guy Orcutt, and Edward Fried and Robert Roosa, to name a few. Discussion was usually hot and heavy at the Suits-Orcutt-Duesenberry apartment on Kingsley Street. "The graduate seminar, so to speak, that [we] would carry on endlessly in that apartment! There would be nights when there would be no more than one person in bed at any one time. The other two were up arguing with each other about something." Duesenberry and Bob Roosa (who stayed on at Michigan when the onset of World War II preempted his Rhodes scholarship) "were the [university] debating team for a while. I don't remember what the proposition was that year, but it was an economic proposition, and they had put together an argument that was so sophisticated that they lost all their debates. The judges couldn't understand it."[93]

Under Sharfman's nurture, the department had pulled itself out of the academic weakness of the late twenties and early thirties. Although the roster of courses changed little between 1930 and 1940, the content and perspective of many of them was considerably altered by the dramatic shifts that had occurred in the discipline. And a creative faculty was inspiring a cohort of excellent students. The department was on its way to becoming a leader again when World War II exploded and, for a time, canceled everything.

The students and younger instructors went off to fight and numbers of faculty members went off to help run the war from Washington. Gardner Ackley, after completing his prelims and most of the dissertation in 1939, had gone to Ohio State for a year, returning to Michigan in 1940 as an instructor in economic history to replace Max Handman, who died that winter. Ackley was actually the first faculty member to leave for wartime Washington, slightly ahead of the opening of American hostilities, in the summer of 1941. He served first at the Office of Price Administration (OPA), then in the Office of Strategic Services (OSS) ("That was a fascinating place. It was full of topnotch economists who have been among the stars of the profession ever since."[94]), ending the war back at OPA.

Carl Remer left next, in 1942, to go to the Federal Coordinator of Information, then to the Office of Strategic Services as chief of the Far Eastern Section, finally to the Department of State as Advisor on Far Eastern Affairs. In the last post he was sent to Chungking in the winter of 1945 to work on planning for China's postwar economic development. He wrote prophetically from there "I am sure that our dealing with China in the next few years will be one test and a highly important one of the liberalism and intelligence of our policies."[95]

Edgar Hoover left in 1942 to work first for the Office of Price Administration, designing the nation's gas rationing system, then for the War Production Board, and finally going overseas with the Office of Strategic Services. The year 1942 also saw Edward Simmons depart for the navy, and William Haber go first to the Bureau of the Budget, then to the War Manpower Commission, and lastly to the White House as advisor on manpower to the Director of War Mobilization and Reconversion. Haber returned to campus in the fall of 1945, but was recalled in 1947 to another year and a half of service that was actually an extension of wartime activity, as special advisor on Jewish affairs to General Lucius Clay, the commander in chief of the United States forces in Germany and Austria.

In 1943 Arthur Smithies departed for the Bureau of the Budget, Robert Ford was appointed by Governor Harry F. Kelly as director of the state Department of Administration, dubbed "vice-governor," and Leo Sharfman went on leave to serve as chairman of the Railroad Emergency Board.

By the fall of 1944 the professorial staff was reduced to eleven people, striving to mount a full program for the civilian students who were left and to serve the military units that crammed the principles course. It was a difficult job for the chairman to assign courses, but he had a valuable asset in the intellectual versatility and teaching virtuosity of William Palmer.

Palmer had come to the university as an undergraduate in 1925, and was captivated by economics in the introductory course. It was not only the intriguing spectacle of his instructor, Bill Selby, who "used to sit with his feet on the desk and sort of aim at students by looking through the V made by his two shoes on the desk," but "there was something about economics that appealed to me in much the same way as a game of chess at the time appealed to me."[96] He was a man of wide intellectual interests, however (and still counsels students to take a broad spectrum of liberal arts courses as undergraduates), and had made no plans to become an economist when, in the last week of his senior year, he received an unsolicited offer of an

instructorship from Fred Taylor. It was an attractive idea, the more
so

> because of my experience as an undergraduate in finding that
> the best way for me to be sure that I had a subject well in my
> mind was to try to explain it to some dumb fraternity brother of
> mine. I spent a good deal of time . . . putting many fraternity
> brothers through various courses in economics . . . and I always
> enjoyed this. It seemed to be fun."[97]

He took a year to earn his master's degree before taking up the
instructorship in 1930, and, although continuing graduate study, "never
bothered to write a dissertation. . . . It's hard to explain precisely why
this happened." Among other reasons was

> this feeling on my part that my first responsibility was the teach-
> ing that led me always, when I had to make a choice as to
> whether to think of preparing a new course or writing an article
> or writing a chapter in a dissertation, I always have chosen to
> prepare the course. . . . So I went on teaching . . . in a variety of
> fields. Enjoying it. Never was bored with teaching. Never found
> it anything but exciting. Every class was a new experience .[98]

The department, reaping the benefit from this instructor who could
and did teach in almost every field offered, recognized his contribution
in successive promotions without the badge of "Doctor." The university at large paid tribute to Bill Palmer's teaching when the first
Outstanding Teaching Award, a one-thousand-dollar annual gift of
the class of 1919, was conferred upon him in 1949.

The difficult war years of knotty administrative problems, combined with anxiety about the war itself, sorely tested Leo Sharfman's
commitment to public service. He firmly believed that an economist
should be a public servant as well. He himself served on numerous
boards and commissions dealing with railroad problems. Moreover

> Leo was very much persuaded, as I am, that it was a two-way
> street. . . . I'll give you the best illustration I know. Something
> that can only happen in a great department. I came in September
> 1936. . . . The chairman said, "Is there some special course you'd
> like to teach?" I said, "Yes. I spent the last five years dealing
> with unemployment." "Write it up." I wrote up the description

... and the course ... was introduced. .... I left in 1942 to join many colleagues in Washington in the war. I came back. The same chairman, "Is there anything in your Washington experience that you think might make an interesting course in the economics department?" I said, "Yes. I'd like to teach a course in manpower utilization." By golly, it was introduced.[99]

There was no question as to choices between the department and public service during the wartime emergency. But when some of the leaves extended beyond the end of the war, attended by vacillation as to a faculty member's return, then Sharfman's deep loyalty to the department and the university took over. He was as committed to university service as to public. He served on numerous committees and rarely missed a college faculty meeting. "Those were the days when there were real debates at faculty meetings. Leo was one of those who always participated and always had something to say. Always had a point of view that he expressed with great fervor and eloquence."[100] His eloquence, his professional stature and his importance to the university were attested by numerous honors bestowed in the mid-1940s. In 1943 he was awarded the Russel Lectureship, the highest honor the university confers on its faculty. In the same year he gave the commencement address, entitled "The Challenge of the World Crisis." And in 1945 the economics profession conferred its highest honor, the presidency of the American Economic Association. It was a good year to be president. The long, hideous war was over and economists could once more turn their full attention to improvement of people's lives.

New Directions, 1946–62

When peace was restored in late 1945 the discipline of economics frothed with new ideas and techniques that would transform its appearance during the next couple of decades as an array of new component fields emerged. The Michigan economics department would assume national leadership in several important aspects of this development.

First, the tenets of the Keynesian revolution were institutionalized in the Full Employment Act of 1946, and national income accounting moved from the academic journals to the White House. Macroeconomics emerged as a major new field in the curriculum, at once theoretical and applied. It arose not only from the Keynesian theoretical structure, but, especially in its applied aspects, from over a decade of struggle to master the economic complexities of depression and "total war."

Arthur Smithies was expected to return to the university in the fall of 1946 to continue and enlarge upon the teaching in this field that he had begun eight years earlier. On that understanding Leo Sharfman put through his promotion to full professor, although the salary negotiated was something of a disappointment to Smithies. Then, an eleventh-hour round of correspondence among Budget Director Harold Smith, Sharfman, Smithies, and Dean Lloyd Woodburne during the summer of 1946, reminiscent of the Copeland episode, concluded with Smithies's resignation on August 7, in favor of staying on at the Bureau of the Budget. Like Copeland before him, perhaps the infection of "Potomac Fever" was irresistible, although he did join the Harvard faculty two years later. Sharfman, ever just, wrote a glowing letter of recommendation, despite his dismay and distress at the circumstances of Smithies's departure from Michigan.

Fortunately, he had negotiated that same summer to rehire one of the department's promising "favorite sons," Gardner Ackley. Ackley had briefly toyed with the idea of going into business from Washington, but "in the end I decided maybe, after all, I was an economist . . . I had thought of myself entirely as a microeconomist and my wartime experience had essentially been in microeconomics. But somebody had to teach macro [in place of Smithies] and Leo Sharfman decided I was it."[101] Thus was launched a career that became the exemplar of the Michigan dual tradition of scholarship and public service.

Stabilization policy was another derivative of Keynesian theory. Its fiscal aspects entered the Michigan curriculum when Richard Musgrave joined the faculty in the winter of 1948. Musgrave, born and raised in Germany, had earned his doctorate at Harvard in 1937 and, after a few years of teaching there, had spent six years on the staff of the Board of Governors of the Federal Reserve System. In July, 1947, he wrote to Sharfman expressing his desire to return to teaching. Sharfman replied on the twenty-sixth that the department was "amply staffed" at the moment, but he would be kept in mind. Two weeks later Musgrave was in Ann Arbor for an interview, and on August 22 the request for his appointment went to the dean. Another of those

quick-change-of-plans staffing headaches that seemed to dog Leo
Sharfman was thereby solved; he now had a superb replacement for
Ed Simmons, who had suddenly resigned on August 9.

Musgrave was a valuable addition to the faculty, not only for the
scholarly eminence he would achieve, but for his lively personal interest and participation in all aspects of department life. For example,
he was a guiding spirit in organizing the Little Seminar, an informal
weekly meeting of graduate students and several of the younger faculty. Named after a similar institution at Harvard, it was open to anyone who cared to come and

> present problems . . . analyses of papers and things like that, and
> . . . fight with each other intellectually . . . I remember Dick and
> I used to get up at the blackboard and just argue endlessly about
> some obscure point in his book. . . . I can remember, at one
> point, that we wanted a translation of a piece of work by a Dutch-
> man. I have forgotten now what it was, but we turned it over to
> [graduate student] Muriel Converse . . . [who] had a Dutch boy-
> friend . . . or somebody. Anyhow, she came up with a translation.
> She said, "There's just one word in this that I can't understand,
> and he can't understand it either. It's this word 'four-side.' They
> keep talking about the four-sided root of this and the four-sided
> root of that." And of course it was the square root, which in
> Dutch is the four-sided root.[102]

Harold Levinson recalls an even more informal discussion setting, which he refers to as the Basement Debating Society. "The
various and sundry slaves who were working on the Ph.D. would just
be in the back, in the bowels of the building there, and . . . sit around
and talk about Keynesian analysis or whatever." He found Suits, who
became a close friend, to be "extraordinarily helpful to just play off
ideas. . . . And every morning he would come in and say, 'What's the
P for T?' What's the Problem for Today?"[103]

Of the many unusual agencies in wartime Washington, one that
would come to exert a profound influence on the Michigan economics
department was the Division of Program Surveys, tucked away in a
corner of the gargantuan Department of Agriculture. Under the direction of Rensis Likert, a collection of psychologists and sociologists
conducted studies for a variety of policy agencies and experimented
with survey methods of research. In 1944 George Katona joined the

division to work on projects that linked psychology and economic issues, and to develop methods for applying microdata to macroeconomic analysis and prediction.

Katona had begun his higher education in the study of law in his native Hungary, but a Communist putsch by Bela Kuhn in 1919 closed the university and propelled him to Gottingen, Germany. There he changed fields to earn his doctorate in psychology, entering the labor force in time to meet Germany's runaway inflation. This got him interested in studying economics, and a few years later he joined the staff of Gustav Stolper's new weekly, *The German Economist*. In 1933 Adolph Hitler's accession to power propelled both men to New York, where they conducted a successful investment advisory business. A long illness then forced Katona to yet another career change, and he decided to return to academia, as both a psychologist and an economist. He pursued the infant field of behavioral economics in research, in teaching at the New School for Social Research, and in a stint at the Cowles Commission, before joining the Division of Program Surveys.

At war's end the division decided to move from the federal government to a university setting. Likert negotiated with his alma mater, the University of Michigan, and in 1946, under the new name Survey Research Center, some twenty people moved to Ann Arbor. The arrangement was unique at the time. The center was to be financially independent of the university in that it was funded by its own grants and contracts. It was governed by an executive committee appointed by the university executive officers, with representation from university departments as well as institute executives. (By 1948 the Survey Research Center and the Center for Research in Group Dynamics, which moved to Michigan from MIT that year, were subsumed under the new umbrella of the Institute for Social Research (ISR); later other centers were added.)

Finally, senior members of the center staff received part-time, nontenured teaching appointments in the departments of their respective disciplines. A special Dean's Fund was created to pay their salaries, in order to encourage interdisciplinary studies in the departments. Thus George Katona was appointed professor in both the psychology and economics departments and his course, "Psychological Foundations of Economics," was cross-listed in both departments. He taught, as well, a graduate economics seminar on survey research methods. He and his future economist colleagues at ISR would come to supervise a substantial number of graduate students, who found direct research experience at the Survey Research Center invaluable to their doctoral training.

After the move to Ann Arbor the economic behavior section of the center, directed by Katona, began to grow rapidly. Over a period of five or six years the Carnegie Corporation awarded twelve one-year fellowships to economists interested in survey research. The first Carnegie Fellow, in 1948, was James Morgan, a 1947 Harvard Ph.D. who had been teaching at Brown. After a second year as a fellow he stayed on permanently at the center, and came into the economics department as a lecturer in 1950, to teach consumer economics, and later the survey methods course.

Another of the Carnegie Fellows was Lawrence Klein, who came to the Survey Research Center in 1949, and also joined the department as a lecturer in 1950. He was a little further along in his career, having earned the Ph.D. at Harvard in 1944, followed by three years as a research associate at the Cowles Commission and one at the National Bureau of Economic Research. Although it was survey research that had attracted Klein to Ann Arbor, he was already active in the relatively new field of econometrics. When Sharfman told him that he had long wanted "to get something started in a very modest way"[104] in that area, Klein introduced the department's first course.

John Lansing joined the Survey Research Center staff in 1949. He had been with the Division of Program Survey early in the war period, before returning to graduate school to earn his doctorate from Harvard in 1949. He didn't join the department until 1956, however, as an associate professor, sharing the work in a number of areas.

Katona had begun the annual Survey of Consumer Finances in 1946, even before the move from Washington, and Morgan and Lansing were deeply involved in the development of that project, which continued for some twenty-five years. A few years later the quarterly Survey of Consumer Attitudes was initiated, and another new Harvard Ph.D., Eva Mueller, joined the center staff in 1951 to work on that. She and Katona developed the Index of Consumer Sentiment, which is now produced monthly. Mueller came into the department as a part-time assistant professor in 1957, teaching a variety of courses other than those connected with survey research.

This kind of association between a research institute and an academic department was an innovation at the time, one that is unanimously considered a success.

> The Survey Research Center is . . . a major research resource [that] lends an air of uniqueness to Michigan, a unique kind of opportunity . . . that . . . few universities can match. These people have contributed . . . perhaps, a great deal more to the status of the department than the department has contributed to them. And I think we've been fortunate in having access . . . to [them].[105]

By 1950–51 there were some important new features in the economics curriculum. Macroeconomics was a full-fledged field, with course offerings at all levels; the undergraduate theory sequence was now clearly divided between macro and micro. Stabilization policy, behavioral economics, and econometrics completed the roster of new fields. In addition, faculty growth enlarged and enriched the curriculum in traditional fields, such as labor, international trade, and public finance. More important, perhaps, changes in course titles since the 1940 catalog listing indicated a more theoretical cast to the content of the curriculum as a whole, even as the empirical and policy orientation of the department remained strong.

Registration data by field reveal interesting shifts in field popularity, if not curriculum focus. Whereas courses in monetary and banking problems had enrolled the largest proportion of students, 28 percent, in 1940–41, by 1952–53 this percentage had declined to 13, with a slight bulge in the 1946–48 period. Labor, on the other hand, grew from 17 percent of course elections in 1940–41 to 24 percent by 1952–53, peaking at 34 percent in 1946–47. International economic relations showed a more dramatic growth, from a low of 3 percent in 1941–42 to 10.5 percent in 1952–53. Oddly, statistics declined from 6 percent at the beginning of the period to 3 percent at the end. Economic history declined more drastically from 7 percent to 2 percent. Theory enrollments, as a proportion of the total, fluctuated widely throughout the period, from 8.5 to 22 percent. Public finance remained remarkably steady at the 4–6 percent level. Industrial organization and public control was also fairly steady between 11 and 16 percent, except for one wild 26 percent year in 1944–45. The area that showed the strongest growth was "other," from 0.6 percent in 1940–41 to 9 percent in 1952–53. This consisted mostly of new advanced seminars, although one undergraduate course and the new undergraduate honors seminar were included as well.

As for the total number of economics students, the big jump, 120 percent, came in 1945–46, followed by a second record year at 89 percent. Enrollments actually peaked in 1947–48 at 9,100, when the largest number of veterans crowded the nation's colleges and universities to take advantage of the unprecedented education benefits offered in the Servicemen's Readjustment Act, popularly known as the G.I. Bill of Rights.[106]

The G.I.'s who came back to college, or were attending for the first time, were a mature and serious lot, who made teaching an especially stimulating experience at that time. Then there were those who didn't make it back. In the economics department they are all represented by the annual prize awarded in memory of Lieutenant Harold D. Osterweil. Osterweil was an outstanding economics honors graduate of 1941, who entered the army after a year at Harvard Law School. He was killed in action in Normandy, on July 30, 1944. Loved and admired by his friends, a committee to establish a memorial in his name was established within a couple of months of his death— an unusual occurrence at a time when so many vibrant young men were dying. The group was chaired by fellow alumnus Evsey Domar, and among its most active members were the wives of other classmates still overseas, Edward Fried and Philip Trezise. For various logistical reasons the first award was not made until 1949, but every year since then the fifty-dollar Osterweil Prize has been conferred on the graduating economics major who is "the most outstanding and promising student in the field of economics and who has also shown the greatest degree of social awareness."[107]

In the 1950 catalog the description of economics which had stood for almost fifty years was drastically revised. The new text emphasized the importance of an understanding of economics for enlightened citizenship, the value of a concentration in economics for students intending to pursue careers in law, business, government, and journalism, and the need for graduate study "to attain professional competence as economists." The concentration was described to require a course in either accounting or statistics and contact with at least four of the major substantive fields in at least seven courses, as well as six hours of cognates.

In 1951 the honors program was introduced in economics, under the direction of Shorey Peterson. At first it consisted of a one-semester seminar for superior senior concentrators. Then, as the decade wore on, it was expanded to a two-semester senior honors proseminar, and by the end of the decade the second semester junior honors tutorial was in effect. From among this group the winner has usually been selected for the annual Sims Senior Honor Scholarship, awarded at the end of the junior year and carrying a stipend of $500. Ernest Sims was a 1906 graduate of the LSA, who obtained a subsequent degree in mechanical engineering and went on to a business and engineering consultant's career in Elkhart, Indiana. He and his wife established the award in 1949 as an outgrowth of Sims's interest in the economics of industrial production.

While the vast majority of returning servicemen who flooded the classrooms between 1946 and 1949 were undergraduates, a record number of graduate students entered the department during these years as well. Whereas each decade from 1920 to 1950 had produced about twenty Ph.D.'s in economics, in the decade of the 1950s fifty-eight were awarded. The small crop of immediate prewar candidates returned to finish their dissertations between 1947 and 1950. This period in American educational history was unique in the maturity of its students, many of whom were married and raising families. Among them was one who would become very important to the department, and whose story was, in many respects, representative of his generation.

Warren Smith came late to higher education. He was graduated from high school into the 1932 depths of the Depression, and was lucky just to find work to support himself and his aging parents. Ultimately, he came under the supervision of a University of Michigan graduate at General Electric Corporation, who recognized the intellectual superiority of this employee. By the end of the decade Social Security helped ease the parental burden and Smith was able to save enough to start college. At his boss's urging he enrolled at Michigan as a twenty-six-year-old freshman in 1940. A victim of the Depression and, like most of his generation, deeply affected by it intellectually, he knew that he wanted to study social science. Economics 51 and 52 with Shorey Peterson convinced him it would be economics, but Uncle Sam had other things in mind for him—three and a half years in the Army Air Force, marriage on a three-day pass to the girl who had sat in front of him in economics 51–52, and, finally, return to the university in 1946. Like much of his cohort, the G.I. Bill and his wife's earnings as an accountant enabled him to finish his undergraduate studies and go on to the Ph.D.

So outstanding a student was Warren Smith that he actually began his teaching career as a senior undergraduate in 1947, helping to relieve the shortage of graduate teaching fellows in the bulging principles sections. With record numbers of students going through, true-false exams were introduced, and the teaching fellows' wives could grade them while their husbands studied. The Smith family (first child arrived in 1947 along with the teaching job) was, in respect to housing, better off than most. Ann's grandmother had built a house on the outskirts of town, on Olivia Street near Burns Park, in 1908, and they moved into it on Warren's return from service. They shared its subdivided second story with his parents and three successive economics graduate student couples. Helen and Joseph Crafton, who were both in graduate study, were the first. The arrangement lay somewhere between landlord-tenancy and commune because the esprit de corps among postwar teaching fellows was very strong.

> I think the first time we got together as teaching fellows and wives was when the Craftons were married. . . . Then there were times . . . that we got together for baby showers. . . . The time that we always got together was when Shorey . . . had the teaching fellows and their wives over for an evening in his house. . . . Eleanor Peterson . . . was sort of the mother or grandmother figure of the department for the teaching fellows and their wives and children.

These struggling student/teachers pooled their resources in many ways.

> During that period, just before the prelims, I did the cooking and we sort of combined our groceries . . . so that Helen and Joe would not have the bother of preparing meals. They could all study. At that time I also had a play school in the back yard, and quite a few of our friends sent their children so that we would get through a summer [and] Warren didn't have to teach.
>
> There must have been eight or ten different families over the period of teaching fellow time that would get together, . . . four or six people [for] "you bring the pie, I'll bring the soup" kind of dinners, because none of us could really afford the kind of entertaining that many people think of now. I remember Betty

Stevens always brought butter because Bob wouldn't eat margarine and none of us ever bought butter. . . . You made toys and you had hand-me-down clothes, and you were sort of proud of the fact that you would borrow diapers or whatever from your friends and neighbors. . . . A big social event was getting together and having coffee and making cake.[108]

Baseball was the major athletic diversion, and Warren Smith was an enthusiastic member of the economics department team as it met the challenge of other graduate student teams at Ferry Field.

The early to mid-1950s saw a number of especially outstanding graduate students in addition to Warren Smith. Jim Morgan recalls what it was like to teach graduate macro theory to them. He was substituting during an Ackley leave of absence.

I was . . . teaching it for the first time and here were these three geniuses in there. . . . Stefan Valavanis-Vail . . . Artie Goldberger . . . and Mordechai Kreinin . . . plus a bunch of clods . . . who could hardly understand national income accounting. . . . Mordechai Kreinin was still using a dictionary; he was a native born Israeli who had come over.[109]

Two of those three had nearly been lost to the department before they even started.

The early 1950s was the beginning of the great foundation bonanza. The Ford Foundation, like the Rockefeller and the Carnegie and other such family tax shelters, had been accumulating the excess of several fortunes, but unlike its bretheren had not been distributing same for the public good. New federal regulations decreed that it begin to give as well as get, and Ford sought out universities for get-rid-of-it-quick schemes to the tune of about ten million dollars. A million-dollar offer that came to Michigan proposed "the development of research resources in 'behavioral science.' "[110]

In those days a million dollars looked very big. There were discussions in Ann Arbor about what to do with that money. And the economists . . . almost . . . didn't know how to spend the money. Psychologists and sociologists, I think, were more attuned to project work and knew how to spend it. . . . The economists were not. They were all . . . the lone scholar in his study working, and they did very fine work, but they didn't operate through projects ... except for the economists who were associated with the Survey Research Center.[111]

Larry Klein and Kenneth Boulding were discussing the problem and came up with an idea. "I think the idea of a research seminar was Kenneth Boulding's suggestion, quantitative economics was mine, and we put it together."[112] Thus was born the Research Seminar in Quantitative Economics (RSQE), which would put the Michigan economics department into a position of national leadership in econometrics.

Ford came through with a $60,000 grant for three years in the late spring of 1951, after "the graduate student [fellowship] awards had already been made. I went over to Rackham and culled through the rejects. There I found Stefan Valavanis-Vail and Arthur Goldberger, and then we took some people who were [already] on campus. The rejects turned out to be powerhouses."[113] Goldberger would go on to a distinquished career. Vail would meet a tragic death the summer after completing his degree, when he returned to his native Greece for a visit before taking up his new teaching job at Harvard. While camping in the mountains he was assassinated by a rifle bullet—mistaken identity.

The seminar conformed to its research title from the start and immediately undertook the building of a model of the United States economy. Its tools consisted mainly of pencils and brains, but there was one bit of new technology which would greatly facilitate the work—an electric desk calculator. The Ford grant included an equipment budget that was administered by the chairman of the psychology department, who told Klein he could spend up to $750 on a calculator. When he filed his request through channels in the economics department, Sharfman wanted assurance that the expenditure would be approved. "That's a lot of money," he told Klein. "I've been chairman in this department for twenty-five years, and I've never been turned down in any request I've made, and I'm not going to make a request unless I know it's going to be granted."[114] To reinforce Klein's assurance that it was all fixed up, Sharfman, in his memo of request to the dean for an electric Monroe calculator at $637.50, strengthened the case for such a large expenditure by pointing out that the research seminar would share the new machine with the statistics classes, to which it would be carried for demonstration, and that it would also be available on request to other faculty members in the department.

Supplementing the new Monroe desk calculator was the university's infant computation center.

> In those days if you wanted to analyze data you went over in the basement of Rackham, where they had a tabulator, so-called, which was programmed by sticking wires in a board, and wouldn't handle negative numbers. You had to add a constant of 7,000 to everything so that all the numbers were positive. And [there was] something called the 602-A, which was a Rube Goldberg machine that flashed lights when it multiplied and would read an IBM card, do something, punch answers into the same card, then kick the card out to the other end of the machine."[115]

It was tedious work. "When we wanted to make a calculation on the model, make a projection, it took us one or two days . . . and then if we wanted to study an alternative . . . it took us another one or two days. Of course, now . . . you do it in the next ten minutes."[116] But after two years the pioneering econometric model of the United States was produced—the soon-to-be-famous Klein-Goldberger model.

Meanwhile the department had been talking about ways of contributing to public affairs and thereby attracting more research money. A committee consisting of Klein, Musgrave, Ackley, Suits, Katona, and Smith spawned the idea of a conference on the economic outlook, to which economists from business and government would be invited to learn about the quantitative research going on at the University of Michigan. This kind of conference was a unique concept at the time— the reaching out of an academic unit to educate business and government leaders about developments at the frontiers of social science research. It was most favorably received by the executives of firms large and small. The first of these annual events took place in the fall of 1953. From the beginning the program featured presentations by both ISR and RSQE; in the early years the Index of Consumer Sentiment took top billing. The debut of the Klein-Goldberger model at the first conference was probably the first public forecast made from an econometric model. It was fortuitously timed.

Shortly before, in an article in the *Manchester Guardian* Colin Clark had predicted that the end of the Korean War would precipitate a major depression in the United States. The new Michigan model, on the other hand, predicted no such thing. It foresaw only a mild recession. After the model was unveiled Klein and his colleagues sent the *Manchester Guardian* a rejoinder to Clark, which was published along with an appropriate Low cartoon. In this way the new model received instant world recognition—and turned out to be correct in the bargain.

While these exciting developments were taking place in new areas of economics, some of the more traditional segments of the discipline were being strengthened as well. Ed Hoover returned from Washington for only one year, and the department was sorry to lose him to the Cowles Commission in 1946. At about the same time Dan Suits returned from four years of civilian public service as a conscientious objector to complete his Ph.D. Although he had had only one graduate course in statistics, with Hoover, he had started his higher education as a physics major and

> my training in physics, plus Smithies's . . . mathematical and quantitative orientation . . . together determined the way that I approached economics. That is, I had always thought of it as a science. . . . When Bump [Hoover] left, Sharfman called me in and asked me if I would take over his [teaching] program, which I did. So that's how I started teaching in mathematical economics and economic statistics.[117]

Harold Levinson had remained in Ann Arbor during the war years, teaching principles and pursuing his graduate studies. He wrote his doctoral dissertation in labor under Shorey Peterson's chairmanship, as Haber was away from campus during virtually all of Levinson's graduate student years. It was Haber's 1947–48 leave to assist Clay in Germany that gave the younger man his first opportunity to teach labor courses. "I remember teaching in a huge room up at the top floor of the West Engineering Building to about . . . 200 people. That was the first time I . . . stepped up from principles of economics . . . and I worked very hard at it."[118] The hard work paid off and Levinson was appointed an assistant professor in 1950 to replace Margaret Elliott Tracy, who had retired the year before.

America's involvement in World War II had changed its self-image with respect to world affairs, and the study of international economics rapidly expanded. When the department began to look for an addition in the field Musgrave suggested his old friend, Wolfgang

Stolper. They had first met as teenagers in Germany, then Stolper arrived at Harvard about half a year after Musgrave did, and obtained his Ph.D. a few months later. From Harvard Stolper went to Swarthmore College to teach. Later his friend, Musgrave, replaced him during a sabbatical. A year and a half later the academic leap-frogging friends became colleagues when Stolper joined the faculty at Michigan in the fall of 1949, to teach international trade and take over Hoover's course in location theory. Stolper found another old acquaintance in the Michigan economics department—George Katona, who had worked so closely with his father, Gustav Stolper, in the 1920s and 1930s.

During the 1948–49 year the department ran a series of guest lectures by prominent economists, including Fritz Machlup, David McCord Wright, John H. Williams, Theodore Schultz, Howard Ellis, Abram Bergson, Jacob Viner, and Kenneth Boulding. Boulding, born in Liverpool, had received his B.A. from Oxford in 1931 and his M.A. in 1938, and had had a distinquished teaching and research career in the British Commonwealth and the United States. He joined the Michigan faculty in the fall of 1949, and was awarded the John Bates Clark Medal by the American Economic Association a few months later. Boulding's major teaching assignments were in theory, and for some years he also taught a course in agricultural economics. But by the early 1950s his interests were moving beyond economics, to general systems analysis and to interdisciplinary scholarship. During the first five years of his tenure he ran a seminar in "Problems in the Integration of the Social Sciences," funded by the Ford Foundation, and attended by faculty from the physical sciences and engineering as well as the social sciences. Each year focused on a different theme, the final one entitled "Conflict and Conflict Resolution." The *Journal of Conflict Resolution,* and later the Center for Research in Conflict Resolution, grew out of that seminar.

Boulding's concern for conflict resolution was more than intellectual. As a devout Quaker he was a passionate pacifist. Pacificism was not as respectable in 1951 as it would come to be during a different war twenty years later, and Boulding's views precipitated a near-crisis in the economics department. The *Michigan Daily* distributed a questionnaire to faculty members in May of 1951, asking them to answer a series of yes/no questions on "the effect of the draft on the University . . . student deferment . . . and UMT [Universal Military Training]."

Additional comments were invited and Boulding added some, which read in part,

> Military Conscription is a form of slavery. It represents the use of a coercive power of the state against its own citizens. I disapprove of it in any form and for any purpose. . . . I think the best service the youth of America can perform for the country and for the world today is to refuse to be conscripted at whatever personal cost.[119]

With the nation almost a year into the Korean War this would be considered inflammatory language indeed. As the questionnaires were to be returned through each department office, the content of Boulding's reply came to Leo Sharfman's attention. He was profoundly disturbed. This sensitive matter, teetering between academic freedom and public irresponsibility, seemed to present the ultimate test of his leadership skills. "Recognizing immediately . . . both its essential impropriety and the serious consequences it might bring if published . . . I sought . . . the counsel of my colleagues in the Department."[120] It was late afternoon and only Musgrave and Suits were still in the building. They agreed to visit Boulding at home and try to persuade him to withdraw the statement.

The next day they reported to Sharfman that he "had taken the whole matter rather lightly but agreed to modify it."[121] From the chairman's point of view the result, if anything, was worse, as a heavy irony was superimposed upon the straightforward seriousness of the earlier version. Sharfman, in greater distress, called Peterson, Haber, Palmer, and Stolper to his office to discuss the problem. Boulding then met with this group. He listened to Sharfman's opinion that the statement was inciting students to break the law and might bring disastrous consequences to both the department and the university. Boulding responded with an explanation of his Quaker position and his belief in the right of civil disobedience, but agreed not to forward the offending statement to the *Daily*. The crisis was over and Sharfman's faith in governance by persuasion of reasonable men was vindicated.

The arrival of Richard Musgrave in 1947 revived and gave new luster to the somewhat flagging Michigan tradition in public finance. Bob Ford had never been a full-time member of the department. Nor did he provide academic leadership in the field, although he was an able administrator, published extensively, and rendered much public service on a pragmatic level, including presidency of the National Tax Association. He served as director of the Bureau of Reference and Research in Government from 1937 to 1950, when he became assistant dean of the graduate school, with a one-sixth appointment in the department. By that time the Bureau of Government was a unit within a larger Institute of Public Administration. In 1957 Ford went on inactive status in the department to devote full time to the graduate school, where he served as associate dean until his retirement in 1968.

His withdrawal from the department left the field of state and local finance uncovered. This was a rapidly growing sector of the economy and of government, however, and John Lederle, director of the Institute of Public Administration "was, perhaps more determined than the economics department was"[122] to fill the university's gap in the field. Harvey Brazer came in 1957 as an associate professor, half-time in the department and half-time at the institute. Born and raised in Montreal, he had returned from military service to earn his doctorate at Columbia in 1951, and had taught at several universities. From his arrival he furthered the department's public service tradition, as he had already been appointment director of a special Michigan tax study. This two-year project involved Professors Musgrave and Stolper, as well as a number of graduate students.

In 1957 Leonard Watkins did what he had always promised himself he would do. He retired early to the gentle southland and the fishing that he loved. Warren Smith, who had gone to the University of Virginia after completing his degree in 1952, and then to Ohio State, was invited to replace him, at the rank of associate professor. Watkins had been such a star that his was deemed a hard act to follow. There was no need for worry. In the classroom Warren Smith took second billing to nobody.

The best teacher I have ever had in economics was Warren Smith. . . . Warren knew the theory, Warren knew the math, and Warren knew why you wanted to know it. . . . Warren was the most fantastic teacher. And when you came into Warren's class, from the minute you got there you wrote like crazy . . . because he said that when he was a graduate student he didn't want people to waste his time. He wanted to come there and they should talk. He didn't like discussion groups. He was there to listen to the professor and he wanted to hear it. And so that's the way he did it. You could ask questions, but not a foolish question. You thought twice before you asked a foolish question of Warren.[123]

Warren Smith

was a warm, amiable, quick to laugh, quick to anger, kind of person, [but] he had little tolerance for fools. He had strong opinions about people, about issues. Probably wasn't always right, but in terms of policy issues, in terms of theoretical issues, always able to offer thoroughly reasoned . . . decisive bases for positions taken. [He was] always able to gain the respect of those he worked with, whether they be students, colleagues, fellow government officials, congressional committees. Before all such groups Warren commanded nothing but the highest respect. . . . In the classroom he was absolutely revered. Students . . . would audit his course time after time. And some of his contributions to the literature clearly have become classics.[124]

By 1946 the faculty ranks had returned to their prewar level, at about fifteen. Expansion to meet the postwar influx of students raised the total to twenty by 1950, where it remained for several years. By this time enrollments had fallen off considerably as the G.I.'s passed through the system and the low-birth-rate cohort of the Depression years attained college age. Economics enrollments halved between 1948 and 1953, levelling off at about 4,500 until the closing years of the decade. The faculty continued to grow slowly, however, to the benefit of the student body in that most fields were covered by at least two faculty members, who tended to complement each other's strengths and share the graduate and undergraduate responsibilities.

The slow growth of the faculty also meant that new members were welcomed and absorbed into the group, much as children, arriving one by one, are integrated into the family. They were a diverse group, to be sure, highly individual in their personalities, histories, research interests. But the analogy to family is apt, for it was a spirit of belonging, a sense of family, that animated the loyalty and harmony of the economics department. Newcomers like Dick Musgrave, Wolf Stolper, and Kenneth Boulding, quickly adopted this spirit and were enthusiastic participants in every phase of department life from their arrival. The people whose primary appointment was at the Survey Research Center shared in the warmth and devotion. Jack Lansing, for example, rarely missed a department meeting.

Leo Sharfman set an example of "official" humaneness that carried individuals and the group as a whole over some very rough terrain. Like a family the department rallied around those in trouble. And trouble struck the newest assistant professor in the late fall of 1950. As the weather turned cooler, and anxious parents breathed relief that another hazardous summer had passed, Harold Levinson was stricken with poliomyelitis. "I was in the hospital . . . for about five months. . . . I remember Sharfman coming up to the hospital and giving me a short lecture on Franklin Delano Roosevelt. . . . But the other thing that Sharfman did . . . was [get] an agreement from the dean of the college to give me full sick pay for a year rather than for a semester," which was all a new assistant professor was entitled to. When Levinson returned to work in the fall of 1951 he was on crutches. "I used to come up to the front steps and I would call Mrs. Uhlendorf, who was the department secretary, and she would come down and sort of stay in back of me while I got up the steps with my crutches."[125]

Of course to Mrs. Uhlendorf, Hal Levinson was one of "her boys." She called "faculty members who were former Michigan graduate students by their first names, but contemporaries who came from outside were Mister. I was Mr. Brazer, but Suits was always Dan. Levinson was always Harold, but Musgrave was Mr. Musgrave, and so on."[126] Mrs. Uhlendorf thereby established something of an economics department tradition. Unlike many, if not most, other units around the university, secretaries in the department continue to address the faculty as Mister or Mrs. or Ms. Sharfman, himself, was a rather formal man, of course. But the degree of formality which prevailed twenty to thirty years ago was, perhaps, conducive to the respect and courtesy with which this diverse group of people interacted. And it in no way diminished the department's vibrant social life.

The softball games begun in the twenties fell by the wayside during the war, but the annual picnic for faculty and teaching fellow families became a regular feature. For years it took place at the Winans Lake home of George and Adele Anderson, where swimming and boating were featured activities along with volleyball, beer, and a variety of potluck foods. Later on additional picnics at local parks were often scheduled by graduate students and faculty were invited.

The esprit de corps of the teaching staff carried over to their wives. Most of the teaching fellows during this period were married, and during the 1950s regular gatherings of teaching fellow wives were

initiated by Marion Carroll, whose husband, John, took over supervision of the TFs for one year while Shorey Peterson was acting
chairman. (Mary Alice Shulman lays claim to being the first female
teaching fellow in the mid-1950s, although Marion Engle had been
a predoctoral instructor thirty years earlier.) Later, the faculty wives
joined the group, which met one evening a month in each other's
homes, sometimes with a planned program, sometimes just to talk,
always with cake and coffee.

Home parties were the mainstay of department social life, dinners being the most common variety, usually in subsets of two to six
couples. But for the Stolpers a living room concert was their unique
style of entertaining. An accomplished pianist, Wolf Stolper's greatest
joy was (and is) to make music with his friends—duets with Elise
Boulding on the cello, or graduate student violinist Arthur Benavie
(who had trained early for the concert stage, then switched to economics), or baritone Ronald Teigen, and two-piano work with a great number of talented noneconomist musicians. Nonperforming members of
the department were always invited to listen, and on one memorable
occasion they found, on arrival, that Stolper's living room had been
transformed into the setting for a full chamber orchestra, to be conducted in their impromptu performance by music professor Hans David
(the father of a department graduate student).

The annual department Christmas party for faculty and teaching
fellows was inaugurated at the Brazer's house in 1958. An after-dinner
hors d'oeuvre potluck, often accompanied by records and dancing, it
rotated among people's homes until numbers burst the bounds of anyone's living room. Then for the remainder of its approximate ten-year
life, the party consisted of a potluck dinner-dance, held often at a
sorority house that Lois Levinson "mothered," after the girls had left
for the Christmas break.

The social climax of the 1950s was undisputably the gala that
marked the retirement of Leo Sharfman on January 15, 1954. Here
was the opportunity to pay tribute to the man who, more than any
other individual, had devoted his life to creating a department of intellectual stature, mutual respect for diversity, humaneness, and harmony. The outpouring of affection and esteem was expressed in a
masterwork of theatrical creation that took place at the Michigan
Union on that winter night.

Act I   Now to the Banquet We Press—
Entire Company

Act II   Under the Sign of Leo—
The Lord High Executioner, William Paton

Act III   My Boy, You May Take it From Me—
The Lord Chancellor, Shorey Peterson

Act IV   Ileolanthe—
An Almost Entirely Unoriginal Comic Opera in
One (That's Enough) Act

Words by A. Random Sample, with posthumous assistance
of W. S. Gilbert
Music by Arthur Sullivan, with occasional notes by Wolfgang
Amadeus Schumpeter
Cast, Castoffs, and Castaways—
Adam David Maynard Marshall Taylor, a would-be student
Mrs. Butterdorf, the department secretary
I Leo Lanthe, the department chairman
Pennyworth Beholding, an economic theorist
Mike MacAggregate, an econometrician
Do Re Ma, an academic counselor
George the First, King-pin of Survey Research

This performance by an indigenous troupe of economist-musicians introduced such characters as the Maundering Theorist and the Model of a Man Econometrical.[127] It was, to understate, well received.

From the euphoria of the Sharfman dinner the department was soon plunged to the nadir of its experience as a collegium, and much of the burden would fall on the new chairman, Gardner Ackley. The virus loosed by Joseph McCarthy invaded the University of Michigan campus via a subcommittee of the House Un-American Activities Committee. That subcommittee, under Congressman Kit Clardy from East Lansing (the "Clardy Committee"), held an "Investigation of Communist Activities in the State of Michigan" in the spring of 1954.

Three suspected faculty members were questioned—a zoologist, a pharmacologist, and a mathematician. Bill Palmer was chairman of the Senate Advisory Committee on University Affairs (SACUA) during the critical years of 1952 and 1953. They could see what was coming and appointed a subcommittee to draw a bylaw to deal with this novel problem. Under the lengthy procedures adopted, two of the "investigated" professors were exonerated by the faculty; the third, an instructor, was asked to leave, largely because of his belligerent, uncooperative attitude with those trying to be supportive of him. Of the two men whom the SACUA committee had endorsed, one left the university for other reasons; in the second case President Harlan Hatcher overruled the faculty committee decision. Tempers and fears were rising on the campus.

In addition to faculty members appearing before the Clardy Committee, students were called for interrogation. Two of these were graduate students in economics who were about to be admitted to doctoral candidacy. They refused to testify. Pressure was brought to bear on the department from the central administration of the university to deny these men candidacy on three grounds: their behavior at the committee hearing had been insolent and uncooperative; there were allegations that their presence on campus was part of a conspiratorial Communist network and that they were not, in fact, bona fide students; and their preconceived, doctrinaire position would prevent the scientific objectivity necessary for research. These issues were fully debated at department staff meetings.

Ackley's letter to Dean Ralph Sawyer of the graduate school upheld in ringing terms the department's lifelong commitment to academic freedom. While the apparent convictions of these two were held in contempt by the department, there was no evidence of dishonest or illegal behavior and the department rejected the notion of going beyond behavior to "look into their souls." We cannot create new character requirements for the degree and then apply them ex post, the chairman reported to the graduate dean.

> If they have violated reasonable standards of student conduct, they should be expelled. If they have violated the law, they should be jailed. Our whole concern is with the integrity of our academic process and our degree requirements. If we tamper with these to achieve the dismissal of Communists, we might someday find ourselves tampering again . . . to disqualify a McCarthyite, a Socialist, a Catholic, or a Negro. When we do this we have forfeited our right to be part of a great university.[128]

The department sustained its principle, although the two candidates never finished their dissertations.

At the time that the three aforementioned professors were under investigation the *Michigan Daily* kept on top of the story. Included in their reports about these men were allusions to an additional suspect, a mysterious Mr. X. It turned out that Mr. X was Survey Research Center Research associate and economics department lecturer Lawrence Klein. As he was not a regular member of the faculty his case did not go through the SACUA process. But it had, for some time, been understood that Klein was to be appointed a regular member of the faculty. Moreover, his stature as an economist and his importance to the department were such that Sharfman had stated his intention early in 1953 to leapfrog the lower professorial ranks and recommend a full professorship. But the time was not yet, he told Klein. In keeping with his policy of ensuring success before he made a move, he advised waiting for one more year of seniority, as it were. This was agreeable to Klein, but by the fall of 1953 he had been served with a subpoena to appear before the Clardy Committee when, in its own good time, it would convene in Detroit.

Klein then went to Sharfman and requested that he not be considered for appointment because he was under subpoena. It was a distressing circumstance for Sharfman's last months in office. Klein went on to explain the nature of his involvement with the Communist party, as he would later describe it to the committee. While he was a graduate student at MIT he had taught at the Samuel Adams School, since declared subversive. When he moved to Chicago in 1944 to work for the Cowles Commission he taught at the Abraham Lincoln School, since declared subversive. He was asked by the latter group to join the party, apparently as a condition of employment, and he did so, attending altogether about six meetings in the homes of various members. After his marriage in 1947 he lost interest and dropped permanently out of all party activity. That was the entire story, which he confided to Sharfman, to incoming chairman Gardner Ackley, to Rensis Likert, director of ISR, and to the Clardy Committee when he appeared before them on April 30, 1954. His testimony, offered in executive session, was supposed to be privileged, but on September 4 the committee made it public. By this time Klein was out of the country, having earlier accepted a visiting appointment at Oxford for 1954–55.

As far as both ISR and the economics department were concerned, however, Klein was a highly valued staff member who deserved promotion. An indiscreet impulse of seven years earlier in no way diminished his stature as an economist or his respect as a colleague. There was no discernable communism in his teaching, nor in his coversation for that matter. In recognition of the temper of the times, however, the department held thorough discussions at two meetings, then voted on November 19, 1954, to recommend him for appointment in 1955–56 as a full professor with tenure, three-quarters time in the department and one-quarter time in the Survey Research Center. The vote tally was fifteen to one, with three absences. The dissenting vote came from Bill Paton, with whom Klein was barely acquainted. Boulding was on leave in California, and Sharfman recuperating in Florida from the illness that had necessitated his sudden midyear retirement, but both wrote letters of support.

Bob Ford, absent from the meeting, explained the reasons for his opposition in response to a request from Dean Odegaard. They are representative of the doubts and timidities of many otherwise reasonable people during this dark episode in American history. He had had very little contact with Klein, but based his view on Klein's testimony.

> How much time is required for a person to become de-communized, I do not know. . . . The story of Dr. Klein's activities . . . is a sordid one involving clandestine meetings, contacts with persons who were known only by their first names. . . . I have serious misgivings as to the objectivity of one who has been a party to such proceedings. . . . Appointment as a full professor . . . is very rapid progress that is hardly warranted under the circumstances.

The regents were not likely to approve this appointment, in Ford's opinion, and to put it before them would "simply aggravate the situation that existed at the time disciplinary action was taken against two members of the faculty last year. . . . I see no reason in deliberately creating an incident that would reopen this controversy."[129]

Paton answered Odegaard's letter with some of the same arguments, but in much more strident tones. He was a man of strong reactions to personal characteristics—appearance, voice, origins, mannerisms—and had vehement likes and dislikes. Apparently he found in Klein an unacceptable number of the "angles" he had chided other colleagues for criticizing in Smithies sixteen years before, and he didn't hesitate to point out these personal idiosyncracies in his letter. In addition to reiterating Ford's arguments, he further questioned the need for a full professor in econometrics, naming the other members of the department whom he believed thoroughly competent to teach in the field. "Fourth, there is the important point that Mr. Klein is aggressively Socialist in his entire outlook. . . . there is very little economics in it. . . . We have no need for a thoroughgoing Socialist professor at this juncture." Fifth, of his six elaborated points, was his conviction that not all economists had such a high opinion of Klein and he offered to supply the Dean with ten well-known names who might "balance the scales."[130] In a later letter Paton wrote that he "regarded his [Klein's] conversion as only skin deep, because he currently states that he espouses the Norwegian brand of socialism (regarded by most economists . . . as the most extreme case of statism in Europe . . . outside of Russia and the satellites.)"[131]

In submitting the recommendation Ackley had attached enthusiastic testimonial letters from Arthur F. Burns (then chairman of the Council of Economic Advisors), Tjalling Koopmans, Wassily Leontief, and Jan Tinbergen. This was unusual procedure, but the department anticipated, correctly, that the appointment would not go through easily. Paton had made his opposition clear from the outset, although Ackley pointed out in the twenty-two-page appointment submission that he taught no economics courses (and, indeed, was the last of the accountants still to be listed in the department) and that Ford had only a one-sixth appointment in the department.

Odegaard, himself, had written to Simon Kuznets, Jacob Marschak, Charles Roos, Paul Samuelson, Richard Stone, and James Tobin on the same day he wrote Ford and Paton, January 27, 1955. Five of them replied in superlatives; Kuznets expressed doubts only about the usefulness of advanced mathematical techniques in understanding complex historical processes. Nevertheless, the dean wrote to all ten of Paton's names (although he had requested that only five be supplied): Yale Brozen, Howard Ellis, Friedrich Hayek, Gottfried Haberler, Frank Knight, Emerson Schmidt, Ernst Swanson, Leo Wolman, David McCord Wright, John Van Sickle. Four replied that they didn't know Klein, two were unfavorable, and the remaining four ranged from complimentary to expression of doubt about the modernity and usefulness of this approach to economics.

Much discussion of the issue took place among all parties in the unrecorded form of personal conversations and telephone calls, and on March 2, Odegaard requested final comment from the department.

A meeting was called for the fourteenth, in which the whole issue was once more reexamined. No one changed position. But tempers flared, culminating in a stormy altercation between Bill Paton and George Katona when "Katona challenges Paton's statement . . . that L. K. is 'aggressively socialist in his entire outlook.' "[132] As a consequence, each of them wrote letters to the dean, and circulated copies, concerning the Socialist views and American loyalties of Lawrence Klein.

On March 18, Ackley transmitted another long memo to the dean, confirming the department's strong recommendation, and refuting the arguments raised by the opposition with respect to the importance of econometrics, the availability of this expertise elsewhere in the department, Klein's teaching ability, and the merits of Keynesianism.

A few weeks later the "recommendation received strong and unanimous support from the Dean and Executive Committee"[133] of the College, was accepted by Vice President Marvin Niehuss, and was forwarded to the regents. The proposal was slightly modified, however, as the result of a strategy session among Niehuss, Likert, Odegaard, and Ackley. The appointment was modeled on ISR appointments, like Katona's, a full professorship but without tenure.

On June 24, Ackley happily cabled Klein that his appointment was official. Klein's letter of acceptance expressed his disappointment on the tenure question, but his deepest gratitude for the efforts made by Ackley and the other department members on his behalf. The decision came too late for him to cancel commitments he had made to Oxford for the fall term, however, so his return to Michigan was put off to the spring term, 1956. Everyone was relieved by the satisfactory resolution of this difficult matter.

Then, in late October of 1955, Ackley received a deeply distressing letter from Klein.

A few weeks ago [he wrote], I received an anonymous letter outlining Paton's recent moves against my appointment. I am not certain whether this tip was sent as a warning by a friend of what to expect on my return or as a threat by a foe against my returning at all. Should I take seriously Paton's activities? He now approaches the Regents and administration directly to let my appointment expire at the end of the current year and makes the veiled threat of carrying the case to the public if he gets no satisfaction from University authorities. I had planned to come back full of enthusiasm . . . but I don't look forward to the bother of carrying on this fight once again.[134]

In light of this shocking new development Ackley asked Odegaard and Niehuss for clarification and reaffirmation of the assurances given to Klein that, although untenured in the department, he was "permanent" at ISR and department tenure could be expected in future. On November 14, Niehuss wrote directly to Klein that there was no question about his status at ISR or at the rank of lecturer in the department. The objections of Paton and "one other member of the Economics Department" had recently been transmitted to the regents in a letter from Paton. They discussed the matter informally, but took no action. Niehuss's personal evaluation of the situation was that Klein could count on continuation at the Survey Research Center. "I will join with the Department and School in recommending a renewal of your present appointment as Professor of Economics without tenure at the end of the current academic year. I cannot predict the action of the Board of Regents on this recommendation." If they should not approve, Niehuss was certain they would renew the appointment at the lecturer level. He expressed regret that he couldn't give more assurances and went on to conclude, "We are all aware of the fine contributions you have made to your field . . . and of the high esteem in which you are held by the great majority of your colleagues in the Department of Economics. It is my personal hope that you will decide to return to Michigan and rely upon time and your own accomplishments to overcome the problems that now exist."[135] An ambiguous message, at best.

After another staff meeting on November 18, Ackley wrote to Klein that prior to his letter of October 18, "none of us in the Department had any inkling that the question of your status had been reopened." The meeting reaffirmed the department's commitment, and voting with the majority this time was Bob Ford, who now "fully supports the present appointment."[136] The letter concluded with the hope that the unfortunate turn of events would not change Klein's decision to return.

Meanwhile Ackley, learning more of the nature of Paton's activities with respect to the executive officers and the regents, could not let them pass unchallenged. In as calm a mood as he could command in the circumstances he wrote Paton a trenchant letter, deploring his methods and the insult to his colleagues. Paton answered with equal asperity to justify his behavior and censure Ackley's. The seething anger of both men showed through their measured phrases. From that time William Paton no longer participated in department affairs or had any personal association with more than one or two of its members, although upon retirement in 1959 he was designated Professor Emeritus of Economics.

Klein's response to Ackley's letter of reaffirmation might have been expected.

> Your letter is very kind and certainly makes me hesitate, yet I can't banish the feeling . . . that there is a serious deficiency of academic freedom in the summation made by Niehuss. It isn't the risk of uncertainty . . . that bothers me so much . . . and it isn't any fear of Paton's actions. It is simply a feeling that it is wrong for the Regents to pay heed to Paton and also to weaken what was already a less than satisfying offer. I don't put much value in tenure as such; I simply don't like the reasons for which it is withheld. [With much regret he submitted his resignation] to accept a newly created post (for my benefit) at Oxford as Reader in Econometrics. . . . I find it hard to make this decision, to give up all that I worked so hard on at Michigan, and especially to refuse acceptance of the very best fruits of the magnificent efforts you and other dear friends made on my behalf.[137]

Upon receipt of this letter Ackley made a last-ditch effort, on December 14, appealing to Odegaard to resubmit the original tenure proposal to that day's executive committee meeting, so that it could be forwarded to Niehuss in time for the January regents' meeting. Odegaard did, the college executive committee endorsed it unanimously, and it was on its way to Niehuss the next day. Niehuss's reply to Odegaard: after discussion with President Hatcher "we do not believe that we are warranted in asking the Regents to make such an appointment or commitment at this time." It was best, he said, simply to accept the resignation.[138]

In late January of 1956 Rensis Likert, regretful at losing Klein from the Institute for Social Research, revived the whole matter once again, and set in motion another submission to the regents. In yet another flurry of excitement Ackley telephoned Klein asking him to postpone final commitments. But after thinking it over once more Klein replied with regret that arrangements, both at Oxford and in the family's personal lives, had gone too far to reverse at the last moment. Ackley's letter to Odegaard closing the record lamented that

> the University, through unnecessary bungling has lost the services of a unique and distinguished scholar. If only the Regents had dismissed the Paton letter ... as an unauthorized, ex parte rehash of ideas and arguments fully considered by the responsible administrative officers at every level Klein would he here today.[139]

In a postscript to Niehuss on April 11, 1959, Ackley reported, without comment, that the American Economic Association would award Lawrence Klein the John Bates Clark Medal for 1959. But the final irony of this entire episode occurred in 1977, when the University of Michigan bestowed upon Lawrence Klein an honorary Doctor of Laws degree. At a party the night before commencement, the valedictory was delivered when Leslie Kish walked into the room and "congratulated Klein on his fourth degree. To Klein's puzzled look, [Kish explained] 'We gave you, in 1955, the third degree.' "[140]

Larry Klein's verdict twenty-five years later about the department and the university:

> I feel very attached.... I did a lot of good research in those years. It was a very formative period in terms of my professional career, and I look back on it very fondly. I often go back, and I always enjoy being there.... One of my children was educated there ... and so I have good feelings.[141]

The department and the college came through the Klein affair with honor, but the episode had been painful to everybody, and was rarely discussed afterward except by oblique allusions. Only a few actors in the drama knew all the details, and they preferred to put it behind them. For Leo Sharfman it must have been a wrenching experience to see his beloved department sore distressed, to see the division from it of his lifetime colleague, to see the unanimity he had always striven for, especially in dealing with the world beyond the department, impossible to achieve. Yet there was never any doubt expressed by Sharfman as to where justice and honor lay. Could he, had he been here, have mollified Paton and avoided a public showdown, as he had done for twenty-six years? Or were the fears and passions of the times too strong even for the master persuader?

For the new chairman, Gardner Ackley, the affair was an initiation by fire. At its conclusion he could know the satisfaction of having upheld the precious principle of academic freedom, although the skirmish itself was ultimately lost. Now he faced a more pragmatic problem—finding a new director for the Quant seminar, as RSQE came to be known. The most logical internal choice, Dan Suits, had filled in for the year Klein had planned to be at Oxford, and took the emergency second year, as well, upon Klein's resignation. But he didn't want to be the sole entrepreneur for the seminar. When Jack Lansing agreed to share the responsibility with him Suits agreed to the directorship.

Lansing was an economist of considerable versatility, whose research talents had won the respect of his colleagues and whose warm, unflappable personality had won their affection. "He was very loyal to the Survey Research Center . . . and very involved in it. . . . There was almost nothing that he didn't make a major contribution to."[142] He was also a participant in the department even before his part-time appointment as associate professor in 1956 to help direct the seminar. He regularly attended the Economics Club, the Little Seminar, and the staff luncheons, as well, by invitation. He stayed with the seminar for five years, until he began teaching in industrial organization and in transportation. By then Locke Anderson had come into the department, mainly as a macro theorist, and had joined the staff of RSQE as well.

Under Suits's direction the parade of excellent graduate students continued, including a strong Japanese contingent. The camaraderie which had characterized the seminar from the start continued and was even strengthened. Six to twelve students might be working in the seminar in any one year, "but usually no more than six were highly active." Their theater of operations was a large room at the far end of the basement hallway. The students

lived down there. The real pros lived down there. They argued with each other . . . and settled all the problems of the universe.

The seminar would tool up in September when the students arrived and the assignment was to take the model apart and see where it had functioned poorly last year and what should be done about it to improve it, with the notion that come the second or third week of November . . . somebody had to stand up in front of that Conference on the Economic Outlook and produce a forecast from this model. . . . Then for the next semester we'd do whatever came to our heads to do.

The first calculations . . . were all done by hand. . . . you had to iterate with a desk calculator . . . and the first forecast I ever made with it I was working until about four o'clock in the morning and I couldn't get the iteration to converge. And it happened that [Susumu] Koizumi was coming home from a date . . . and . . . he saw the light on in the seminar. He came in to see what was going on, and here I was trying to get this darn thing to converge . . . this is four o'clock in the morning [and] four o'clock this afternoon I've got to be on. And so he said, "Well, I'll get on one calculator and you get on the other one, and I'll start low and you start high, and . . . we'll converge on it." So we kept on going . . . and, by God, if we didn't pass each other and it still hadn't converged. And then I discovered that the calculator that I was using, an old Monroematic . . . was making an error.

So then we got more sophisticated, of course, and began to do the forecasting with a computer. And I remember one time . . . when Saul Hymans was in Washington at the Council . . . he called me up to find out what [the forecast] was . . . just as I got the sheet out of the computer. I looked at it, and somebody had got a big blooper in it. And I said, "Saul, this shows that the increase in GNP next year is going to be about 200 . . . trillion dollars." There was a pause on the end of the line, and then Saul said, "Is that current or constant dollars?"[143]

As RSQE and the Economic Outlook Conference continued to flourish, one more new field was being readied to join the economics curriculum. When the industrial nations adopted a new stance of economic and technical assistance to the undeveloped nations and former colonial territories after World War II, the new field of economic development was born. Michigan didn't get around to organizing the interests of its faculty in this area until the end of the decade.

In 1959, a special part-time appointment was made to direct a departmental committee in designing a teaching and research program. Samuel P. Hayes, a 1934 Yale Ph.D. in social psychology, had come to Michigan in 1953 as director of the Foundation for Research in Human Behavior, after an extensive career in teaching and in foreign economic service with the federal government, including an instrumental role in developing the Point Four Program. He had been a sometime lecturer in the economics department when Ackley requested his appointment to chair the committee. By the spring of 1960, seven National Defense Education Act fellowships had been obtained to launch the new Ph.D. program. A series of faculty seminars, that would include some noneconomists, was projected for the following academic year "to go carefully over the whole field and to figure out what its real content is, and what we should be doing in our research program and in the doctoral program after the first year."[144] Hayes was now given a full-time tenured professorship to organize the seminar, obtain financing for, and then direct the proposed Center for Research in Economic Development, which would integrate the graduate teaching program with its research agenda. Funds were obtained from the Ford Foundation and from the Agency for International Development (AID), but Hayes felt that the center did not get the kind of support from the university it should have, and in the summer of 1962 he resigned to accept the presidency of the Foreign Policy Association.

Leo Sharfman's retirement in 1954 had been a milestone in several respects. It not only closed a forty-four-year career in the teaching of economics, but it opened a new era in the organization of the Michigan economics department. In 1945, and again in 1951, the college requested its departments to reexamine their organizational structure "to the end of improving administrative efficiency and safeguarding democratic procedures."[145] Sharfman's orderly and literary response on both occasions reproduced his 1934 memo as a still valid description. In the later response he identified the membership of several administrative and advisory committees, as well as the individual faculty members responsible for specified administrative tasks, such as registration, announcements, and Economics Club. Once more, at a regular monthly meeting the "staff agreed, without dissent, that the present organization . . . functions effectively, and that no formal modifications . . . are either necessary or desirable."[146]

While Sharfman's skill at autocratic democracy was admired,

and people were not actively dissatisfied with his decisions, there was a restive desire, especially among younger faculty members, for a more explicit, less hierarchical, participatory democracy (although the last phrase had not yet been coined).

> I'm not aware that there was any real revolutionary spirit in the department. I think nobody was really ready to challenge Leo. . . . Everybody had to agree that he ran the department very, very well. . . . But there was no organized method of anyone's partic-ipation other than through the meetings. And in the meetings . . . we kept talking until we finally agreed to do it Leo's way. And . . . after a while you got tired of fighting and his way usually was not so bad [although] it may not have been exactly the way the rest of us would have done it. So I don't think there was a great resentment, but there was a considerable relief when the method of running the department changed.[147]

Change it did, almost immediately upon Ackley's accession to the chairmanship. A meeting of the upper staff (defined as lecturer through all professorial ranks, including part-time) on March 8, 1954, decided, with little argument, to establish an elective three-man ex-ecutive committee, to be reviewed one year hence. Shorey Peterson, Dick Musgrave, and Harold Levinson composed the first group, and would decide which matters should be referred to the full staff. Be-cause "it is important that the Executive Committee not take the place of full staff participation in the discussion and determination of significant matters of departmental policy,"[148] the monthly staff lunch-eons at the Michigan Union were continued and a minimum of two upper staff meetings per semester were mandated. (The luncheons included instructors and teaching fellows.)

When the review came up a year later the chairman reported that the executive committee had met sixteen times, and dealt mostly with recommendations on budget, salary increases, promotions, new ap-pointments, changes in teaching assignments, and appointment of teaching fellows. The system was unanimously endorsed, and has remained in force to the present day. As the department has grown in size and complexity various standing and ad hoc committees have been appointed to assist the chairman and the executive committee. But the respective policy roles of the chairman, the executive com-mittee, and the full faculty have remained essentially as defined at that time. The chairman takes full responsibility for budget and salary, while appointments, promotions, and significant curricular changes are decided by the faculty as a whole.

One of the most difficult administrative questions facing the department in those years was the problem of staffing. Gaps were filled to some extent during the 1958–60 years by a series of distinguished visiting lectureships, which provided the opportunity to "look over" some very senior people for possible recruitment, while at the same time enriching the undergraduate and graduate programs. But this did not begin to solve the problem caused by the retirement between 1954 and 1959 of four long-time faculty members, and the resignation in 1959 of Dick Musgrave to accept an appointment at Johns Hopkins was a heavy blow. The most glaring deficiencies were in public control, international economics, and the perennial economic history gap. Furthermore, Shorey Peterson wanted to divest himself of the principles responsibility, which, in effect, created another gap there. All this was going on in the face of rising enrollments that in the 1960s would overwhelm the department, the university and higher educational institutions in general, beyond all projections of the late 1950s.

With all these openings the department ended the decade of the 1950s with a faculty very little larger than when it began. But, as in 1929, the character of the group had been transformed during the decade. The "gentlemen of the old school"—Sharfman, Dickinson, Watkins, Remer—were retired, and with Paton, who also retired in 1959, went a continuity stretching back forty-five years to the department's youth. By and large the newer group, who now became the "senior" figures of the department's leadership, were more research-oriented than the older ones had been, and the new quantitative cast to the discipline was becoming firmly seated in the curriculum. But the tradition of public service was continued in its familiar form, and the legacy of mutual respect, humaneness, and unity left by these particular four retirees was received and carried forward to define the department spirit ever since.

The Turbulent Years, 1963–73

The rifle shot that closed the life of John F. Kennedy on November 22, 1963, opened a decade of turmoil on the nation's college and university campuses. The University of Michigan, its economics department in particular, would come to play a significant role in the events of that unique period.

The opening years of the 1960s were conventional enough, and gave little hint of what the second half would bring. With the election of President Kennedy in 1960, the economics department's Washington connection was reforged after eight years of weakness. Not that the members of the department were ever uniform in their political views. The story is told that at a department luncheon after the election of 1940, Leo Sharfman

> in his very cautious fashion said, "Now I'm very curious . . . I don't want to embarrass anyone, and you don't have to respond to what I'm going to ask, but . . . I'm curious as to how the members of this department voted." . . . There were eighteen people who responded. . . . Six of the eighteen had voted for Norman Thomas, six had voted for [Wendell] Wilkie, and six had voted for [Franklin] Roosevelt.[149]

As for Sharfman himself, he perhaps typified many of the faculty when asked

> what his political affiliation was. He said he's independent. He does not believe in so-called party loyalty. He'd vote for the best man, be he Democrat or Republican. Coming to think of it, he said, he'd never yet seen his way clear to vote for a Republican candidate.[150]

For whatever reason, during the Eisenhower years there was not a great deal of federal government involvement. The first to leave for Washington in 1961 was Harvey Brazer, who joined the Kennedy administration for a two-year stint as deputy assistant secretary of the treasury for tax policy. A year later Gardner Ackley was appointed by Kennedy as a member of the Council of Economic Advisors. He would not return to the university for seven years, for his membership on the council was followed by the chairmanship of it from 1964 to 1968, and in 1968 President Lyndon Johnson appointed him Ambassador to Italy (a country in which he had done a good deal of research.) In 1962 Warren Smith went to Washington to serve a year on the council staff; he returned in 1968 as a member of the council. In addition to these public service leaves among the senior faculty various junior members served in government agencies throughout the 1960s, and many of the faculty regularly contributed congressional testimony.

This active period of public service coincided with two other circumstances to place great strain on the teaching resources of the department. Grant money, from both private foundations and government sponsors, began to flow in accelerating amounts and there was a marked increase in the number and frequency of research leaves. During the winter of 1960–61 the chairman was faced with no less than eight faculty leaves requested for the 1961–62 year. At the same time the dam broke on student enrollments. Unfortunately, even this quantitative economics department does not have course election data for every year, so it is not certain precisely when the numbers began to climb. By 1963–64 course enrollments, at 4,072, had not yet recovered to their 1953 level of 4,462. But the following year, 1964–65, they went over 5,000 and continued to climb to a peak of 6,622 in 1967–68. Enrollments may have gone higher yet in 1968–69, but the data for that year are missing, and by 1969–70 the slide had begun (although graduate course elections actually didn't peak until 1970–71, at 858) to a low of 5,600 in 1972–73. Again two years are missing, but by 1975–76 undergraduate elections alone were back to 5,000 and since then they have continued to rise steadily to 6,400 in 1978–79, while graduate registrations have fluctuated in the 950 to 1,000 range. The "ideal" section size of 20 students rose steadily after World War II to 30 and more, and in the late seventies advanced undergraduate classes seated more than 100 students.

Thus the staffing deficiencies noted at the end of the 1950s plagued department chairmen all through the 1960s. Faculty recruitment dominated most staff meetings and most of the chairman's work day. Gardner Ackley had requested relief from the chairmanship in 1959, and in 1961 it was granted, when Harold Levinson agreed to take the post for one year on an acting basis. The college had established a succession procedure, "recommending chairmanships . . . for a maximum term of five years. This policy assumes neither automatic rotation nor automatic reappointment. It does imply periodic assessment of the department situation based on extensive consultation with members of the department."[151] A statement of the department's situation, problems and plans was expected at the time of change, and each member was invited to submit recommendations for the chairmanship by personal letter to the dean, a practice still in effect.

The department statement emphasized its precarious position with respect to its national standing of probably sixth to tenth rank, unless several senior appointments were made along with recruitment of a number of promising younger people.

> Because of the frequency of outside demands for our staff, we are greatly in need of reserve strength, or depth of personnel. . . . Emergency substitute appointments . . . are seldom fully satisfactory; and while reserve staffing involves extra cost when it happens that all staff members are here, it should involve no extra cost on the average. Perhaps department budgets, like those of government, cannot be balanced wisely on a year-to-year basis.[152]

It was not merely a question of funding that made faculty recruitment a trying task, however. Every other university was active in the market during this time of growing enrollments and the bidding for the most reputable senior people and the most promising new Ph.D.'s was hectic and sophisticated.

The furious pace of faculty recruitment during the period looked like this:

	New Hires	Departures	Net Additions
1961–64	19	4	15
1965–69	23	11	12
1970–74	16	12	4

These figures refer only to people on the staff three years or more. In addition a substantial number of people moved in and out in less than three years. Of the fifty-eight hires listed above twenty-eight remained in the department in 1979. While a good deal of the recruiting effort was necessitated by attrition and turnover, and while growing enrollments demanded a larger staff through the late sixties, of greatest importance was the need to add depth in individual fields. Thus selective recruitment continued into the 1970s, even during the recession in enrollments. Moreover, depth in fields was especially important to the burgeoning number of graduate students during this period, which rose at a faster rate than undergraduate. Whereas in the eleven years 1950–60 65 Ph.D.'s had been awarded, in the following eleven years, 1961–71, more than double that number, 137, were conferred. Because of lengthy time-to-degree the all-time record years occurred in the 1970s, when the high graduate enrollments of the 1960s produced 33 new Ph.D.'s in 1974, followed by a second place year in 1977 with 24 degrees awarded.

Building on the momentum generated in the 1950s, international economics was the first to see a substantial expansion of faculty in the several branches of that field. Robert Stern, a 1958 Columbia Ph.D., joined the department in 1961 in international trade theory and finance; Alan Deardorff came in 1970 from his graduate study at Cornell. Morris Bornstein, a 1952 Michigan Ph.D., returned to the department in 1958 to introduce Soviet economics into the curriculum. Michael Manove joined him in this field from 1969 to 1975. The offering in Eastern European economics was greatly enriched from 1964 to 1974 by a series of nine visiting professors and research scientists from four of those countries, under Ford Foundation and United States Office of Education grants, "hosted" by Bornstein.

After Carl Remer's retirement, the China connection was picked up again when Alexander Eckstein joined the department as a full professor in 1961. A native of Yugoslavia, he had earned his Ph.D. at the University of California at Berkeley in 1952. He was active in the Center for Chinese Studies, serving as its director on more than one occasion, and participated widely on the national level in the affairs of "China watchers" during the strange period when mainland China was virtually a closed book. He was serving as chairman of the National Committee on United States–China Relations when it arranged the famous "ping-pong diplomacy" of 1972 that helped to end the two decades of estrangement. Alex Eckstein was an exuberant man, who cared deeply about public affairs and private relationships, and he played an active role in the department's business. His untimely death in 1976, from a series of heart attacks, was a shock and a great loss.

Robert Dernberger, also in the field of Chinese economics, joined the department in 1968 as an associate professor. A Michigan B.A. in Asian studies, he had taken a master's degree under Carl Remer, who inspired him to become an economist. Then, in light of Remer's imminent retirement, he went on to Harvard for his Ph.D. in 1965. Gary Saxonhouse, a Japan specialist with a 1971 Yale Ph.D., came in 1970 to complete the roster of area specialists. All four of these men taught in the field of comparative economics systems introduced during the 1960s with a substantial Ford Foundation grant.

When Sam Hayes left in 1962 the Center for Research in Economic Development (CRED) had barely gotten started, although it had both Ford and AID money. Wolf Stolper had by then moved firmly into the field of economic development with a two-year stint in Nigeria, and after his return he became director of the center in 1963. Stolper had very definite ideas about how such a center should be run. In particular

> I wanted two associate directors, who are essentially equals . . . to build it up on the principle of interchangeable parts. . . . I thought what was necessary [was] to concentrate on field work. I had no objections whatsoever to theory, quite on the contrary, but I thought the most important thing was to do field work. And that meant two people would always be abroad. And it meant that there should always be somebody here who could make decisions for all three, was informed. And I remember Bill Haber said, "Look, I'm dean and two other people are deans. There are three deans for 11,000 students and you want three directors for five people."[153]

Gradually the center acquired a pronounced Africa emphasis, and while the field work was important for the staff, the teaching function under Stolper also got a good deal of attention. "I got a lot of fellowship money for our students and never wanted to see them. I said, 'First become good economists, and then I want to see you.' So even people I financed I didn't see for two years, until after the prelims. Then I wanted to send them abroad."[154] He did see them, of course, as the teaching program grew under his instruction, and that of new faculty. Richard Porter, a 1957 Yale Ph.D., came in 1964 as an associate professor and Elliot Berg, Harvard 1960, arrived at Michigan as a full professor in 1966. Both of them filled the associate director roles that Stolper wanted for them, and from 1970 to 1977 Berg was the formal director. Susan Ranney joined the department and the center in 1978, after receiving her doctorate at Wisconsin.

There were a couple of appointments to the CRED staff that didn't work out so well. Montague Yudelman was a dashing person, with valuable experience to offer students, whom Stolper refers to as the "phantom professor." Although he was technically on the staff for several years, he went from one leave to another and never taught a course. Peter Newman, here only two years, left behind a substantial research project on malaria control when he decided not to stay. This was picked up and completed by Robin Barlow, a Michigan Ph.D., who had joined the staff upon completing his degree in 1961 in the field of public finance. But his work on the CRED project brought him into that field as well. He has continued to teach in both fields and became director of CRED in 1977.

The center had always been technically an interdepartmental agency, answerable to the dean of LSA, but its ties were closest to the economics department and during the first half of its life, at least, all economists in the center also held professorial appointments in the department. As it grew, however, the center's research needs exceeded the department's requirements for teaching faculty, so that a number of research associateships were established, along the same lines as the Survey Research Center (SRC). In addition, CRED, like SRC, provides an invaluable research environment for doctoral students.

Money and banking had been a staple in the Michigan curriculum since the turn of the century, but in the late fifties and sixties, under Warren Smith, the traditional approach shifted in emphasis to macroeconomics and stabilization policy. Thus the two people who joined the department in this field in the 1960s were macroeconomists, specializing in money. Ronald Teigen came in 1962, after completing his Ph.D. at MIT, and Robert Holbrook arrived in 1965 with a Berkeley doctorate. A third man in money, Harold Shapiro, joined the department in 1964, but soon thereafter his primary focus shifted to econometrics.

Shapiro had just completed his Ph.D. at Princeton.

> I really came to Michigan working in two areas, econometrics and money and banking. . . . I came here primarily because Warren Smith was here, and only secondarily because Dan Suits and the Quant seminar were located here. But as things developed my interests kind of flip-flopped. . . . I began attending . . . the Friday afternoon seminar that Dan Suits had been giving for many . . . years and became quite intrigued at the idea of macroeconometric model building and forecasting. . . . Before I knew it, in another year and a half or so I was producing the forecasts with Dan . . . in the fall of 1967.[155]

Locke Anderson, who had been working closely with RSQE, was turning his attention to other things at about this time, and so Shapiro, in effect, took over his role. This was also the time when the technology was changing rapidly and the 1967 forecast was the first one that really began to exploit the capacity of the computer, using some of the techniques Shapiro brought back from research experiences elsewhere.

Six months before Harold Shapiro arrived in Ann Arbor Saul Hymans had joined the department, in January of 1964, after completing his Ph.D. at Berkeley in econometrics. He was more interested in theory and formalism than was Suits, the pragmatist, who "had always approached [economics] as a physicist does. . . . I believe theory is something that goes somewhere and does something."[156]

Hymans, on the other hand, believed "from the perspective of [teaching] a fresh graduate student [that] you had to do econometrics by formally writing down what it was you were doing, and deriving what it was you were going to do as a result of that."[157] Yet Hymans was as deeply interested as Suits in the application of econometrics to economic problem solving, and when he returned in 1968 from a stint at the Council of Economic Advisors he got more closely involved with RSQE.

While at the council, Hymans had developed, with Tom Dernburg and David Lusher, a quarterly model of the economy, and he proposed that Michigan shift from the annual to the quarterly basis. Suits resisted. "He had some doubts about how productive that . . . could be, whether the accuracy of the data we had would be sufficient to support quarterly modeling."[158] Shapiro agreed that quarterly modeling was desirable, but he recognized the merit of Suits's arguments as well. As a consequence, in 1968 he worked with Suits to produce the annual model and with Hymans to produce a quarterly model. "We kind of maneuvered both of them around so that they were consistent with each other in . . . a gross way."[159] Both models were presented at the Economic Outlook Conference in 1969, but by 1970 the Michigan Quarterly Econometric Model stood alone. At that time Hymans and Shapiro had become codirectors of RSQE, when Dan Suits resigned from the department to accept an appointment at the University of California at Santa Cruz.

In the 1970s the Quant seminar "moved away from [its] almost exclusive emphasis on macroeconometric forecasting models and began to use one of the semesters in the sequence for . . . general problems in econometrics."[160] At the same time more econometric theory was introduced into the curriculum. Lester Taylor was a member of the faculty from 1968 to 1974. And the arrival in 1973 of E. Philip Howrey and Jan Kmenta (1964 Ph.D.'s from North Carolina and Stanford, respectively, and both at the full professor level) not only enlarged the econometrics faculty, but by the nature of their interests, gave it a more theoretical cast.

In the early 1960s Suits had developed a model of the Michigan economy for use of the state Department of Commerce. Shortly after Hymans and Shapiro took over direction of the Quant seminar the state, and the university itself, requested production of a periodic state forecast, to assist their respective planning efforts. In the summer of 1971 the new codirectors developed a rough working model, primarily as part of a feasibility study. Although it was a crude model of the state, the seminar worked with that model for about a year or two. Then in January of 1974 the president of the university authorized $12,500 a year for up to five years from nongeneral fund sources for construction of a quarterly state of Michigan model. Additional funds were provided to support a dissertation fellowship for Joan Weiss who, expanding on the earlier work, developed a more extensive and refined state econometric model. That was about the time the Michigan House Fiscal Agency came along and offered to finance an ongoing state forecast. The timing was fortuitous because the National Science Foundation, which had succeeded the Ford Foundation in support of RSQE, had decided that the building of econometric models was no longer basic research and declined to renew such grants. The directors were able to convince the state legislature that they couldn't have a decent state forecast without a national model. So between the state and the university the financing of the forecast activity has been assured since 1974. The model and forecast part of RSQE's work now costs about $70,000 a year.

The Economic Outlook Conference underwent some changes during this period too. During the 1950s George Anderson had done the organizing work for it and was "hired" as director. By the early 1970s, however, paid attendance fell from its peak of almost 125 to 49. The educational value of the conference had diminished as econometric model building became more widely used and understood among business and government economists. In 1973 a department committee recommended discontinuance because the benefits to the department and RSQE were less than the opportunity costs. But, under some pressure from the university administration to retain it, modifications of format and the addition of speakers on timely topics in addition to presentation of the national and state forecasts and results of the Survey of Consumer Attitudes have combined to keep the conference viable, self-supporting, and useful to its participants. Attendance is now back up again.

Just as the field of money broadened its scope during this period, so labor economics took on new dimensions under the concept of human capital. John Parker, a Wisconsin Ph.D., was in the department from 1963 to 1967. In 1966 George Johnson came from Berkeley, where he had just completed his doctorate, and Frank Stafford arrived the same year, after completing his graduate studies at Chicago.

The field of industrial organization was deepened with the arrival of William (Geoff) Shepherd from his graduate studies at Yale, in 1963, and Frederic (Mike) Scherer, a Michigan B.A. and Harvard Ph.D., at the associate professor level in 1966. He was here until 1973, replaced in 1974 by William (Jim) Adams, a 1973 Harvard Ph.D. In the meantime Peter Steiner, a 1950 Harvard Ph.D., had joined the department in 1968. Steiner revived a Michigan tradition going back to Henry Carter Adams—connection with the Law School. Adams and Sharfman had both taught courses there. Steiner, who had come onto the faculty with a joint appointment, now worked with his Law School colleagues to establish a joint graduate program in law and economics, which allowed a student, in four to five years' time, to attain the J.D. and the Ph.D. degrees. This program was established in 1970, and has produced eight dual degree holders, with another half-dozen or more still in the pipeline. Moreover, the teaching of economics in the Law School has expanded, with Jim Adams and Daniel Rubinfeld now holding part-time appointments there as well.

Dick Musgrave's departure in 1959 and Harvey Brazer's two years in Washington left public finance extremely short-handed. Robin Barlow completed his degree at Michigan in 1961 and joined the staff that year. William Neenan, also a Michigan doctorate in 1966, came in on a joint appointment with the School of Social Work in 1967.

One new field was introduced during the 1960s. Paul Demeny came in 1966 to launch the program in economic demography under a National Institutes of Health grant for traineeships. He remained only three years. In the meanwhile Eva Mueller's interests had shifted strongly to this area, in conjunction with her work in development and Southeast Asia. Deborah Freedman joined the staff in 1968, after

completing her degree here in this field. George Simmons was in the
department from 1969–74, and Ronald Lee was here from 1970–79.
There are close associations between this program and the Population
Studies center, where graduate students in the field conduct their
dissertation research.

As the department moved into the 1960s its greatest weakness
was in theory. In macro theory Ackley was gone through most of the
decade and the burden fell on Locke Anderson, with Smith, Teigen,
and later Holbrook handling the monetary and stabilization aspects.
Micro theory was in even worse shape because Boulding's newer interests frequently took him away from campus. John Cross, a 1964
Princeton Ph.D., joined the department in 1965, and Sidney Winter
was here from 1968–76. But real faculty depth in this field was not
achieved until the 1970s, after Theodore Bergstrom, Stanford 1967,
and Hal Varian, Berkeley 1973, came in as full professors in 1975 and
1977, respectively. John Laitner also came in 1975, after completing
his work at Harvard, and Lawrence Blume in 1977 when he attained
his Ph.D. at Berkeley. In 1979 Glenn Loury, a 1976 MIT Ph.D.,
joined the department at the associate professor level. Carl Simon
moved over half-time from the mathematics department in 1977. Thus
the department is currently stronger in theory than at any other time
in its history.

When the decade opened the principles course, which accounted
for the lion's share of enrollments, had a problem. Since the late 1950s
Shorey Peterson had wanted to be relieved from responsibility for it,
in order to devote his time to the honors program and his advanced
courses. One reason for difficulty in finding a replacement was that
the course, as taught in the Peterson style, required a time and effort commitment to teaching which the academic world of the mid-
twentieth century did not value as highly as it did research and publishing. The emphasis in this department, as in every other, had shifted
strongly, with respect to hiring, promotion, and salary increases, from
the teaching function to research productivity. Principles, as traditionally taught at Michigan, was too demanding to be compatible with
the other career interests of most faculty, although there has always
been virtually unanimous agreement that principles is the most important course of all.

When Daniel Fusfeld, a 1953 Columbia Ph.D., came into the
department in 1960 he agreed to assume responsibility for the course.

Economics Building as the Chemical Laboratory, ca. 1874

Pharmacology wing of the Economics Building, 1950

Economics Building in 1979

Henry Carter Adams, ca. 1888

David Friday, ca. 1918

I. Leo Sharfman, ca. 1918

William A. Paton, ca. 1918

Fred Manville Taylor, chairman, 1921–24

Edmund Ezra Day, chairman, 1924–28

Howard S. Ellis, ca. 1925

Z. Clark Dickinson, ca. 1925

I. Leo Sharfman,
chairman, 1928–54

Leonard L. Watkins, William B. Palmer,
George R. Anderson, 1938

Teaching fellows, 1939. *Left to right:* Judd Polk,
George Anderson, Clay Anderson, Gardner
Patterson, Marshall Colberg, Floyd Bond,
Dean Bowman.

Kenneth Boulding lecturing in room 101, ca. 1950

Shorey Peterson, acting chairman in various years, 1930s through 1950s

George Katona, 1951

Lawrence Klein, ca. 1952

Gardner Ackley, chairman, 1954–61

Harold M. Levinson, acting chairman, 1961–62

William Haber, chairman, 1962–63

Warren L. Smith, chairman, 1963–67, 1970–71

Harvey E. Brazer, chairman, 1967–70

Peter O. Steiner, chairman, 1971–74

Harold T. Shapiro, chairman, 1974–77

Saul H. Hymans, chairman, 1977–80

I. Leo Sharfman retirement dinner, January, 1954. *Left to right:*
Z. Clark Dickinson, William Paton, Kenneth Boulding (partially
hidden), Minnie Sharfman, Leo Sharfman.

Shorey Peterson retirement dinner, April 15, 1967: the head table.
Left to right: Warren Smith, Mrs. Ben Lewis, Shorey Peterson,
Leo Sharfman, Eleanor Peterson.

William Haber retirement dinner, April 4, 1968: the head table.
Left to right: Mary Palmer, William Palmer, Fannie Haber,
William Haber, Marjorie Brazer, Harvey Brazer.

But Fusfeld's style was much looser and did not perpetuate the Taylor-Peterson tradition. He adopted a different stance toward the teaching fellows than had his predecessors at Michigan. By sharing the course with them, rather than supervising all its details, he was able to manage it with a less consuming time commitment.

> My position has always been that these people are instructors in the department, and . . . that I have to treat them as I would a full professor colleague, who might be teaching a section of that course. It's theirs to develop within the framework of the things that the department needs to have done with that course, which are laid out very clearly [in conference] at the beginning. . . . We sort of have a social contract that they've taken the job of teaching assistant, these are the things that they're expected to do, and now go ahead and do it. . . . So I give them a lot of flexibility.[161]

The teaching fellows could change the order of topics, emphasize mathematics, teach the course from any ideological perspective they wish, so long as the "students are prepared to take the midterm exam and the final." The examinations are common, drawn up by a committee of teaching assistants, and given final approval by Fusfeld.

On one occasion when Dan Fusfeld went on leave Harold Levinson took over for him. An admirer of the Peterson model, who believes that "the teaching of principles is a crucially important function, [he] tried very hard to . . . go back to the old system. . . . I had eighteen teaching fellows, I remember. . . . But . . . there was just no way. I had to compromise on what I thought ought to be done."[162] As a consequence of differences in approach among faculty members, and of various committee studies, lengthy debates, and curricular decisions taken by the department, principles has since the early 1970s been taught in two formats. In one case, there is a big lecture addressed to 500 or 600 students once a week by a senior faculty member, usually Fusfeld, and teaching fellows take three discussion sessions per week. In the other model, the senior faculty member lectures three times a week to a smaller group, about 160, which then breaks up into discussion sections to meet with teaching fellows once a week.

To help carry the immense burden of teaching principles to mushrooming numbers of undergraduates during the 1960s, former Michigan graduate students Mary Alice Shulman and Helen Crafton joined the department as lecturers, in 1962 and 1967, respectively. Mrs. Shulman left in 1975 and Ann Anderson, who had earned her doctorate here in 1974, joined the staff in 1977. These people might teach the principles course under either format, depending primarily on the availability of teaching fellows in any given year.

Almost all of the recruitment we have discussed took place under five chairmanships from 1961 to 1974. At the close of Levinson's one-year term, Bill Haber accepted the post. He had barely warmed the office chair when he was appointed dean of the College of Literature, Science, and the Arts in 1963. The department choice was then Warren Smith, who served from 1963–67 and 1970–71. His first term was followed by Harvey Brazer, who elected to reduce the term to three years with a presumption of no succession, where it has remained since then. Peter Steiner was chairman from 1971–74. Each of these men conducted department affairs in a different style, but all agreed that the most important function of the chairman was the strengthening of the department through effective faculty recruitment and carefully orchestrated salary adjustments. They continued the same basic form of department organization, although under Brazer brown bag lunches in room 301 were substituted for the more formal Union luncheons—a sign of the elaborately informal times during which he served.

While appointment to the chairmanship was considered an honor, in that it signified the trust and respect of one's colleagues, it no longer represented the level of academic aspiration that it had in pre–World War II days. Rather, it has come to be viewed as an honorific obligation, to be fulfilled for the benefit of the institution, usually at considerable sacrifice to the incumbent's research career. Therefore, a term specific was an inducement to acceptance of the responsibility. Another incentive was having some power to exercise. One might say there has been a consensus among chairmen since Sharfman's day that the introduction of more formalized democratic procedures has assisted the chairman in performing his functions rather than serving to reduce his power.

We have a situation that I've described as serial autocracy, the three year rotating chairman. The chairman has a great deal of power. Not that things don't get voted on, but the chairman controls the agenda. . . . It's on the personnel side, both in terms of who you hire and who you let go, and how you reward people and motivate them [that] is the main thing a chairman does.[163]

Interestingly . . . despite the short tenure of the chairman, we have retained the tradition that the chairman controls the budget. The chairman decides how to allocate among members of the department funds available for salary increase . . . and he does this unilaterally, in cahoots, of course, with the dean's office. . . . The power of the chairman . . . is enhanced by his access to the dean. . . . If [the dean's] going to solve the problem of keeping chairmanships filled, [he] has to have a good relationship with the chairmen . . . and . . . one way in which he maintains a good relationship . . . is by supporting the chairman in his requests or demands as nearly as he possibly can. . . . While there is often dissatisfaction with the [salary] decision of any particular chairman one always has the consolation of knowing that it can't go on for more than three years before someone else will be making the decisions. And, of course, what often happens is that an incoming chairmen views the salary sheet with some dismay, arguing that his predecessor has made substantial errors of judgment. And he proceeds . . . to make corrections. . . . It means that over a period of five or ten years in an individual's career there will have been two or three opportunities for adjustment if he should have been treated unfairly by any one chairman.[164]

In the crucial matters of appointment and promotion, however, the entire department is involved. Prospects for appointment at tenure ranks had long been invited to address the Economics Club, in order to allow the entire group to form a judgment and then discuss it in a department meeting, before the chairman opened negotiations. Nontenured assistant professors were traditionally hired much more informally, however. They might address a seminar, after which the chairman would poll the attending faculty informally, and make the offer or not according to the degree of enthusiasm he found. In the late sixties a new member of the executive committee took exception to this procedure, and for several years these appointments were debated by that body. Somewhat later, and currently, appointments at all ranks came to be debated in full department meeting. This change in procedure recognizes that an initial three-year appointment can be just as critical as a tenured one, because when that individual comes up for promotion he may have made a place for himself among his colleagues that makes it difficult to refuse tenure on hard-nosed academic grounds.

About 1967 the practice was begun of appointing an ad hoc committee to consider the work of each candidate for promotion, two members in the field and one outside. Their report is presented to the senior faculty for discussion. After full debate a "significant minority" vote opposed to the promotion is sufficient to block it. Nevertheless, the chairman retains considerable power, for he is the one to decide what proportion constitutes a "significant minority." Even when there is little or no opposition by the group,

> the chairman is in an excellent position to control that issue because it's the chairman's obligation to draft the statement . . . that goes to the dean. And obviously a promotion will or will not go through, in large part, depending upon the strength and content of the chairman's statement . . . doing the best he can in good conscience.[165]

This question came to a head during Peter Steiner's administration, 1971–74.

> I was chairman at . . . a turning point in time . . . in the sense that we were just ending the period of rapid expansion. . . . One of the traditions that Michigan has had as a wonderful place to be is because it hired good people, and it was very nice to them, and it tended to be very humane and to, by and large, promote people if they met threshold standards. . . . It was right in the middle of my chairmanship that the issue came up as to whether we could afford to do that. . . . We were pretty much against . . . a budget constraint that would mean we were going to have very few new positions in the future. . . . As my colleagues looked at the situation they saw pretty much the same picture, and decided that they would have to take a tougher attitude on the promotions of the then junior people than they had taken in the past. . . . And we had what is known in the department as Bloody Saturday, on which we made a decision to let seven people go on the same day. One of my least pleasant moments as chairman was to tell them all.[166]

As department life became more complex with the faculty/student growth of this period, and as an enormous amount of time was required for personnel decisions, the administrative structure of the department expanded to meet these needs. In 1963, the same year the university moved to a trimester time schedule, the post of associate chairman was established, with Bill Palmer as its first incumbent. That job, too, now rotates for three years, with a reduction in teaching load. The keeping of formal minutes of executive committee and department meetings was also begun in this period, and the secretarial staff was enlarged. In February of 1963, Evelyn Uhlendorf retired. She had already acquired a couple of stenographers to assist her, and by the fall of 1963 a room was set aside for a stenographic pool of three. Another was added in the spring of 1964, but by 1969 the pool idea had been abandoned in favor in individual assignments, three to eight faculty members to a secretary, depending on their work loads. In the spring of 1973 Donna Henderson became administrative assistant, and by the following fall there were ten secretaries in the department.

While each of the chairmen of this period had his own style of running the department, they all confronted, in greater or lesser degree, the academic turmoil for which the sixties is remembered. The problems they faced were unfamiliar; there was no precedent for coping. Student activism was actually a world-wide phenomenon, which began in the early 1960s and gathered momentum as additional public controversies heated up. Its strength varied from campus to campus, but it was at Michigan that the most widely known organization, Students for a Democratic Society (SDS), was founded in 1961. Among the early leaders of that group were economics graduate students, including Sander Kelman, Howard Wachtel, and Michael Zweig, who now teach economics at Cornell, American University, and Stonybrook, respectively. Alan Haber, another leader, was not a student in economics, but he had filial links to the department.

The Port Huron Statement, which set forth the purposes of SDS, declared the principle of participatory democracy, and identified the links between the civil rights movement, the antiwar movement, and the antinuclear movement, a coalition of interests that had inspired the organization's founding. The local chapter, one of the largest in the nation, numbering 400–500 at its peak, was called Voice Political

Party (Voice), and played an active role in local campus and community affairs as well as the national movements.

By the middle 1960s Voice was involved at the local level in students' rights, welfare rights, a student employees' union, and so on. But by then the war in Vietnam was beginning to overshadow all other issues in the passionate feelings it aroused. The nation's first teach-in against the war opened on the campus right outside the Economics Building. The teach-in, as well as the many demonstrations both local and in Washington, involved groups and unaffiliated individuals far beyond SDS and the student body. Antidraft feeling ran high in the community as well, but the occupation of the ROTC (Reserve Officers Training Corp) building, in protest of the university's cooperation, was led by economics graduate student Barry Bluestone, an active member of Voice and SDS.

The draft issue took on more sinister implications at the university than the presence of ROTC. When the law was amended to condition deferments for college students upon grades and class standing, a wholly irrelevant criterion for academic achievement was imposed on the university. Some of the economist leaders of SDS were also among the better graduate students in the department, and many of them were teaching fellows. "A group of them got together and decided that they would not turn in their final grades, because those grades would be used as part of the draft process, and they did not want to participate in anything to do with carrying on the war in Vietnam." Although Dan Fusfeld did not agree with their strategy,

> and I told them that, . . . we spent our weekly staff sessions for about six weeks discussing that issue. . . . Well, as soon as the graduate students announced . . . their intention there was a tremendous uproar among the faculty in the economics department. We had one full faculty meeting that was devoted to nothing but a discussion of that. Proposals were made to take away the teaching fellowships . . . to seize their grade books . . . [for] faculty to grade the exams. Meanwhile . . . my position was nobody's done anything yet. All we've done is talk.[167]

Fusfeld's relaxed style and infinite patience with teaching fellows was well suited to the period. He debated with them the consequences for the students involved if they were deprived of grades on their transcripts, the issues of academic freedom and the intervention of politics in the classroom.

> The day before the final exam, I come home after . . . a full day meeting with the teaching assistants . . . and I'm terribly discouraged because they're adamant. . . . Then about ten o'clock that night the doorbell rings. There are four of the teaching assistants, the leaders of the group, with a big bottle of champagne, and as I open the door they hold up the bottle of champagne and say, "We've decided to turn in our grades." . . . What a relief![168]

One of the antiwar organizations, the New Mobilization Committee, called for a university strike against the war in Vietnam on Moratorium Day, October 15, 1969. Support for this antiwar effort was so widespread that Vice President Allan Smith circulated a memo to deans and department chairmen stating that the university had no policy on the cancellation of classes, but left to individual faculty member's discretion the question of whether to reschedule their classes or hold a substitute event in order to participate in some appropriate way. The Department of Economics decided at its October 7 meeting to offer a two-part "Symposium of the Economics of Vietnam and the Military-Industrial Complex" in room 101 on the afternoon of the strike day. Part 1 was a presentation by Professor Sidney Winter and graduate student Richard England, with graduate student Darius Gaskins as commentator. Part 2 presented a panel of professors Mike Scherer and Daniel Fusfeld, and graduate student Barry Bluestone (now a professor at Boston College), with graduate student Irwin Garfinkel (now teaching at Wisconsin) as discussant.

The students who were politically active through SDS also sought answers to their social concerns through their intellectual life and their study of economics. But

> many of us who were graduate students in economics . . . felt that increasingly the economics profession, as it was being taught not only at the University of Michigan but everywhere else, was out of touch with the real world. It had nothing to do with Marxism versus neoclassical theory. It had to do with the fact that neoclassical theory did not seem to be able to give any decent answers to questions about racism, imperialism, the kinds of

issues that we'd been involved in in the student movement during most of the 1960s.[169]

And so a group of Michigan graduate students—Michael Zweig, Howard Wachtel, John Weeks, Sander Kelman, Barry Bluestone, Eric Chester, and others—organized the Union for Radical Political Economics (URPE). They called friends at a few other universities and held their first meeting in Ann Arbor in August of 1968.

> URPE was bred out of a frustration with a profession that seemed to be mired in neoclassical thought, and unable to deal with what we felt were the pressing issues of the day. URPE was therefore established to try and . . . use our economics tools to attack some of those issues in a new way. . . . It had very few members who would be considered Marxists. It really wasn't until almost the mid-1970s that . . . people began to turn to Marxism and to study it rigorously. . . . During all the sixties there was very, very little understanding of Marxism or Marxist thought.[170]

The initial meeting of about a dozen people decided to sponsor a conference at the December meetings of the American Economic Association, to see if there was enough national interest to start a new organization. But that was the summer of the disastrous Democratic convention in Chicago, and the association was severely split over the question of boycotting that city for its planned December meetings. Kenneth Boulding was president that year (he had just left Michigan); he and the other leaders declined to move the convention. A group led by Larry Klein arranged alternative meetings in Philadelphia. It was there that URPE organized a session, sending advance notices to schools around the country. To the amazement of the founders about 300 people showed up, and the new organization was launched on the national scene.

Their interest in alternative approaches to the study of economics led these students to push for a new course in the curriculum. At a department meeting in December of 1969, Economics 205, titled "Topics in Political Economics," was approved on a trial basis, to be taught by graduate student Paul Gingrich, then evaluated by the Undergraduate Curriculum Committee. A year later a joint memorandum from the Graduate and Undergraduate Curriculum committees implied not only approval of the experiment, but proposed a joint course with political science, establishment of Economics 558 on Marxian and neo-Marxian economics, and hiring of a new staff member with alternative approaches to economics to offer an 800-level seminar. Meanwhile Dan Fusfeld and Locke Anderson, the members of the department most interested in exploring these new approaches, were including some of this material in their courses and have continued to teach in this area. In 1972, Thomas Weisskopf, a 1966 MIT Ph.D., joined the department at the associate professor level to teach political economy, which in the spring of 1973 was recognized as a doctoral field with the addition of two 600-level courses. This whole course of events raised considerable controversy in the department, and the debates in curriculum committees, in executive committee, and in department meetings were long and sometimes impassioned. But when it was over, as has been traditional in the department, no acrimony was perpetuated into other affairs.

While the student movement was most conspicuous in the arena of national issues, on campus it focused with greatest tenacity on the demand for student participation at all levels of university affairs. Economists were well represented at the higher levels of university governance called upon to deal with these matters, with Bill Haber serving as dean of the college 1963–68 and Jim Morgan as chairman of SACUA 1965–66. On November 19, 1965, the executive committee of the department met with a group of graduate students, under the leadership of Michael Zweig, to explore the opening of channels. They wanted to be involved in decisions directly affecting graduate training, like degree requirements, prelims, etc. The faculty were receptive in varying degrees to some measure of student participation in department affairs, and for the next several years different models were tried on an informal basis—primarily observer status for students in certain meetings, and parallel student committees to serve as counterparts to major faculty standing committees.

In April, 1969, the department directed Chairman Brazer to appoint a committee of four faculty members, two undergraduates, and two graduate students to consider methods of student participation. That group reported in September, recommending equal representation of students and faculty members on those standing committees concerned with the educational program and its environment, such as the graduate and undergraduate curriculum committees. Operating committees, such as graduate student placement, fellowships and admissions, and faculty recruitment, should consist entirely of faculty members, but with a means of registering student reactions to visitors who are staff prospects. The presidents of the Graduate Economics Society (reactivated about 1966) and the undergraduate student association (newly formed) should be appointed as voting members of the executive committee, although excluded from participation when delicate personnel matters are on the agenda. Two graduate and two undergraduate students should attend department meetings as voting members, except where an individual student is being evaluated, honors and awards are being selected, or sensitive personnel matters are being decided; in the last case the students should have the opportunity to present their views before leaving the meeting. The report further stated that the recommendations were predicated upon the belief that the positive benefits accruing to the department from greater student participation would be greater success in implementing policies which have had the benefit of student input, and enhancement of a sense of community in the department as a whole. The report also recognized that a prerequisite to implementation of its recommendations was the existence of democratic and informed student organizations to select representatives. This "Report of the Committee on the Role of Students in Economics Department Decision Making" was endorsed by the full department, faculty and students, and has functioned as the department "constitution" ever since.

Nor were the students alone in requesting an opening of department channels for decision making. In September of 1968 the department voted a requirement that one of the three members of the executive committee be a nontenured member of the faculty, and in November of 1971 they passed a resolution that two teaching fellows, nominated from the membership of a new teaching fellows' organization, participate in department meetings without vote.

This whole series of actions was codified in the 1971 report of a faculty committee on governance, which defined the economics department as "the total educational community directly concerned with the study and teaching of economics, including the senior faculty, graduate students and undergraduates."[171] The duties and responsibilities of department officials and committees were spelled out, and quorums were defined. In the seventeen years since Leo Sharfman's retirement, department governance had come a long way. But even the two major detailed committee reports didn't resolve all student participation issues. New questions arose, were debated at length, and ultimately resolved for several years into the seventies.

While the radical students were seeking access to university governance, the black students were seeking access to the system. The university in general, and the economics department in particular, had sought to increase black enrollments and recruit black faculty, but with little conspicuous success. The department had produced one black Ph.D., in 1962; a second would obtain his degree in 1976; they were not successful in recruiting a black faculty member until 1979. Nor have many black undergraduates elected to major in economics. In the spirit of demanding and demonstrating times, however, the black students of 1970 organized the Black Action Movement (BAM) and called a strike in the spring of that year to call attention to the issues of increasing black enrollments at the university and creating a more hospitable environment here for black students. As with the radical students their ultimate goals were admirable, but their methods portended violence. The Black Action Movement stated its objectives as a set of nonnegotiable demands for black quotas among students, faculty, and administrators, as well as other amenities and perquisites, called for a university-wide strike against classes to continue until their demands were met, demanded amnesty in advance for all strikers, and intimated violence, even if they did not intend it.

> Most of us, I think, were in favor of some kind of negotiation, some kind of settlement. Most of us regretted that it took this kind of action to get us to move. . . . [But] the Black Action Movement was unfortunate . . . in that it involved what I regarded at the time as extortion. . . . Here we were in this little Economics Building, I sitting in my chairman's office, thinking as the young men in black skin with lead pipes, in number perhaps sixty to eighty, entered the building, . . . "well, everyone can leave by the fire escape or the back door except me. I have to stay." It was a frightening experience.[172]

The economics department had not canceled classes, as the strike call had demanded, and the BAM students occupied the building for the express purpose of disrupting those classes. Their major tool for the purpose was trash can lids, which they banged with sticks and pipes to make an intolerable racket in the old building, which reverberated in the best of circumstances to the march of tramping feet and the echo of voices at class changes. Economics was fortunate in that there was little actual destruction of property beyond a couple of broken chairs. Chemistry fared worse, for example, with a badly "trashed" lab. But the presence of this large crowd, and the fierce aspect they presented, was intimidating to the coolest of faculty members. Dan Fusfeld recalls an episode that occurred on his way to the department meeting at which the BAM demands were to be discussed.

> As I came up from my basement office . . . I saw the following layout . . . in the lobby. . . . A group of faculty members were standing by the bulletin board on the right-hand side of the lobby as you walk up those stairs from the basement. The meeting was being held in the department offices, [then] over on the left-hand side of the lobby. . . . Standing at the entrance to the department office was a great big black student carrying a club, an axe handle, with a grim look on his face . . . and there were others . . . loitering around the door. . . . I figured, "What the hell. These guys are afraid of nothing," so I walked over to the student and I said to him, "You don't intend to use that club, do you?" And he said, in a very mild voice, "No sir." So I said to him, "Well, why don't you go outside with it and wait so that the people will feel free to enter the meeting." And he said, "Yes sir," and he walked out the front door. . . . My feeling was that they were more interested in giving the appearance of fierceness than in being fierce. And, hell, this was a seventeen- or eighteen-year-old kid, and he wasn't going to hit a fifty-year-old man over the head with a club who comes up and talks to him in a gentle voice. But that gives you some idea of the kinds of tensions.[173]

In an effort to reach some satisfactory settlement of the immediate crisis, Rufus Brown was invited to present the BAM position at the meeting. All male BAM students, when asked, were named Rufus Brown. After lengthy discussion "The department agreed—the department agreed! Here we were sitting under seige, and we agreed that in some reasonable way their demands should be met."[174] The faculty also passed a motion that "Classes will not be held in the Economics Building until the Department determines that conditions are conducive to teaching and learning."[175] The vote was twenty-two to two, with one abstention. Five days later, the department passed a motion that conditions were now conducive.

As an outcome of that meeting thirty-one members of the economics faculty signed a memo to the regents urging resumption of "full and reasoned discussion with members of the Black Action Movement and other concerned members of the University community. Furthermore, we are anxious to discuss the role we can play in increasing the resources available for minority education."[176]

This period is remembered as a time of strenuous contention between students and faculty, one which emphasized the generation gap and displayed defiance of "the establishment," from the trivialities of hair and dress to the cosmic issues of nuclear holocaust. But by and large, the economics faculty was sympathetic to the ideals and objectives of the students, if not all their methods. In December of 1966, forty-five faculty members signed a letter to the *Michigan Daily* opposing the compiling of class ranks for the use of the Selective Service System. And, while the department did not officially boycott the Chicago AEA meetings of 1968, it did resolve only to "window shop" for faculty at Chicago, but to do its buying and selling (recruitment and placement) at the alternative meetings in Philadelphia. Most students were appropriately respectful of faculty views, even when they disagreed. Although the economics department was, in important ways, a center and leader of radical activity at Michigan, there were no mindless or violent confrontations. Anger perhaps, but expressed within the context of intellectual debate. Once again, in a time of crisis, the department, students and faculty, acquitted itself well.

> I think there were probably several times when a number of us were on the verge of being kicked out of school that Harvey came to support us, and did what was necessary to solve the situation. ... There was a general feeling that, indeed, we weren't all crazy, that some of the work we would do would eventually be useful. ... I'm not sure we would have found that same kind of support on other campuses, where I think there would have ... been almost a total revulsion of the kind of thing that we were trying to do. ... I always felt that I was very fairly treated by the economics department and that it was a supportive environment, even though I was marching, perhaps, to a different drummer. ... The preconditions for a radical political economics came

because of what the University of Michigan was. The incubation
for that came from what the economics department was. It gave
us the room and the space to develop our ideas.[177]

Unlike the gradual enlargement of the 1950s, the hectic growth
of the 1960s, which saw as many as seven or eight new faculty members come in in a year, didn't permit easy absorption of these people
into the social fabric of the department. Warren and Ann Smith were
very conscious of this, and they began the annual faculty cocktail party
in the fall, to introduce new members and to bring old friends together
to start the season. They lived near the stadium and often had department people in for drinks after the football games. A block of seats,
purchased every year by a large contingent of the economics department, fostered closeness—physical as well as spiritual.
Ann Smith, as the chairman's wife, assumed a special role.

I thought it important to welcome new faculty and staff and their
wives. And so I tried to get together with the wife, usually, and
take her to the Farmer's Market, and show her around town, and
see that she had maps and things like that. . . . I tried to remember Christmas and birthdays . . . I remember I had the secretary
check on all the children's birthdays and their names, so that
when I talked to the faculty wives I'd get the right name and the
right age. At my telephone I had a list with the children's names
and their sex.[178]

The Smiths and the Brazers also held receptions in their homes
for graduate students, directed especially toward integrating new ones.
Attendance might run one-third to one-half, perhaps because of the
alienation many students felt from the older generation, but for those
who attended it established a tradition, and the more informal picnics
in the park, fall and spring, continued during these years.
If this period of political and organizational tension was not
trying enough, for a time personal tragedy stalked the economics department. An uncanny number of untimely deaths occurred in the
five years from 1967 to 1972. John Parker, thirty-three years old, universally well-liked, an economist of promise, was stricken with mel-
anoma in the spring of 1967 and was gone before Christmas. An
equally promising young man, Joseph Mooney, was hired to replace
him in the field of human capital, and within six months of his arrival

at Michigan in the fall of 1968 he, too, died of cancer. In June of 1970, genial, soft-spoken Arthur Ross, who had come to Michigan as a vice-president and economics professor in 1968, for reasons known to himself wearied of life and took his exit.

Nineteen-seventy was a year of department chairman turnover, and the popular appointment to succeed Harvey Brazer was John Lansing. Before he could assume his office, Lansing was stricken with a malignant brain tumor and died within three months. Warren Smith quickly volunteered to fill the breach, because he felt that he owed the department a year, having served for only four rather than five years of his earlier term. Less than a year after he had fulfilled this service Warren Smith, too, was gone. In an almost poetic circumstance, just as this superb teacher was completing his lecture on the very last day of class, in April of 1972, he collapsed with a massive brain hemorrhage and died a few days later.

> Warren's death was really a major blow. . . . In many ways Warren represented a focus around whom the department rotated intellectually. . . . And I think he provided a certain degree of . . . cohesiveness. It's very difficult to explain, but somehow or other he was at the center of intellectual activity. . . . We all felt . . . that . . . he gave us intellectual support and intellectual feedback and that kind of thing. . . . I have the feeling that when Warren died something a lot more than Warren went with him.[179]

The grim fate that seemed to overhang the economics department during these years extended even to the families. The Barlows and the Levinsons each lost a precious daughter, one aged four, the other aged nineteen, and Wolf Stolper's beloved wife, Vögi, passed away. By another twist of fate, one new member of the staff appointed in the year the tragedies began, 1967, was an ordained priest. Bill Neenan's warmth and understanding suited him well to that calling, and the department found it had much need of him beyond the classroom, as its chaplain in residence.

In the midst of the stress of student activism, and before the time of sadness set in, there were occasions to celebrate. In 1963 Kenneth Boulding received a university Distinguished Faculty Achievement Award; George Katona was a 1967 recipient. Meanwhile, in 1964, Joseph A. Livingston, 1929 baccalaureate, was awarded an Outstanding Achievement Award for alumni, as was Edward L. Cushman, class of 1937, in 1966. In 1966 Gardner Ackley gave the university's commencement address; on his return to the university in 1969 he was named Henry Carter Adams University Professor.

In addition to honors such as these, two memorable department events reinforced the sense of family once more. The first was the retirement dinner for Shorey Peterson. The planning for it began early because it was to be a surprise for the guest of honor, though Eleanor, his wife, was brought into the plot. The dinner, held at the Union on April 15, 1967, was preceded by a cocktail party at Bill and Fannie Haber's. Since there was nothing unusual in that, it was easy to steer an unsuspecting honoree to the ready-made party. What may have been an even bigger surprise was the number of former students and teaching fellows who assembled in Ann Arbor to pay tribute to the man who had taught them so much, of humanity as of economics. It was hard to keep the after dinner speaker's list to six. The testimonial letters from all those unable to attend were bound in a special book.

A year later the department was at it again. For Bill Haber a completely different sort of program. No speeches. Rather, a presentation to a man of far-flung interests and activities, the university's resident humorist, of a "This is Your Life" recapitulation in multimedia format. A slide show, opening with little Bill Haber hawking newspapers on the streets of Milwaukee at the age of ten, was accompanied by running patter from Dan Fusfeld, interrupted at strategic moments with a return engagement of those musical talents of the fifties, Levinson, Suits, and Stolper, joined this year by John Cross, performing unauthorized versions of selections from *Fiddler on the Roof*. These entertainments were undertaken only after ingestion of a substantial dinner, of course, at the Washtenaw Country Club (one could not yet serve wine at the Michigan Union), which, in turn, had been preceded by a cocktail party at Bill and Mary Palmer's.

In that same year of 1968, Bob Ford retired and Kenneth Boulding resigned to accept an appointment at the University of Colorado. In September of 1969, word came from Washington of the passing of Leo Sharfman on the ninth. Clark Dickinson died in 1966, and in 1972 news came of Carl Remer's death in California. Thus the 1960s closed, as had the 1920s and the 1950s, with the departure of a number of the old-timers. Peterson and Haber would not depart very far, and continued to be active participants in the life of the department. The irrepressible Bill Haber, in fact, merely shifted gears to become advisor to the executive officers of the university, and in the mid-seventies returned to teach a special course in the Residential College.

Yesterday, 1974–80

If the 1960s was a period of expansion and excitement, the 1970s might be described as a time of consolidation. Enrollments declined from 1968 to 1973, easing the pressures from that direction, although since the mid-seventies undergraduate numbers have climbed back up again well beyond earlier expectations. There were a few left-over burning issues in the early seventies that the department grappled with. The Economics Teaching Fellows Association, under the leadership of Everett Ehrlich, in the fall of 1972 asked for greater participation of teaching fellows in the definition of core material in the principles course, selection of texts, and so on. This was denied, as being beyond the rights and responsibilities of teaching fellows defined the previous spring.

The problem of minority affairs was less readily dealt with. In settling the BAM strike the regents committed the university to a target of 10 percent black enrollment by 1973–74, coupled with provisions for financial aid, more vigorous recruitment, and so on. The economics department took the effort seriously, although people were dubious about whether the target figure was realistic. Especially in economics, where a strong mathematical background was rapidly becoming critical to success at the undergraduate as well as the graduate level, the pool of adequately prepared minority students was small indeed. Moreover, tutorial arrangements the department set up were not judged very successful, largely because of nonattendance. Nevertheless, at its meeting in December, 1972, the department passed an affirmative action resolution with respect to admissions and fellowships that recognized the "strong bias against minority-group applicants that may be inherent in most formal measures of ability or past performance,"[180] and incorporated the use of additional kinds of information in making these decisions.

Decision on an affirmative action program for women was postponed, although the sense of the meeting asserted that an effort should be made to increase that pool, as well, and adopt an explicit admissions policy that would enhance the probability of larger female enrollments. Actually, Michigan had a better record than most economics departments in the training of women, at least since the mid-1950s.

Leo Sharfman had discouraged them from going on to graduate study. One, who did anyway, was advised, gently, by Sharfman that " 'We do not encourage women. You will not find this a field receptive to women.' I was flabbergasted, not offended, [but] I never felt unfairly treated in the department."[181] There was always a sprinkling of female undergraduate majors, and the first Ph.D. awarded to a woman came in 1922, the second in 1930, and the third in 1953. A letter from the last named credits Harold Levinson with "tempting me to switch my major to economics in Graduate School. . . . The professors were very kind and helpful. . . . It was a shock to me later when I experienced discrimination because of being a woman. I had not felt any at Michigan."[182]

Over the next decade five women earned the doctorate, then the pace stepped up rapidly. From 1966–73 sixteen Ph.D.'s were awarded to women. Nineteen sixty-eight was the unique year of the Gails. All three of those who received the degree that year were named Gail, each was an outstanding student, and each went on to a rewarding career: Gail Cook to teach at the University of Toronto, and later to be the first woman to serve on the board of directors of a Canadian chartered bank; Gail Pierson to become the first female economics professor at Harvard; and Gail Wilensky to a number of government appointments, mainly in the Department of Health, Education, and Welfare. In the six years 1974–79 another fourteen Ph.D.'s were earned by women. And the Michigan economics department has managed to have at least one woman on the senior faculty almost every year since 1924.

Student life calmed down by the mid-seventies and became depoliticized in favor of academic pursuits, but economics students continued to take seriously their participation in department affairs. Representation on department committees gave the student body an important reason for organizing themselves, but the undergraduates had a hard time maintaining continuity. The present Michigan Economics Society (MES) dates from about 1975, but has had a conspicuous program only since the 1978–79 year. An office in the basement of the Economics Building has given them a place to meet and exchange messages; they hold weekly meetings in room 301, the student lounge; publish a monthly newsletter; numerous fundraising sales and social events through the year have enabled them to sponsor speakers; and they offer a tutorial service to their fellow students. At a wine and cheese party each semester unaffiliated economics students are encouraged to join, and as the number of concentrators has increased, so has the membership in MES, to a 1979 level of about 130.

In 1973 the then Michigan Undergraduate Economics Association requested help from the executive committee in sponsoring a journal, but the venture was not much of a success. The idea was revived several years later, however, and the first issue of the *Michigan Journal of Economics* came off the duplicating machine in April of 1979. The editorial board of six student editors, which is not connected with MES, has in mind an interdisciplinary journal, with the major focus on economics, that would allow students to submit papers they have written for courses in history, philosophy, and the like. The ten faculty advisors come from several social science departments. Forty submissions were received for the spring 1980 issue, of which six were selected after a screening by the student editors and review by the faculty advisors for major errors. The student editors work with the authors through a revision process, in an effort to publish work of truly high quality. With budget support from Michigan Student Assembly, LSA, business administration, and the vice president for academic affairs, the journal has a print run of 1,500, of which 300 go to libraries, and the remainder are distributed free in the associated departments.

The Graduate Economics Society has, likewise, had a history of intermittence, with more formalized continuity dating from the 1971 department "constitution." An annual meeting selects the delegate to the department meetings and the representatives to the committees to which they are entitled. The president is automatically a member of the department executive committee. Otherwise the society meetings are held in response to particular issues that arise. It does sponsor social events, however, primarily as a means of integrating new students. This function is especially active in summer, with two picnics, distribution of information packets, and orientation meetings. Second-year students tend to be most active; once graduate students have completed their course work they tend to interact less with their fellow students beyond personal friendships.

The late 1960s and early 1970s were years marked by frequent, spirited, and lengthy department meetings. Not only were there numerous personnel decisions to be made, and crises brought on by student activism to be debated, but during those years the entire curriculum was reexamined by the undergraduate and graduate program committees. The last major review had taken place in the mid-1950s. At the undergraduate level this resulted primarily in the two-model principles course discussed earlier; a restructuring of the 400-numbered field courses to provide levels of advancement (renumbering had occurred again in 1961 to the 200, 400, and 600-up level format for beginning, advanced undergraduate, and graduate); a requirement that concentrators take a two-course sequence in one field; and a mathematics prerequisite for intermediate theory for concentrators. At the graduate level, among other things, a two-track system was introduced, based on the mathematical preparedness of the entering student, and provision was made for the required theory prelim to be taken at a different time from the two field prelims, if the student so desires. (The total number of prelims had been reduced from five to three in the 1950s revision.) The master's degree in applied economics was established in 1974, as a terminal degree for students headed for nonacademic careers in economics, or who want advanced training in economics in conjunction with another professional field, such as law, public health, or natural resources.

All of these developments are quickly told, but they involved, at the time, hours of discussion. Consequently, when Harold Shapiro became chairman in 1974, "quite aside from the so-called care and feeding of the department . . . I had two objectives. . . . The most important one was to recruit people in economic theory. . . . The other . . . was to decrease the length and frequency of department meetings."[183] And he did. Saul Hymans, chairman since 1977, similarly calls meetings only when specific issues arise, although the weekly noon-hour time is kept clear for that purpose. Under both chairmen the executive committee continued to meet with approximately semimonthly frequency, if not more often.

In the mid-1970s one problem that had plagued the economics department for many years was resolved, although in a manner considered by an ad hoc committee to be the fourth-best solution. The Economics Building was rather middle-aged when the department moved into it in 1909, and for the next fifty years few, if any, structural changes were made. Indeed, there weren't too many cosmetic changes either. Moves by business administration, sociology and political science to other buildings had provided the breathing room the department needed during the 1920s and 1930s. In June of 1928, the department expected to move into the still new Angell Hall, but for some reason never did. An unusual solution was found to one problem created by the hordes of returning veterans after World War II.

> I was impressed by the fact that . . . there wasn't easy ingress and egress from the building, and so . . . I said, "Leo, when people are coming in, that's fine, but let's have a door where people who have finished their classes can get out." . . . And so it was I who suggested that an additional door be put into the front of the building, which has since disappeared.[184]

Thus the building managed to weather the immediate postwar influx with one new, rather incongruous front door, but by the mid-1950s problems with the antiquated quarters were assuming desperate proportions. Not only did many faculty members share offices, but the ancient wiring did not permit use of such new-fangled devices as electric fans or desk calculators without special transformers, and there was no way to correct the midwinter steam bath conditions that might prevail in one office while next door's occupant shivered in his overcoat. A ray of hope flickered in the spring of 1956, when the executive committee went so far as to pore over a blueprint of Angell Hall, where some space on three different floors might be opening up. Did the department want to give up its rickety, self-contained building for scattered space in one that was old enough to have a few disadvantages of its own? Apparently not. It settled for 110-volt wiring, and new furniture. Oh, but that new furniture would be welcome. Gardner Ackley expressed the hope that when it arrived "we can dispose, once and for all, of every stick of the disgraceful old furniture that is now in the building. A search party should be found to make certain that all of the old stuff is carted away."[185]

They got a remodelled basement men's room thrown in too, but the few women who haunted the building would be confined for another fifteen years to the renovated storage closet beneath the back stairs, with its 1914 plumbing. In August, Ackley was pleading for correction of another deplorable situation, the insufficiency of telephone lines. In one illustrative case, three full professors and one associate professor were on one line "with no means other than wall pounding, loud shouting, or a trip down the hall, for the person answering to call another to the telephone or to find out that he is not in his office."[186]

The next bit of improvement occurred in 1963, when an effort was made to turn room 301, the quaint tower room up the steep Sleeping Beauty stairs, into a student-faculty lounge. It was suggested that faculty members might donate furnishings. This they did, but the result was something less than satisfactory, particularly the ancient and mangy carpet the Brazers had inherited with their house six years earlier. In 1969 Chairman Brazer was again asking for "good" castoffs, plus a cash contribution to defray the costs of carpet and of paint. The students would contribute their labor to apply same.

Budgetary munificence offered new visual possibilities in 1964 when some of the walls were washed and painted and new florescent lights were installed in some of the worst dungeons. But the best treat of all that year was that, at last, new valves were installed on the radiators. The Centrex telephone system went in then, too, a mixed blessing. Then in 1969, two new corridors of offices were opened up in the basement, one through the old classroom and quant seminar quarters, the other through the old accounting lab, to relieve some of the office pressure. Students got new furniture and lighting in the classrooms.

In 1971 Ackley and Brazer were at the barricades again, joined this time by Peter Steiner, as a special committee to report on the status of the Economics Building. Steiner, about to take office as chairman when the committee reported, made decent quarters a crusade of his administration. Their report summarized conditions: "noisy, cluttered, inefficient, ugly inside, impossible to keep clean, subject to frequent leaks and heating failures, and it is undeniably a serious fire hazard."[187] The committee estimated a deficiency of thirty units of office space, and deplored the fact that people with joint appointments were given the least adequate space, if any, if they were housed elsewhere as well, and so they rarely spent time among their colleagues in the building. The committee ordered its preferences for a long-term solution to the space problem: a new building; a new addition to the existing building; occupation of remodelled space vacated by a larger unit elsewhere on campus. What happened was none of the above.

There were several months of hopeful planning for a possible new Center for Public Policy Studies that would include the departments of economics and political science, the Center for Research in Economic Development, and the Institute for Public Policy Studies, to be housed in one glorious new building. All four units went so far as to detail their space needs in square footage by function, but by the summer of 1972 it became obvious that the reality of such a proposal lay so far in the future that the plans wilted in the drawer.

The "interim" solution for economics was implemented, over a period of two and a half years from the fall of 1972 to the winter of 1975. It involved extensive renovation of the interior to convert most of the remaining classrooms to offices. Thus the department was forced to accept a change it had long resisted, removal of the teaching function, except for a few small classes and seminars, from the building which would now perform only an office and meeting function. The architectural changes were so drastic that an old-timer returning might get lost.

After no little controversy, room 101, the big lecture hall, was turned into a block of offices, including a new suite for the chairman. After sixty-five years one no longer turned right to room 105 upon entering the building to visit the chairman, but left to a modernistic place called 101H. Furthermore, these quarters were refurnished with comfortable couches and chairs for conferences. A far cry from the austere old days of 1967 when Warren Smith was chairman and his secretary, Penelope Carr, wanted to surprise him for his birthday with a couch in his office. After a few phone calls to the department in charge of couches she discovered that mere chairmen were not entitled to this luxury, only deans. When the birthday arrived she could only present him with a little doll house couch and the wistful observation that "This is the best we can do."[188]

Throughout the building, ceilings were dropped, transoms covered over, florescent lighting installed, carpeting laid, air-conditioning units strategically located, the entire heating system replaced, new 1964 valves and all, bright colors and graphics painted, and even new furniture ordered. All that remained of the historic interior was the skillfully joined wood paneling of the stairwell and a glimpse of the unique iron trusses peeking through the ceiling tiles in the lobby. And all of it, according to one chairman's memo, was intended only to buy five years' time until a "permanent" solution could be found.

Two rooms in the renovated building are of special significance in the department's tradition. In September, 1972, the old classroom 207 was opened officially as the Lansing Lounge, decorated and furnished as a comfortable gathering place for faculty, in memory of their late colleague. And in 1978, the Warren L. Smith Memorial Seminar

Room, specifically designed and decorated, was dedicated to the memory of the friend to whom stimulating intellectual interchange was the essence of life.

The curriculum did not change greatly during the 1970s, but two important fields were greatly strengthened. Economic history has been taught virtually since the earliest years of the department's life, but has had periods of abeyance when the role was either unfilled or occupied by transient personnel. Dan Fusfeld taught in the field along with his other work, and in 1972 Gavin Wright, a 1969 Yale Ph.D., joined the staff. Steven Webb came in 1978, from his doctoral work at Chicago.

Urban economics is an area that grew in importance during the 1950s and 1960s, with close ties to the field of public finance. Daniel Rubinfeld came in 1972, having earned his Ph.D. from MIT that year; Paul Courant joined the department the following year, after completing his doctoral work at Princeton; and Edward Gramlich, a 1965 Yale Ph.D., came as a full professor in 1976. All of these men have taught in public finance as well, and their research, as well as teaching, interests have been furthered through association with the Institute for Public Policy Studies. Gramlich became director of the institute in 1979.

These joint appointments are indicative of the branching out of the economics department to links with a number of other units around the university. Indeed, joint appointments and interdepartmental arrangements as a whole in the university have increased considerably in the past fifteen years. The Institute for Public Policy Studies is actually the successor to the Institute for Public Administration. The name was changed in 1968 when there was a major shift in the teaching and research program, away from the practitioner–civil servant orientation of the earlier institute, with a heavy emphasis on state and local government, to the more technical, policy analysis orientation of the newer organization, with a heavy emphasis on economics. With the new focus the institute's need for economists was substantially enlarged, and a number of new courses have been developed in economics for the master's degree in public policy studies.

The other institute with which the economics department continues the closest association is, of course, the Institute for Social Research, which offers no teaching program of its own. Survey research became a doctoral field in economics in 1965. F. Thomas Juster, a 1956 Columbia Ph.D., joined the economics faculty in 1973 and became director of ISR in 1976. Greg Duncan and Richard Curtin, both Michigan Ph.D.'s, joined the institute staff and the economics department in 1975 and 1976, respectively.

In addition to the law and economics program discussed earlier, a joint economics and natural resources Ph.D. was authorized in 1964; the social work/social science Ph.D. program produces some doctorates in economics; and a formal link to the School of Public Health was established in 1968 with the joint appointment of Paul Feldstein, a 1961 Chicago Ph.D. Joint arrangements with business administration, so long a tradition, waned during the past two decades. The economics department at one time carried 50 percent of the accounting budget, but this was shifted entirely to business administration when the school and the department divided on the question of tenure for a joint appointee whom business administration wished to promote. Although accounting is still cross-listed and recommended for economics students, it is no longer required.

Two retirements took place in the 1970s. George Katona retired in 1972, but remained active in research and in ISR affairs throughout the 1970s. William Palmer retired in 1976, but returned shortly thereafter to continue on a part-time basis the undergraduate counseling which he had conducted with great skill for many years.

Economics' participation in college and university affairs has continued during these years, with Eva Mueller serving as associate dean of LSA, 1974–78, and Robert Holbrook in the same capacity since then. Service by economics department faculty on university committees has been too frequent and too widespread to list.

Department social life took a new twist in the early 1970s—to the tennis court. Along with the national trend of reviving interest in the game and the opening of new tennis clubs, department members began entertaining at tennis parties and various twosomes and foursomes scheduled regular games. By mid-decade the big round table at the east end of the Michigan League cafeteria, first occupied in the mid-sixties, had become a hallowed luncheon tradition. No other university group risked usurpation of the place, and no matter how many economists show up for lunch, there is always room for one more. Conversation at this noontime (ten minutes before noon to avoid the line) rendezvous touches on all the important affairs of the day—the standings of the college football teams, the latest follies of corrupt congressmen, the standings of the National Football League, the follies of university administration, the standings of the hockey teams, the follies of Ann Arbor street maintenance, the standings of the National and American League baseball teams, and so on until football season returns.

More dignified professional discussion and debate is reserved for the Faculty Seminar, a 1970s version of the Little Seminar and Economics Club combined. At each monthly meeting a member of the faculty presents an aspect of his or her current research, followed by general discussion on a technical level. And the period saw continuing university recognition of the achievements of department members. Distinguished Faculty Achievements awards were conferred upon Gardner Ackley in 1975 and James Morgan in 1976. Peter Steiner received the University Press Book Award in 1977. Alumnus James Duesenberry, B.A. 1939, Ph.D. 1948, was recognized by the university for outstanding achievement in 1979. In national affairs, Michigan alumna Nancy Teeters, M.A. 1954, became the first woman to serve as a member of the Federal Reserve Board in 1978. And in 1979 Darius Gaskins, Ph.D. 1970, revived Michigan's ninety-year connection to the Interstate Commerce Commission when he was appointed its chairman.

Approximately every thirteen to sixteen years of the past fifty-five the Michigan economics department has found reason to throw a special fête. The occasion of its centennial birthday has, perhaps, capped them all. A year in the planning, it balanced a serious tribute to the intellectual achievements of the department with fitting acknowledgement of its equally strong tradition of festivity. A two-day symposium of papers presented by distinguished former faculty members or students was introduced by an overview of the department's intellectual development. Intermission on the first evening of the centennial celebration once more demonstrated the prodigious, if shy, theatrical talents of department faculty, wives, and students, in an original (not to say fanciful), irreverent, multimedia presentation of one hundred years of department history. The climax of the entire event occurred on the second night, at a dinner dance which featured an address by television-renowned alumnus (and nephew of Leo Sharfman) Mike Wallace and presentation of alumni awards to six graduates of the past fifty years who have gone on to high achievement. To cap the evening Chairman Saul Hymans announced that once more the discipline's highest honor will be bestowed upon a University of Michigan economics department faculty member, when Gardner Ackley becomes president of the American Economic Association in 1981.

It was a quiet Monday morning in the world at large. A new cabinet was formed in Liberia; European capitals considered imposing economic sanctions against Iran; the Soviets reacted angrily to the United States boycott of the Moscow Olympic games; an assasin's knife missed Indian Prime Minister Indira Gandhi; the Vietnamese expressed concern over the weakness of the Cambodian regime; rising gasoline prices posed a threat to the expansion of cities in New Mexico; in Cleveland the Citizens Party nominated Barry Commoner and La-Donna Harris for president and vice president of the United States, while Edward Kennedy won the Arizona Democratic caucus; the sale of Treasury Bills set a $7 billion record; Penn Central closed at 15⅞— and in the vaulted splendor of Hill Auditorium the University of Michigan inaugurated its tenth president, economics professor Harold T. Shapiro. The date was April 14, 1980, one hundred years to the day since this story began.

NOTES

1. *Proceedings of the Board of Regents*, 1876–81, p. 497, The minutes are in error in one respect; Adams had earned the Ph.D. in 1878.
2. A. W. Coats, "Henry Carter Adams: A Case Study in the Emergence of the Social Sciences in the United States, 1850–1900," *American Studies* 2, no. 2, p. 181.
3. Ibid., p. 187.
4. Ibid.
5. Ibid., pp. 187–88.
6. Z. Clark Dickinson, manuscript biography of Fred M. Taylor, chap. 3, p. 12n. in Michigan Historical Collections, Dickinson Papers.
7. Coats, p. 195.
8. Interview with Shorey Peterson.
9. *President's Report*, September 1892, p. 22.
10. *President's Report*, 1907, p. 10.
11. *President's Report*, 1909, p. 10.
12. Individual faculty members are discussed in the text and listed in the appendix only if they taught at Michigan three years or more, at the rank

of instructor or lecturer or above. Teaching assistants are not included, not because they are unworthy but because they are too numerous.

13. Dickinson, chap. 13, p. 23.
14. Interview with William A. Paton.
15. *University of Michigan Catalogue*, 1913–14, p. 188.
16. Memo to Howard Ellis and Edward Chamberlin, April, 1920, quoted in Dickinson, chap. 10, pp. 32–33.
17. William A. Paton, "Fred Manville Taylor," *Michigan Alumnus*, April 22, 1933, p. 4.
18. Interview with William Palmer.
19. Interview with Shorey Peterson.
20. It was common practice for university faculty to publish notes and essays for the instruction of their students in this way, which were priced at marginal cost. Frequently these collections evolved into major publications.
21. Paton, "Fred Manville Taylor," p. 4.
22. William A. Paton, "Recollections re a Kindred Spirit," in F. A. von Hayek, ed., *Toward Liberty: Essays in Honor of Ludwig von Mises* (Menlo Park, Calif.: Institute for Humane Studies, 1971), vol. 2, p. 251.
23. Letter from Fred M. Taylor to Leonard L. Watkins, August 22, 1922, in Watkins department file.
24. Interview with William Palmer.
25. Dickinson, chap. 10, pp. 40–41.
26. Paton, "Kindred Spirit," p. 260.
27. Interview with Shorey Peterson.
28. *President's Report*, 1920–21, p. 176.
29. "Memorandum from C. E. Griffin to Professor Henry C. Adams on the Teaching of Economics and the Establishment of a School of Commerce," n. d., in Michigan Historical Collections, Henry Carter Adams Papers, Box 24.
30. Interview with Shorey Peterson.
31. Letter of March 3, 1923, in department files.
32. Interview with Shorey Peterson.
33. Letter from Margaret Elliott to I. Leo Sharfman, February 11, 1938, in Sharfman department file.
34. Interview with Shorey Peterson.
35. Letter from Professor H. A. Mills to Edmund E. Day, January 9, 1924, in Goodrich department file.
36. Interview with Robert C. Angell.
37. Interview with William Palmer.
38. Interview with Shorey Peterson.
39. Letter from Fred M. Taylor to Leonard L. Watkins, August 22, 1922, in Watkins department file.
40. Interview with William Palmer.
41. Interview with Daniel Suits.
42. Interview with William Paton.

43. Paul D. Cahow to I. Leo Sharfman, n.d., in Michigan Historical Collections, Sharfman Papers, Box 6.
44. Interview with William Haber.
45. Interview with Gardner Ackley.
46. Anonymous, quoted by James Duesenberry.
47. Interview with William Palmer.
48. Interview with Nelson Sharfman.
49. Interview with Shorey Peterson.
50. *University of Michigan Catalogue*, 1930, p. 118.
51. Interview with William Palmer.
52. Interview with Robert Dernberger.
53. Interview with William Palmer.
54. Interview with Daniel Suits.
55. Letter of I. Leo Sharfman, June 2, 1931, in Caverly department file.
56. *Proceedings of the Board of Regents*, May 22, 1914, p. 707n.
57. Letter from I. Leo Sharfman to Morris Copeland, June 27, 1933, in Copeland department file.
58. Letter from Carter Goodrich to I. Leo Sharfman, December 16, 1929, in Goodrich department file.
59. Letter from Frank Knight to I. Leo Sharfman, February 28, 1931, in Handman department file.
60. Interview with William Haber.
61. Interview with Gardner Ackley.
62. Interview with William Haber.
63. Interview with Shorey Peterson.
64. Interview with William Haber.
65. Interview with William Palmer.
66. Interview with William Haber.
67. Interview with William Palmer.
68. Michigan Historical Collections, Economics Department Papers, Box 2.
69. Letter from I. Leo Sharfman to Dean E. H. Kraus, October 6, 1934, in Michigan Historical Collections, Economics Department Papers, Box 2.
70. Interview with Robert C. Angell.
71. Interview with Shorey Peterson.
72. Interview with Gardner Ackley.
73. Interview with William Palmer.
74. Ibid.
75. Interview with Daniel Suits.
76. Interview with Shorey Peterson.
77. Interview with William Palmer.
78. Interview with William Haber.
79. Letter from Margaret Elliott to I. Leo Sharfman, February 11, 1938, in Michigan Historical Collections, Sharfman Papers, Box 8.
80. Interview with William Haber.
81. Interview with Shorey Peterson.

82. Letter to the Centennial Planning Committee from Richard L. Pinkerton, July 13, 1979.
83. Interview with Harold Levinson.
84. Letter from Arthur Smithies to I. Leo Sharfman, March 15, 1936, in Smithies department file.
85. Interview with Shorey Peterson.
86. Interview with William Palmer.
87. Letter from I. Leo Sharfman to William Paton, January 22, 1939, in Paton department file.
88. Letter from William Paton to I. Leo Sharfman, January 24, 1938, in Smithies department file.
89. Interview with Gardner Ackley.
90. Interview with Daniel Suits.
91. Ibid.
92. Interview with Harold Levinson.
93. Interview with Daniel Suits.
94. Interview with Gardner Ackley.
95. Letter from Carl Remer to I. Leo Sharfman, February 1, 1945, in Remer department file.
96. Interview with William Palmer.
97. Ibid.
98. Ibid.
99. Interview with William Haber.
100. Interview with Gardner Ackley.
101. Ibid.
102. Interview with Daniel Suits.
103. Interview with Harold Levinson.
104. Interview with Lawrence Klein.
105. Interview with Harvey Brazer.
106. Tables of enrollment data, numbered I–V by year 1940–41 through 1952–53 for LSA and the Department of Economics, in Michigan Historical Collections, Economics Department Papers, Box 4.
107. Mimeographed statement in Michigan Historical Collections, Economics Department Papers, Box 4, "Department Luncheons" folder.
108. Interview with Ann Smith Fowler.
109. Interview with James Morgan.
110. Memo from Gardner Ackley to Dean Charles E. Odegaard, May 22, 1956, in Lansing department file.
111. Interview with Lawrence Klein.
112. Ibid.
113. Ibid.
114. Ibid.
115. Interview with James Morgan.
116. Interview with Lawrence Klein.
117. Interview with Daniel Suits.
118. Interview with Harold Levinson.

119. Questionnaire and response in Boulding department file.
120. "Minutes of Episode During 24 Hours from 4 P.M., Thursday, May 17, 1951, to 4:00 P.M., Friday, May 18," in Boulding department file.
121. Ibid.
122. Interview with Harvey Brazer.
123. Interview with Deborah Freedman.
124. Interview with Harvey Brazer.
125. Interview with Harold Levinson.
126. Interview with Harvey Brazer.
127. The nonstage names of the cast: Allen Mandelstamm, graduate student; Elise Boulding; Kenneth Boulding; Harold Levinson; Daniel Suits; Gardner Ackley; Richard Musgrave; and Wolfgang Stolper on piano.
128. Letter from Gardner Ackley to Dean Ralph A. Sawyer, December 13, 1954, in Michigan Historical Collections, Economics Department Papers, Box 2, "Executive Committee" folder.
129. Letter from Robert S. Ford to Dean Charles E. Odegaard, February 7, 1955, in Klein department file.
130. Letter from William A. Paton to Dean Charles E. Odegaard, February 3, 1955, in Klein department file.
131. Letter from William A. Paton to Dean Charles E. Odegaard, February 23, 1955, in Klein department file.
132. Minutes of economics staff meeting of March 14, 1955, in Michigan Historical Collections, Economics Department Papers, Box 2.
133. Letter from Gardner Ackley to Lawrence Klein, June 4, 1955, in Klein department file.
134. Letter from Lawrence Klein to Gardner Ackley, October 18, 1955, in Klein department file.
135. Letter from Marvin Niehuss to Lawrence Klein, November 14, 1955, copy in Klein department file.
136. Letter from Gardner Ackley to Lawrence Klein, November 21, 1955, in Klein department file.
137. Letter from Lawrence Klein to Gardner Ackley, December 9, 1955, in Klein department file.
138. Letter from Marvin Niehuss to Charles E. Odegaard, December 16, 1955, copy in Klein department file.
139. Letter from Gardner Ackley to Charles E. Odegaard, February 13, 1956, in department files.
140. Interview with George Katona.
141. Interview with Lawrence Klein.
142. Interview with Eva Mueller.
143. Interview with Daniel Suits.
144. Letter from Gardner Ackley to Kenneth Boulding, April 29, 1960, in Boulding department file.
145. Memo from Dean Burton D. Thuma to department chairmen, December 10, 1951, in Michigan Historical Collections, Economics Department Papers, Box 2.

146. Letter from I. Leo Sharfman to Dean Burton D. Thuma, December 18, 1951, in Michigan Historical Collections, Economics Department Papers, Box 2.

147. Interview with Gardner Ackley.

148. Minutes of staff meeting of March 8, 1954, in Michigan Historical Collections, Economics Department Papers, Box 4, "Department Luncheons" folder.

149. Interview with William Palmer.

150. Interview with William Haber.

151. Letter from Roger Heyns to individual faculty members, dated October 17, 1961, in Michigan Historical Collections, Economics Department Papers, Box 3.

152. "Statement by the Economics Department of Its Position and Needs," in Michigan Historical Collections, Economics Department Papers, Box 3.

153. Interview with Wolfgang Stolper.

154. Ibid.

155. Interview with Harold Shapiro.

156. Interview with Daniel Suits.

157. Interview with Saul Hymans.

158. Interview with Harold Shapiro.

159. Ibid.

160. Ibid.

161. Interview with Daniel Fusfeld.

162. Interview with Harold Levinson.

163. Interview with Peter Steiner.

164. Interview with Harvey Brazer.

165. Ibid.

166. Interview with Peter Steiner.

167. Interview with Daniel Fusfeld.

168. Ibid.

169. Interview with Barry Bluestone.

170. Ibid.

171. Report of the faculty committee on governance, 1971, in department files.

172. Interview with Harvey Brazer.

173. Interview with Daniel Fusfeld.

174. Interview with Harvey Brazer.

175. Minutes of the department meeting of March 25, 1970, in department files.

176. Memo to the regents, March 25, 1970, in department files.

177. Interview with Barry Bluestone.

178. Interview with Ann Smith Fowler.

179. Interview with Harold Levinson.

180. Minutes of department meeting of December 7, 1972, in department files.

181. Interview with Jean Danzer Cobb.
182. Letter to the Centennial Planning Committee from Lenore Frane Stern-light, June 28, 1979, in department files.
183. Interview with Harold Shapiro.
184. Interview with William Palmer.
185. Memo from Gardner Ackley to Shorey Peterson, n. d., but probably summer of 1956, in Michigan Historical Collections, Economics Department Papers, Box 2.
186. Letter from Gardner Ackley to Dean Burton D. Thuma, August 10, 1956, in Michigan Historical Collections, Economics Department Papers, Box 2.
187. "The Economics Building and the Economics Department: A Report to the Executive Committee," 1971, in department files.
188. Quoted in interview with Ann Smith Fowler.

Appendix

DEPARTMENT OF ECONOMICS FACULTY

Those listed were in the department three years or more at a rank of lecturer and up. The concluding year for faculty who moved into the business school is shown as 1924; for sociology as 1929. Current (1980) faculty members' names appear in all capital letters.

Henry Carter Adams   1880–1921
Charles H. Cooley   1892–1929
Frank H. Dixon   1892–1898
Fred M. Taylor   1892–1929
Edward D. Jones   1901–19
Harrison S. Smalley   1903–11
David Friday   1908–21
Carl E. Parry   1908–12
Stuart McC. Hamilton   1910–14
Walton H. Hamilton   1910–14
George W. Dowrie   1913–18
Henry Rottschaffer   1913–16
I. Leo Sharfman   1913–54
Warren S. Thompson   1913–18
Paul W. Ivey   1914–17
Frank F. Kolbe   1914–17
Robert G. Rodkey   1914–17
William A. Paton   1915, 1917–59
Rufus S. Tucker   1915–19
Wilbur P. Calhoun   1916–23
Roy V. Leffler   1916–19
Herbert N. Schmitt   1916–23
Russell D. Kilborn   1917–20
Arthur E. Wood   1917, 1920–31
Roy N. Holmes   1918–30

Harcourt L. Caverly   1919–33
Clare E. Griffen   1919–24
Ross G. Walker   1919–24
Paul D. Cahow   1920–24
Charles C. Edmonds   1920–25
Howard S. Ellis   1920–22, 1925–38
Isador Lubin   1919–23
Carroll May   1920–30
Francis E. Ross   1920–24
Lowell J. Carr   1921–30
Seward L. Horner   1921–26
Saul C. Oppenheim   1921–26
Shorey Peterson   1921–67
Herman Wyngaarden   1921–24
Robert C. Angell   1922–29
Ben W. Lewis   1922–25
Perry Mason   1922–30
Leonard L. Watkins   1922–24, 1926–57
George E. Bigge   1923–27
Edmund E. Day   1923–28
Z. Clark Dickinson   1923–59
Floyd E. Devol   1924–36
Margaret Elliott   1924–50
Augustus W. Foscue   1924–27

Carter L. Goodrich   1924–31
Harold K. Selbey   1924–28
John V. Van Sickle   1924–28
Claude J. Whitlow   1925–29
G. Walter Woodworth   1925–30
Leonard W. Adams   1926–29
Nathanael H. Engle   1926–30
Robert P. Briggs   1927–45
Donald C. Horton   1927–35
Charles F. Remer   1928–59
William T. Crandell   1929–35
Robert R. Horner   1929–41
Roland I. Robinson   1929–35
Morris A. Copeland   1930–36
William M. Hoad   1930–34
Lemuel L. Laing   1930–45
William B. Palmer   1930–76
Vladimir Timoshenko   1930–35
Max S. Handman   1931–40
Robert S. Ford   1935–68
William Haber   1936–68
Edgar M. Hoover   1936–47
Edward C. Simmons   1936–47
Arthur Smithies   1938–46
GARDNER ACKLEY   1940–41,
   1945–
Floyd A. Bond   1942–46
George R. Anderson   1943–72
Rufus Wixon   1944–47
Gardner Patterson   1947–50
George Katona   1947–72
HAROLD M. LEVINSON   1947–
Richard A. Musgrave   1947–59
Daniel B. Suits   1947–70
WOLFGANG F. STOLPER   1949–
Kenneth E. Boulding   1950–68
Lawrence R. Klein   1950–54
JAMES N. MORGAN   1950–
Warren L. Smith   1950–53, 1957–72

Tony Brouwer   1952–55
John B. Lansing   1956–70
Stephen W. Rousseas   1956–59
HARVEY E. BRAZER   1957–
Daniel O. Fletcher   1957–60
Harry D. Hutchinson   1957–60
EVA L. MUELLER   1957–
William P. Winger   1957–60
MORRIS BORNSTEIN   1958–
Ronald A. Shearer   1958–62
Samuel P. Hayes   1959–62
W. H. LOCKE
   ANDERSON   1960–
Eliezer B. Ayal   1960–63
DANIEL R. FUSFELD   1960–
David N. Milstein   1960–63
ROBIN BARLOW   1961–
Alexander Eckstein   1961–76
ROBERT M. STERN   1961–
Jarvis M. Babcock   1962–66
Irene Butter   1962–66
Kang Chao   1962–65
Mary Alice Shulman   1962–75
RONALD L. TEIGEN   1962–
Elliott R. Morss   1963–65
John E. Parker   1963–67
WILLIAM G. SHEPHERD   1963–
Richard Tilly   1963–66
SAUL H. HYMANS   1964–
RICHARD C. PORTER   1964–
HAROLD T. SHAPIRO   1964–
JOHN G. CROSS   1965–
ROBERT S. HOLBROOK   1965–
ELLIOT J. BERG   1966–
Paul Demeny   1966–69
GEORGE E. JOHNSON   1966–
Bernard Munk   1966–69
Frederic M. Scherer   1966–73
FRANK P. STAFFORD   1966–

Kunio Yoshihara 1966–69
HELEN P. CRAFTON 1967–
Peter C. Eckstein 1967–71
DEBORAH S.
  FREEDMAN 1967–
WILLIAM B. NEENAN 1967–
Malcolm Cohen 1968–73
ROBERT F.
  DERNBERGER 1968–
PAUL J. FELDSTEIN 1968–
Michael W. Klass 1968–74
Barbara Newell 1968–71
PETER O. STEINER 1968–
Burkhard Strumpel 1968–75
Lester D. Taylor 1968–74
Sidney G. Winter 1968–76
C. Russell Hill 1969–75
Michael E. Manove 1969–75
George B. Simmons 1969–74
ALAN V. DEARDORFF 1970–
Ronald D. Lee 1970–79
GARY R. SAXONHOUSE 1970–
Donald C. Shoup 1970–74
Kenneth E. Wertz 1970–73
Peter Heller 1971–77

Richard B. Mancke 1971–74
Elizabeth Roistacher 1972–75
DANIEL L. RUBINFELD 1972–
THOMAS L. WEISSKOPF 1972–
GAVIN WRIGHT 1972–
PAUL N. COURANT 1973–
E. PHILIP HOWREY 1973–
F. THOMAS JUSTER 1973–
JAN KMENTA 1973–
WILLIAM JAMES
  ADAMS 1974–
THEODORE C.
  BERGSTROM 1975–
GREG J. DUNCAN 1975–
JOHN P. LAITNER 1975–
ANN P. ANDERSON 1976–
RICHARD T. CURTIN 1976–
EDWARD M. GRAMLICH 1976–
LAWRENCE BLUME 1977–
CARL P. SIMON 1977–
HAL R. VARIAN 1977–
SUSAN I. RANNEY 1978–
STEVEN B. WEBB 1978–
GLENN C. LOURY 1979–